MEDIA PRACTICES AND CHANGING AFRICAN SOCIALITIES

Anthropology of Media
Series Editors: Mark Peterson and Sahana Udupa

The ubiquity of media across the globe has led to an explosion of interest in the ways people around the world use media as part of their everyday lives. This series addresses the need for works that describe and theorize multiple, emerging, and sometimes interconnected, media practices in the contemporary world. Interdisciplinary and inclusive, this series offers a forum for ethnographic methodologies, descriptions of non-Western media practices, explorations of transnational connectivity, and studies that link culture and practices across fields of media production and consumption.

Volume 9
Media Practices and Changing African Socialities: Non-media-centric Perspectives
Edited by Jo Helle-Valle and Ardis Storm-Mathisen

Volume 8
Monetising the Dividual Self: The Emergence of the Lifestyle Blog and Influencers in Malaysia
Julian Hopkins

Volume 7
Transborder Media Spaces: Ayuujk Videomaking Between Mexico and the US
Ingrid Kummels

Volume 6
The Making of the Pentecostal Melodrama: Religion, Media and Gender in Kinshasa
Katrien Pype

Volume 5
Localizing the Internet: An Anthropological Account
John Postill

Volume 4
Theorising Media and Practice
Edited by Birgit Bräuchler and John Postill

Volume 3
News as Culture: Journalistic Practices and the Remaking of Indian Leadership Traditions
Ursula Rao

Volume 2
The New Media Nation: Indigenous Peoples and Global Communication
Valerie Alia

Volume 1
Alarming Reports: Communicating Conflict in the Daily News
Andrew Arno

Media Practices and Changing African Socialities

Non-media-centric Perspectives

Edited by Jo Helle-Valle and Ardis Storm-Mathisen

berghahn
NEW YORK • OXFORD
www.berghahnbooks.com

First published in 2020 by

Berghahn Books

www.berghahnbooks.com

Library of Congress Cataloging-in-Publication Data

Names: Helle-Valle, Jo, editor. | Storm-Mathisen, Ardis, editor.
Title: Media practices and changing African socialities : non-media-centric perspectives / edited by Jo Helle-Valle and Ardis Storm-Mathisen.
Other titles: Anthropology of media ; v. 9.
Description: New York : Berghahn Books, 2020. | Series: Anthropology of media; volume 9 | Includes bibliographical references and index.
Identifiers: LCCN 2019048119 (print) | LCCN 2019048120 (ebook) | ISBN 9781789206616 (hardback) | ISBN 9781789206623 (ebook)
Subjects: LCSH: Digital media–Social aspects–Africa. | Digital media–Economic aspects–Africa.
Classification: LCC HM851 .M4245 2020 (print) | LCC HM851 (ebook) | DDC 303.4833096–dc23
LC record available at https://lccn.loc.gov/2019048119
LC ebook record available at https://lccn.loc.gov/2019048120

British Library Cataloguing in Publication Data

A catalogue record for this book is available from the British Library

ISBN 978-1-78920-661-6 hardback
ISBN 978-1-78920-662-3 ebook

Contents

Acknowledgements

This book emanates from the research project New Media Practices in a Changing Africa (see www.mediafrica.no), financed by the Research Council of Norway (project no. 240714 /F10), lasting from 2015 to 2019. The project's goal was to understand to what extent and in what ways the media revolution taking place influences the changes contemporary Africa is going through. All the contributors to this book have been part of the project and have collected data as part of the project work. Simultaneously, all have had long involvements with the sites researched. Almost all of us are also social scientists foremost; our interest in media research is the result of what we have encountered in the fields.

This background explains the approach we take on media in this book: a premise for the studies is that the social impact of media requires a practice perspective and a non-media-centric approach. We need to look at practices in order to see how media actually impact sociality (and vice versa). Thus, the chapters' take is close-up, ethnographically rich analyses of specific socialities. It is from these concrete, lived realities that we can start to point to more general mechanisms and dynamics linked to media uses in Africa – something we attempt to do in the introductory chapter.

We wish first of all to thank the Research Council of Norway. Without its funding this book would never have seen the light of day. Secondly, we – the editors – thank the chapters' authors. Editing an anthology is a long and challenging process but their competence and willingness made the journey interesting and rewarding. The week-long seminar that was held in Marrakech in January 2018 was an especially fruitful event.

We also want to thank Harvard University and the University of Botswana for hosting us as visiting scholars at different stages in the project's life. A special thank you goes to Professor Jean Comaroff for her always friendly and constructive help. We also want to thank Tom Bonnington at Berghahn for his professional and swift support and guidance.

Lastly, we want to thank our families for their non-academic but crucial understanding and support.

Ardis Storm-Mathisen and Jo Helle-Valle
Oslo, October 2019

INTRODUCTION

A Social Science Perspective on Media Practices in Africa

Social Mechanisms, Dynamics and Processes

Jo Helle-Valle and Ardis Storm-Mathisen

The Book and Its Topic

The scope of this book is to contribute to an increased understanding of the social significance of new media in contemporary Africa. For analytical reasons, which will be made clear in this introduction, our approach is to use a few countries for intense, focused, ethnographically based case studies. These are Botswana, South Africa, Zambia and DR Congo. The question about new media's role is a grand one, and in our view it is impossible to ever give a general and definitive answer to it. Still, it is a crucial question to ask, first of all because two occurrences took place more or less at the same time, starting in the mid-1990s: Africa experienced a marked and relatively consistent economic growth (Jerven, 2005, 2015), and during the same period the continent experienced what can only be described as a media revolution. The World Bank, United Nations and other experts on development issues – supported by leading media outlets – declared that the 'Dark Continent' had recovered. This prompted a strong 'Africa Rising' discourse (Jerven, 2005; Taylor, 2016), often closely linked to the growth of new media (see e.g. Amankwah-Amoah, 2019). Statistics showed that most African countries experienced a sustained growth in GDP and other indicators of economic development.[1] As to the media revolution, the changes have been indisputable: computers, mobile phones and the internet came gradually from the early 1990s but the penetration rate for both mobile phones and use of the internet took off in the early 2000s.

Africa's mobile phone adoption curve has been spectacular. In a little over a decade, Africa, and not least the sub-Saharan part of the continent, has witnessed the fastest growth in mobile subscribers in the world. The number of connections in this region has grown by 44 per cent since 2000, compared to an average of 34 per cent for developing regions and 10 per cent for developed regions, and is expected to continue to grow in the years to come (GSMA, 2012). Nevertheless, according to the ICT Development Index 2017 (IDI),[2] Africa remains the region with the lowest ICT (Information and Communication Technology) development, due to a rather low standing in economic terms and limited development of a fixed broadband infrastructure (International Telecommunication Union [ITU], 2017).[3] African countries also score low on the socio-economic impact of ICT according to the Network Readiness Index (NRI) (World Economic Forum [WEF], 2016).[4]

Investigating the relationship between social changes taking place in Africa and the changing media landscape is important for political reasons as well. The global development industry has embraced the discourse of new media being the salvation for poor and struggling countries. The World Bank, various UN agencies, the International Monetary Fund (IMF) and innumerable non-governmental organisations (NGOs) have identified the media revolution as the main route towards development (Murphy and Carmody, 2015). So have almost all governments in Africa. The countries discussed in this book are no exception and the invested hopes for ICT to have positive outcomes are conspicuously present in their national development plans. This means that questions concerning the relationship between (new) media and development are of crucial social and political significance – the topic has entered arenas in which policy decisions are made. Obviously, good policy decisions rely on good knowledge while inadequate knowledge tends to generate bad policies. Our interest is thus not only academic; it is of crucial importance for all to rapidly expand our understanding of this theme. For it is our – as well as many other onlookers' – opinion that the knowledge we have so far is at best inadequate. New media do have developmental potential but they are not a golden ticket to a prosperous future. Policy failures are already evident and critical voices are becoming more numerous by the day, not least within academia.

In this introduction, we will position our own contribution to this enormous and diverse discourse by first expanding on the academic landscape of media and development. This will then lead us to clarify the book's theoretical, analytical and methodological foundation. We will then give short descriptions of the chapters that follow and draw connecting lines between them before we end our introduction with some synthesising reflections.

Development and ICT/New Media

How media use might positively benefit people in the developing world has long been the focus of scholarly work, most importantly with the Chicago School in the 1920s and the Frankfurter School in the 1930s and onwards. Later it evolved as a distinct field of 'Development Communication' in the 1950s and 1960s (Vokes, 2018a, pp. 5ff). With the rapid developments and uptake of ICT[5] since then, the study of media and development has intensified and diversified into various sub-fields of Media and Communication Studies, with labels such as 'Media in/for Development' (M4D), 'Communication in/for Development' (ComDev)' or 'Information and Communication Technology for Development' (ICT4D) (ibid.; Postill, 2010; Tufte, 2016). It is not within the scope of this book to dig into the specificities of these various strands, except to recognise the most dominant contributions in terms of influence and critical perspectives.

ICT4D[6] focuses on 'the ways in which donor governments, multi-lateral aid agencies, NGOs and developing world governments and their citizens may use media in order to advance their economic, political and social goals' (Vokes, 2018a, p. 20). A narrow approach concentrates on media as institutions by focusing on the 'processes through which development agencies and NGOs might try to engage with a developing world in an attempt to strengthen its media sector, and also to improve the socio-legal environment in which that sector operates' (Tufte, 2016, p. 17). A broader approach looks at 'the interplay and convergence between communication and development' (ibid.). Nevertheless, although there is diversity in the thinking within the ICT4D community, its discourse maintains a positive and technology-deterministic perspective on the prospects of ICTs to transform development processes (Murphy and Carmody, 2015, p. xiv). Since the ICT4D community is well organised, has significant levels of participation of stakeholders and receives investments from transnational media-technology corporations, it has become a powerful agenda-setter with respect to the ICT–development link (ibid.).

As Wendy Willems elaborates in her chapter in this book, the optimistic view of the ICT–development link that can be associated with

ICT4D perspectives closely resembles the perspectives argued by the proponents of Modernisation Theory. This inherently ethnocentric and normative theory, emerging from the Bretton-Woods agreement in the late 1940s, argued that development equalled modernisation and that modernisation was the striving towards the socio-economic form that had developed in the USA and Western Europe. The road 'developing countries' needed to take was to let capitalism run its course more or less unhampered because if capital and technology were let loose, all the other problems would solve themselves, such as democratic rule, welfare and a just society. Needless to say, its evolutionist perspective on the mechanisms of social change soon proved to be mostly wrong, and was heavily criticised.

The ICT4D perspective has rightly been met with the same type of criticism. For one, it presents solutions that ignore or neglect key structural inequalities and thereby distorts priorities from core issues of poverty and debt. Secondly, it takes for granted the transformative capacity of technology – hence alerts to a determinism – without investigating how it in fact affects users. Thirdly, its technology-driven solutions in fact perpetuate dependency, inequality and power inequalities, and hamper the development of local economies. Thus, it 'thintegrates' rather than integrates in thick and more sustainable ways (Murphy and Carmody, 2015). Fourthly, there are ethical issues related to the growing power of global corporations that mine data and take control of markets in developing countries. The weakness in the ICT4D approach is, in other words, that it takes a one-sided, optimistic and macro-oriented perspective, and leaves crucial questions unanswered 'regarding whether, and the explicit ways in which, ICTs are transforming multiscalar and embedded power relations, inequalities, and other structural features that have held back African economies for decades' (ibid., p. xv; see also Ojo, 2018). One reason for this, we argue, is that the ICT4D and various related academic approaches have taken a media-centred focus. In this book we argue for the necessity of a more 'society-centred' (Brinkman and de Bruijne, 2018; Miller et al., 2016; Slater, 2013; Willems and Mano, 2017) and 'non-media centric' (Morley, 2009) approach, a theme to which we will now turn.

The Roles of Media in Research

Important reasons for the techno-optimism of the ICT4D-related perspectives are not only that it ideologically resonates well with our neoliberal era but that much of the academic groundwork was delivered not by critical social scientists but by model-oriented economists and media researchers. The former operated with macro models that were based on mechanical relationships between input and output. Thus, to fit well into their models, ICT is seen solely as a technology and a production factor. Rightly assuming that information and communication technologies hold the potential both for faster and less costly information flows, and that it is a production sector in itself, it is expected that the introduction of ICT will start a self-propelling growth, if only the mechanisms of the market are allowed to work uninhibited.

The other academic perspective affecting the views of the ICT4D community is media research. Naturally, media are at the centre of their attention and tend to acquire a life of their own, pushing actors out in the periphery of their research. Thus, early media research operated with ideas about an 'audience' who dutifully purchased the technologies and passively took in media content. With Stuart Hall's seminal conceptual pair 'encoding/decoding' (cf. Hall, 1980), introduced in the first part of the 1970s, a more critical view developed on how media content was received. This set off a very productive turn in parts of media studies, too many-faceted to be reiterated here. However, reception and audience studies bloomed, turning their attention to how people actually related to media, and especially its content. According to media researcher Pertti Alasuutari (1999), such research has gone through three phases. First, in the 1970s it basically followed Hall's ideas about three types of media receptions: a hegemonic position (uncritically taking in media content), a negotiated position (critical but positive) and an oppositional position. Soon proven to be insufficiently sensitive to complex realities, the next phase of reception and audience studies held a more open approach, insisting that one needed to take more seriously the variations in media reception – studying not only the class position of the media consumers but also the contexts in which media were consumed. Thus, the new perspective argued that media consumption needed to be empirically studied as part of their everyday life. As for the third phase of such studies, Alasuutari is conspicuously vague, only highlighting the importance of an even stronger social contextualisation of media practices, in which ethnographic methodology was crucial.

Our interpretation of this vagueness is that media studies had not yet taken in the radical implication of this turn away from media-centred approaches. The discipline is diverse but ethnography is not among its strengths. It was not until David Morley in 2009 introduced the term 'non-media-centric media studies' that the full implication of this 'third phase' was conceptualised. In fact, one could argue that the full consequence of the radical turn has not yet come into full effect. For instance, Shaun Moores, one of the strongest proponents of the non-media-centric perspective, dedicates considerable space in his book *Digital Orientations* to convincing his fellow media researchers of the wisdom of this perspective despite its 'counter-intuitive' content (2018, pp. 4ff). However, we argue that this is far less counter-intuitive for social scientists.

The reason for this being more intuitively graspable for social scientists than media researchers is that the former habitually place the social or the actors at the centre of analysis. In fact, it was not until Arjun Appadurai published the anthology *The Social Life of Things* in 1986 that putting *things* at the centre of the analysis was presented as a novel strategy within interpretive social science.[7] Thus, what Morley has done for media studies is precisely that – to radically shift the understanding of the role of media. His (very short) article about the non-media-centric approach has of course been interpreted in different ways, but we propose a radical understanding of his Copernican turn – the need to shift attention from the media themselves to focus on how sociality shapes media (elegantly phrased by Miller et al. [2016] as 'how the world changes social media'). Then – and only then – can we look at what roles media possibly play in these practices. There are two very good arguments for doing this, one general and one tied to the topic of this book.

First, although there are good reasons to warn against simplified ideas of media merely being a type of technology – which happen to mediate information – we nevertheless wish to emphasise the instrumental and heterotelic quality of media. Media are technologies, infrastructure and content which people make use of because they are, in some way, found to be useful (cf. Silverstone and Hirsch, 1992). From this, it follows that the *social* significance of media is first of all found by focusing on the practices in which the media are put to use. A farmer calling a veterinary officer for help with vaccinating his goats connects very different people and generates entirely different effects than a young man flirting with a girlfriend-to-be. It is one technology – it can even be the same phone – but the difference the phone makes sociologically is worlds apart.

Secondly, the topic of this book – which is about the social effects of media use – makes the point about de-centring media especially relevant. We want to investigate the ways and the extent to which media play a part in the changes that we see Africa going through. The ambition is to look concretely at the relationships between media and various social processes of change in specific localities. Our main interest is not the various meanings media practices convey in themselves, but that media – as technology, infrastructure and content – are crucial parts of social practices. In other words, we are not primarily investigating media as representations of something socio-cultural but as significant parts of processes that make up the social. In this book, media are thus foremost interesting in their non-representational form – we look at their quality as social agents, not as vehicles of meaning (Moores, 2018; Thrift, 1996).

Media being agents makes sense within the analytical framework of Actor Network Theory (ANT). The point is not to endow things in themselves with some sort of magical agency but to insist that agency is about making things happen, making a difference (Latour, 2005, pp. 40ff). Agency should not be fetishised as a force that exists *within* humans but should be seen as various assemblages of humans and non-humans that together bring about a difference in the world. It is the sum of what these assemblages of humans and non-humans actually do that makes up society. Therefore, our job is to trace the various associations between things and people, to study the trails left behind by these associations and then arrive at the social through observations of these assemblages. From this perspective, the social is the result of actions, not their preconditions (ibid.).[8] Media are hence an essential part of making the social happen, just as sociality fundamentally forms media.

From this, two analytical themes that link directly to media and social change emerge, and need to be discussed. First, what does it mean to give analytical primacy to *practices*? Secondly, how do we deal with *change*?

Practice

Hardly anybody would contest that an idea of, and a focus on practice is important in studies of the social. After all, societies are made up of (among other things) people, and most accord the potential for agency to individuals. So why emphasise practice? The obvious point is found in the history of the social sciences. From Durkheim until today, people – and their actions – have been side-lined for the purpose of highlighting the social as a self-contained and self-reproducing system. A consequence was that what people did – practices – really didn't matter (Helle-Valle, 2010). Thus, a rehabilitation of the acting subject was needed. Moreover, there is a banal methodological side to it: we need to look at what people do, and talk with individuals, in order to understand how society works. So also is the case with media and social change: it is people who use media, it is they who intentionally apply ICTs for various reasons. So we need to look at (media) practices.

However, the more controversial side to practice theories is how to *handle* our data on people's actions. There is a strong tradition in the philosophy of science, from Plato onwards, to make sense of reality through a framework, which can be labelled 'vertical ontology' (Bryant, 2011; DeLanda, 2006). This implies that we explain regularities and order by way of principles of another ontological sense. In short, this is to apply what Carl Hempel (1966) calls 'Covering Laws' – evoking some kind of ordering faculty which is of a 'higher' order than the empirical findings we attempt to explain (hence the vertical). This logic was most clearly displayed in structuralism, where the Saussurean principle of *langue* explaining *parole* was brought into the realm of social sciences, and in functionalism and structural functionalism in which 'society', 'culture', 'social structure' was seen to have an existence of its own and was used to explain what was observed on the ground.

Many authors who advocate various strands of practice theory do not necessarily dismiss this type of explanation (e.g. Couldry and Hepp, 2017; Reckwitz, 2002; Schatzki, 2002). It is not our task or privilege to place different practice theorists into this or that category; what we want to do is highlight the form of practice theory that has guided the studies in this book, which we would term a 'flat ontology' stance. In short, the argument is that it is logically flawed to introduce causes that are ontologically different from that which shall be explained. As Latour puts it, '... the ways in which *la parole* meets *la langue* have remained totally mysterious ever since the time of Saussure' (2005, p. 167). The problem with such reasoning is that the assumed structures (or 'culture', or whatever term one introduces to designate collective forces) are not real but constructions that researchers introduce as shorthand for behavioural patterns. In other words, they belong to a different ontological order than what we study – the former the 'raw material', the latter a 'tool'. Therefore, the analytical flaw lies in applying such constructed concepts as *explanations* or *causes* to what is happening within the field of study. As Bourdieu puts it, 'any scientific objectification ought to be preceded by a sign indicating "everything takes place as if ...", which, functioning in the same way as quantifiers in logic, would constantly remind us of the epistemological status of the constructed concepts of objective science' (Bourdieu, 1977, p. 203, n49). In contrast, a flat ontology-guided practice theory argues that what we use to explain should *only* contain elements that ontologically belong to the realm of what is sought to be explained. It is in this sense that the ontology is flat (DeLanda, 2002; Helle-Valle, 2010). This flatness requires that we study sociality as it flows by and attempt to explain by paying attention to action as it unfolds (and has unfolded in the past) by following actors, tracing networks and revealing assemblages (Latour, 2005), thus putting together the details in ways that give better insights into the flow of life. This does not imply that we cannot make use of terms like structure, culture and the like, but we should not use them to explain anything. As Harré formulates it, 'To collect up a set of rules and conventions as an institution is a harmless and useful classificatory device, so long as we do not slip into ascribing causal powers to it' (2009, p. 139).

The significance of this ontological point is that it has analytical implications. First, one needs to contextualise practices. It is not possible to understand an action (including utterances) without thoroughly linking it to the concrete, specific setting of which it is a part. As Malinowski formulated it, 'the conception of meaning as *contained* in an utterance is false and futile. A statement, spoken in real life, is never detached from the situation in which it has been uttered' (Malinowski, 1974, p. 307, emphasis in the original; see also Wittgenstein, 1968, §43). Secondly, if action derives its meaning from the specific setting in which it unfolds, it follows that we need to be extremely wary of generalisations. Patterns and processes found in one setting do not necessarily have relevance in another, seemingly similar situation. The concrete implication of this is the need to make 'thick descriptions' (Geertz, 1984) in order to give sense to the observations described – it is only in their embeddedness that the descriptions make sense.

This then relates to the non-media-centric approach to media-related studies as it highlights the specific setting in which media uses take place. Moreover, it requires a non-representational perspective as the significant forms of media uses we study are not about representations but as practice in themselves. And not least, the perspective demonstrates the significance of case-based studies – it is only through actual events, in their embedded complexity, that insights into the social roles of media can be revealed ('… there is science only in the particular' [Latour, 2005, p. 137]; see also Flyvbjerg, 2006).

How, then, can we make sense of a flat, complicated field of media practices? As we have already indicated, the particularity of practice requires ethnography and thick descriptions (e.g. Storm-Mathisen, 2018). However, if all we could do was tell stories of particular cases, we would not be able to compare, to generalise, or to move beyond the emic perspective. For one, to gaze beyond the particular we need facts and statistics. It is obviously of great importance that we know how large a portion of the adult population in Botswana owns a mobile phone, how many have internet access in Zambia and that perhaps the most limiting factor for Africans to access the internet is economic. This enables us to know something about the conditions in which media-related practices take place. If you cannot afford airtime, it is of no use that vital resources are available on the internet. Thus, although quantitative data from Africa (and elsewhere in the world) should be treated with the utmost scepticism (due to variable reliability), we still need this kind of information. Triangulation is thus crucial, methodological as well as analytical (Denzin, 1989). More challenging, however, is to grasp and present the various forces that are at play, from global connections to interpersonal dynamics – which of course are connected. Thus, we need to analytically unite the vast and the small in valid ways, to understand change, processes, comparison and generalisation (cf. Miller's [Borgerson and Miller, 2016] and Slater's [2013] use of the term 'scaling').

Change, Causality and Social Mechanisms

The scope of this book is to study how media and social change in Africa are connected. We hold that when something 'social' goes from one form to another, the researcher's job is to give a plausible account of how and/or why. But what constitutes an explanation is not clear. For one, the concepts (explanation, cause, understanding, etc.) are polythetic (Needham, 1975), hence not self-explanatory. For instance, the term 'explanation' conventionally refers to causes of another order and the critique is that this violates logic of scientific thought. Thus, Wittgenstein stated that we 'must do away with all *explanation*, and description alone must take its place' (1968, §109, emphasis in the original), and Latour writes that 'the opposition between description and explanation is another of these false dichotomies that should be put to rest … If a description remains in need of an explanation, it means that it is a bad description' (2005, p. 137). The dominant position among quantitatively oriented social scientists who emulate the hard sciences is to apply an analytical framework of variables (not people) and seek to arrive at explanations by testing out hypotheses that, ideally, have been posited before the research starts. A very different position is found among empirically oriented, qualitatively based researchers who strive for particularistic, thick descriptions. Here the aim is to understand and describe what takes place, not necessarily to explain. A third position is post-structuralist, discursively oriented, in which causal explanations are often non-existent, or at least well hidden. Some have even turned this into a virtue, like Jeffrey Alexander who wrote in *Handbook of Sociology* that 'sociology should pay less attention to "explanation" and more to "discourse"' (1988, cited in Hedström and Swedberg, 1996, p. 282). In all cases it can be argued that causality either represents a problem, or is more or less ignored. In the latter case, it tends to be dismissed as uninteresting, while the 'anthropologist' will argue that reality is too complex to be reduced to a set of causal elements. For variable-based research, explanation is considered important but is critiqued for either postulating correlations and suggestive causality, or – because it is quantitative and based on variables – becoming so oversimplified that it does not fit well with the realities on the ground (Hedström and Swedberg, 1998, pp. 15ff).

Thus, given our topic and our theoretical stance, we want to explain but cannot do this in the form of 'laws' or grand connections – simply because we do not believe that such compelling causality exists within the human sciences. However, changes are not haphazard: the fact that people know most of what is happening around them and have good reasons to believe that they know what will happen tomorrow is an indication that most things do in fact stay the same, and that what exists of changes does actually hold a certain predictability. Most of us take for granted that new media will develop further, and that more people will be online and that the world is overheating and will continue to do so unless some radical political efforts are implemented. But we do not know whether such policies will be implemented, nor do we know if Africa will become a better place for most to live.

Men make their own history but they do not make it just as they please (Marx, 1954, p. 10), nor do they necessarily achieve what they want. It is the same with media in Africa; their presence is the result of human action but the ways in which they are used and the effects they have on people's lives are not necessarily intended, or wished for. What happens within the field of media involves billions of people and ICT devices, hence resulting in innumerable processes and dynamics, which are impossible to unequivocally predict. However, with our ambition to provide insights into the roles that media play in a changing Africa, our theoretical perspective's prohibition to apply explanations of a vertical type, and insistence on situational particularity, we believe that an ideal explanation is an account that both makes actions understandable and seeks to suggest minute causal connections between elements within the field of practice. We suggest that the solution to this challenge is to focus on processes, that is, flows of action where a set of actions generate other actions and together form certain types of results (Storm-Mathisen, 2019). This can give a comparative and generalisable potential to our material. Processes have a universality that transcends particular practices and provides a tool for linking our ethnographies and themes in ways that enable us to paint a larger picture. We thus draw attention to the ways in which various concerns and wider dynamics intersect, and tend to generate certain outcomes (cf., e.g., Barth, 1981, pp. 77ff).

What we want to do is to combine the ambitions of the hard sciences, in terms of explanatory rigour, with the reality of the social sciences – heeding the fact that we deal with people, who are reflexive, have free will and are hence in principle unpredictable. One such approach is what is known under the term 'social mechanisms'. This sprang out of analytical sociology, a spin-off from rational choice theories and other 'hard' forms of sociology. However, it also has links to Critical Realism (Bashkar, Harré), which is rooted in much more reflexive, critical forms of philosophy like those of Bakhtin, Vygotski and Wittgenstein. Jon Elster, who is among the early advocates for social mechanism reasoning, defines it as 'frequently occurring and easily recognizable causal patterns that are triggered under generally unknown conditions or with indeterminate consequences' (2007, p. 36; see also Gross, 2009; Helle-Valle, 2019). The crucial point is that it seeks to create an ordered, realistic model of what influences what in a complex social setting by identifying some types of *causal tendencies* that we find occurring with some frequency, and identifying under what conditions the mechanisms are triggered and under what conditions they are suppressed or modified. Thus, we believe we need to discard the very idea of Covering Law types of reasoning and in its place *empirically* investigate the kinds of causal relations that actually do exist. To take an example: ICT4D and Modernisation Theory rest on ideas about causality derived from a Covering Law logic. Had the central theses in these perspectives been treated as mechanisms, not laws, it would have a lot more explanatory force. The tendency that capital generates more capital is empirically and logically a solid one, so is the assumption that ICTs are labour saving. However, the problem is that it is only under certain conditions that these mechanisms actually operate. The critiques from various strands of dependency theories are doing just that – pointing out the conditions that tend to hinder the capital-generating potential of capital. What we argue, then, is that generalisations can only be reached by investigating empirically the processes that media-related practices tend to generate – to make them explicit and analyse how different mechanisms are combined.

Our insistence on letting people's own life worlds and concerns be the starting point of research, and openly exploring the various consequences of their actions, accords well with postcolonial critiques, brought to the fore by reflections on 'theories from the south', decolonisation and indigenous knowledge (e.g. Comaroff and Comaroff, 2012; Denzin et al., 2008; Tomaselli, 2005). The perspectives vary considerably but one thing they all share is the concern for the uneven power relations between those who do the research and those who are studied. In short, conventional academia's tendency to simply reproduce images of 'the Other' and thereby reinforce the objectification and hence powerlessness of people in the Global South calls for a reconfiguration of the very practice of conducting research. Although we can in no way claim to be acquitted of such a role, we believe that this work's theoretical foundation frees us from some of the criticisms. The open, investigative, 'flat' and emic approach (cf. Tomaselli, 2005, ch. 7) is a necessary precondition for building a sound understanding of what is really going on, how sociality actually works.[9]

We are aware of our privileged position in that we have a life-long training in understanding and representing socialities and are linked to institutions and hence power structures that those we study are not. However, in our view this does not by necessity place us in an exploitative position vis-à-vis those we study. We not only hope that our specialised knowledge can be put to use for good purposes, we have also actively sought to give back in ways that we can. To concretise: we – the editors – wanted to disseminate our knowledge in useful ways to the local community in which we spent so much time. The initial idea was that we, in cooperation with local institutions, would arrange an inclusive seminar so that we could find ways to merge our expert knowledge with the villagers' expert knowledge through a dialogical process (cf. Slater, 2013). However, we found through our preparatory dialogues that it would most likely not work in the inclusive and productive ways we had envisaged. Instead, we ended up making a web page with and for the villagers about the village. It became clear that outside competence and money was needed to construct and maintain a web page.[10] Moreover, early in the process of deciding the web page's content, certain local business interests pressed for exploiting the page to their own commercial ends, detrimental to the voiced interests of most villagers.[11] We engaged in open dialogues with different villagers, and ended up using our privileged position to put our foot down on some suggestions; we had the final say on the terms of the web page. Thus, we used the power vested in our position but we believe we used it in a way to exploit what Foucault calls the productive potential of power; to use power to promote a positive sociality.

Our understanding of practice, as well as our empirically founded emphasis on the various social mechanisms that are in operation in the socialities we study, represent the foundation on which we will now seek to draw lines between the different chapters, suggesting some types of causal tendencies that can be found across space and contexts. This, then, should give some room for sensible generalisations. But first we need to give short accounts of the chapters in this book.

The Chapters

The book seeks to cover areas in people's lives that are of concern to them. Of course, with a handful of researchers and data from five different countries in Africa we can only provide samples of the highly diverse socialities that exist in these countries. Still, we believe that they reveal processes and dynamics that have relevance to more than their specific sites. We have organised the chapters along central lines of concern: economy; gender and social relations; and localities.

Chapter 1, 'Digital Development Imaginaries, Informal Business Practices and the Platformisation of Digital Technology in Zambia' by Wendy Willems, which also introduces the section on economy, attends to the relationship between ICT and economic change by looking at how informal traders in the New Soweto Market in Lusaka use their mobile phones for economic gains. She launches critical perspectives to digital imaginaries of the economic development in Africa as well as to understandings of the role of social media through the lens of users, and argues for the need to situate media practices within the systems of power of which they are part. Willems finds that simple phones, smartphones, mobile internet and social media have offered a 'number of opportunities to small-scale informal businesses' for strengthening existing networks and scaling up and developing new business networks, for instance efficient ways of communicating with customers, cheap and instant ways of sharing information with traders and quick money transfers to suppliers. However, she also identifies constraints related to the situation in the market as well as changes in the internet itself, and explains how these work as factors in a dynamic whereby these new technologies have not really transformed informal businesses in significant ways. Firstly, face-to face contact as well as building mutual trust remain important preconditions for scaling up informal business networks in this informal market. However, trust is currently hard to obtain on the social media platforms to which these vendors' internet use is constrained. Secondly, the growing platformisation of the internet in Africa constrains the development of local IT businesses, violates (mobile) net neutrality and raises concerns about threats to privacy.

In Chapter 2, 'Botswana's Digital Revolution: What's in it?' Storm-Mathisen and Helle-Valle discuss different 'scaling devices' for understanding what lies in Botswana's digital revolution: on the one hand macro-level statistical indexes about ICT and business and, on the other, how people actually engage with scaling practices and ICT devices to position themselves in business. By combining insights from quantitative and qualitative data generated through various means by the two authors during fieldwork in Gaborone and a semi-urban village in 2012, 2015–2016, 2017 and 2018, they discuss how, and the extent to which, digital tools and services can be said to have become part of Batswana's business concerns and practices. Despite a general enthusiasm and rather high investments in ICT, the authors find that its socio-economic impact remains low, and they point to how the significant digital divides, the high costs and lack of transparency are factors in a dynamic that produces this outcome.

Introducing the next section, Gender and Social Relations, Katrien Pype's, '*Bolingo ya face*: Digital Marriages, Playfulness and the Search for Change in Kinshasa' (Chapter 3) analyses uses of new media in another realm of sociality, that of dating, romance, sex and matrimony among independent women in Kinshasa. Pype centres on one case – Flavie, a single mother – and describes how her clever, strategic uses of social media have set off a new rhythm in exchanges of affect. Marrying a wealthy man is the ultimate goal but she makes sure that the relationships she engages in will provide monetary returns along the way. Depicting how Flavie uses more than one smartphone and plays with alter egos online, Pype exemplifies activities that aim at enhancing social connectivity, and how communicating in social media requires situated knowledge and different tactics at various stages to gain attention, affect and money from these partners. She argues that notions of work and play better describe these digital performances than ideas of offline vs. online, for two reasons. The ultimate goal of the digital play is the realisation of corporeal relationships, hence the off- and online practices most often are deeply intertwined. Secondly, the terms 'play' and 'work' fit into emic categories of how courting should be finalised into a legally binding relationship. Thus, although Pype highlights the increased responsibility of the individual in urban space, it shows how new media practices fit into and symbolically interact with local (offline) conventions related to sexual relationships.

In Chapter 4, 'Texting Like a State: Knowledge and Change in a National mHealth Programme', Nanna Schneidermann describes and analyses the first national m-health (mobile health) programme in Africa, MomConnect. MomConnect is a free text message broadcast of information by the state to expecting mothers. These mothers receive weekly messages from week five in their pregnancy through to the first year after birth. Although MomConnect can be received on simple phones, the assemblage of actors and technology is complex: phones, computers, databases, representatives of the state apparatus, developers, clinic personnel and not least expecting mothers. Schneidermann critically discusses this intervention from 'different sites': the state, midwives and nurses at clinics, the pregnant mothers, and researchers and politicians. She finds that MomConnect is understood in contrasting ways by different actors. The state and the developers see it as a tool to overcome barriers to health care access and ensure citizen rights; by engaging pregnant women in 'direct conversation', they hope to produce good mothers. Clinic workers partly share this view, but in a situation of understaffing they also judge it as a stress producer. As for the expecting mothers, they respond positively in questionnaires but the fact is that very few use it. Schneidermann points to a number of elements that constrain the intended effects and argues that the intention was never a simple 'transfer of information', but rather to effectively govern the relations between the state and the individual.

The book's Chapter 5, 'New Ways of Making Ends Meet? On Batswana Women, Their Uses of the Mobile Phone – and Connections through Education', Ardis Storm-Mathisen discusses how the mobile phone has entered into the dynamics that create different economic situations for women in Botswana. Drawing on nine months of fieldwork (2015–2017) in the Kalahari village locality and in the capital Gaborone, she focuses on women of different generations and uses three exemplary cases to illustrate how mobile phone use is connected to everyday concerns and life situations. She finds that whereas all three women have increased their use of the mobile phone over the years, and that their different socio-economic frameworks – with education as a core factor – have a strong effect on their use, their mobile phone-related practices have not significantly changed their ways of earning money. These women's uses of their mobile phones (even the simplest kind) nevertheless have a socio-economic impact because they have enabled changes in the ways in which they deal with their concerns. This impact is most significant in that they enable new forms of multitasking. For instance, the ability to cater for children and kin while working elsewhere is made much easier with social media. Changes in women's communication strategies are not only linked to new technologies in themselves, or to changes in their socio-economic situations, but are part of complex dynamics where changing constellations of mobility, new ways of building and upholding social capital and education are important factors.

The section on Localities and New Media starts with 'The Public Inside Out: Facebook, Community and Banal Activism in a Cape Town Suburb' (Chapter 6) by Nanna Schneidermann. She describes how social media are used to construct the space between the private and the public in a relatively wealthy coastal suburb of Cape Town, a city characterised by extreme inequality and spatial segregation. Schneidermann's empirical focus is a Facebook group 'Muizenberg Notice Board', an online 'community' of seven thousand members. She explores the banal online activism of community-making through practices of sharing and boundary-drawing in this group and highlights three cases to demonstrate how unremarkable events become the basis for mobilising and contesting ideas about 'community': litter in public spaces; petty crime; and unaccompanied children in public spaces. She finds that personal experiences and emotions of residents in the Muizenberg area were at the centre of all three cases. She argues that although their mediated context ties in with globally circulated media forms, they are rooted in and given meaning by the specific context of post-apartheid South Africa, where affect and subjectivity dominate the forms that public expression takes, perhaps as a reaction to the apartheid regime where individuality of the self was denied by racial categories. Moreover, she argues that the concept of community in the Muizenberg Notice Board group and the unquestionable objective of wanting to have a 'community' puts at stake the violent ways in which the city continues to be racially, economically and socially divided. Thus, Schneidermann's contribution is a case of wider currents of turning the private and the public inside out in the political realms of the New South Africa.

In Chapter 7, 'From No Media to All Media: Domesticating New Media in a Kalahari Village', Jo Helle-Valle applies insights from fieldwork in one village in the Botswana part of the Kalahari over a period of almost three decades, to focus on changes that have taken place, and discusses the ways in which the media revolution has played a part in these transformations. In short, he finds that new media have indeed changed sociality in many ways – for instance, how people keep up relations to kin and important others, how funerals are conducted and how cows are surveyed. However, Helle-Valle argues that the social impact of people's new media use is less than the ubiquitousness of media ownership suggests. One reason for this is that media use is highly skewed in relation to age and economic standing, another that institutions in the village have so far not been able to utilise opportunities that are supposed to be available. Concerns and perspectives have shown little change and new media seem to have made a difference only within some areas of village life.

In the book's Afterword – 'The Electronic Media in Africa, with an Addendum from Mauritius' – Thomas Hylland Eriksen takes a bird's-eye perspective on the questions the book asks, with a view from the African multi-ethnic island state and small-scale society of Mauritius. He argues that it is obvious that the mobile phone and internet have transformed everyday life for those who can use them, but that it is equally obvious that the great disparities with respect to conditions for use in different places contribute to how these changes take place. Eriksen highlights six structural features of particular relevance to Africa: scarcity of money; weak states; recent but very rapid new media uptake; the significance of the informal sector; distinct and unpredictable uses; and distinct imaginaries and public controversies. According to Eriksen, Mauritius is different from mainland Africa on most features. Firstly, Mauritius 'has always been modern' – it was from the outset a multicultural and global place, it is a relatively wealthy society and the political system shows little resemblance to mainland Africa. Still, the national dream of turning the country into a knowledge economy remains only a dream. Secondly, Eriksen highlights ethnic vs. non-ethnic life worlds as a central tension Mauritians have to negotiate as they navigate their practical challenges of the everyday. He finds that the ways in which Mauritians use the internet strengthen rather than weaken Mauritian identity. The reason for this is that online activities facilitate shared conversations and negotiations about common concerns and group identity across previously separated social and economic boundaries. Nonetheless, kinship has remained important as an organising principle, both in practical matters and in relation to identity. Eriksen argues that new media have entered into this in both transformative and conserving ways. They offer new possibilities for Mauritians to discover their Mauritianness and to be cosmopolitan and inclusive online, but also strengthen the communality in everyday life where crucial resources continue to flow through kin and ethnic networks. Thus, new media offer new possible identifications and ways of transcending time and space so that people can secure their sense of belonging in a complex society by being both cosmopolitan online and communally oriented in the practicalities of the everyday. However, as Eriksen notes, for new identities to be societally important and transformative, the structural arrangements of society will also have to change, which has not yet happened.

Syntheses

A core quality of new media is that they transmit information faster and in more massive and efficient ways than before. People can be reached almost any time and anywhere, people can talk, texts and pictures can be sent, any kind of information can be accessed, people and things can be traced. Thus, it is within connectivity that new media make a difference. This explains why we find in all our research that they affect relationships between people – they simply revolutionise the ways in which people relate to each other. However, how new media are used, by whom and with what effects differs enormously. This diversity can – to some extent – be coupled to differences in competence, concerns, wealth and opportunities in various aspects of life. Still, irrespective of their social position, people try to make the best out of what they have, including new media. Thus, media's quality as a connector and people's (more or less) strategic mind-set mean that the term 'social capital' is especially relevant. Capital is accumulated labour, which has the capacity to produce profits. According to Bourdieu, it is 'impossible to account for the structure and functioning of the social world unless one reintroduces capital in all its forms' (1986, p. 242) because the unequal distribution of it fundamentally structures society. His main contribution to the understanding of capital, and its application in the social sciences, is that it takes many forms; economic capital is only one – albeit in one sense the most important one (ibid., p. 252). It is only when we acknowledge the other forms that we can fully understand the ways in which capital works. Bourdieu singles out economic, cultural and social capital as the main forms. Cultural capital is mainly tied to education (in its widest sense) while social capital is defined as 'the actual or potential resources which are linked to possession of a durable network of more or less institutionalized relationships' (ibid., p. 248). However, people cannot live on relationships and education alone, and the crucial issue is how the different forms of capital can be converted into each other. Herein lies the dynamic and processual quality. On the one hand, different forms of capital tend to reinforce each other; much of one tends to generate more of the others. This works in all directions. There are, on the other hand, obstacles to capital conversions. Successful conversions require competence and resources. Thus, the crucial issue in respect to this book's theme (and the fact that most people lack money) is how people are able to convert the (potential for increased) social capital that comes with new media into economic advantages. All the chapters in this book can (but need not) be seen in this perspective.

For instance, in Chapter 3 Pype uses Flavie, a single mother of three, as a paradigmatic case to reveal the dynamics of 'romance' among independent women in Kinshasa, and the role of social media in these processes. Facebook and other social platforms provide her with new opportunities for getting in contact with men. While pre-social media required face-to-face contact, she can now use social media to establish contact with prospective lovers. It requires skills – not significantly different from those needed in face-to-face encounters, but other skills nonetheless – in balancing a romantic exclusivity on the face of it and at the same time keeping her suitors in ignorance of each other. Obviously, this is an exemplary case of the uses of social capital. Flavie's main aim is to turn her social capital (her network of potential sexual partners) into economic capital – either by marrying a wealthy man or at least by insisting that her lovers be generous.

The parallels to our work in Botswana are striking: the same sexual networking, the same strategic uses of social media and the same concerns about balancing the instrumental and emotional aspects of these relationships. However, there are some notable differences. While Flavie's long-term strategy is to find a husband, the independent women in Botswana have options that their Congolese counterparts lack. Botswana is a wealthier country than DRC, resulting in a net immigration to the country. Thus, the ideal partner in Botswana is not an expat but a local resident. Of greater significance, however, is that because Botswana has a functioning welfare system (albeit very modest compared to Europe), including social security, student grants, government schemes and so on, the risks associated with living as a single woman are bigger in DRC than they are in Botswana. This explains that while Flavie's expressed goal is to find a husband, her Botswana counterpart does not necessarily see this as the ultimate goal. In fact, with the security net in place, pursuing a strategy of establishing her own household, with children but no man, is a realistic and, for many, the preferred choice for Botswana women. Most consider men to be inherently unreliable and prone to adultery and therefore argue that it is better to keep men as generous lovers than cheating husbands (Helle-Valle, 1999, 2004). Their social environment makes the risks smaller, as there are ways to be taken care of in case their choices turn out to be unsuccessful. This is a major factor in explaining that while in DRC we find that 25 per cent of households are female headed (DRC Health Survey, 2014), the number in Botswana is strikingly high – approximately 50 per cent (Statistics Botswana, 2018).

Another point that can be made by comparing romancing of this sort in DRC and Botswana is that it might be argued that new media do not in fact make a big difference. For one, the practice of sexual networking was commonplace thirty years ago (cf. also Cohen, 1969 for similar practices in Nigeria more than fifty years ago) and the same strategies were applied, but of course without social media. Given that the gross number of sexual relationships has not increased significantly due to social media – which there is no reason to believe – the net effect is that the women are forced to purchase smartphones and buy airtime in order to keep up in the race to find men. In economic terms, what has happened is that although the 'production level' remains the same, the costs of entering the game have increased. Thus, although new media have become a necessary and conspicuous part of a field of practice, their effect on the outcome can be close to none. Of course, new vulnerabilities emerge and dynamics are altered, but it illustrates what we consider an important warning when studying the significance of media on African sociality: it is important not to confuse a conspicuous presence with assumptions about its significance for changing sociality. The latter is something that needs to be empirically investigated, not taken for granted.

A striking issue in Flavie's dealings is trust. She can certainly not take promises made by romantic partners at face value, but the game she plays implies deceit also on her part. The language game of romance requires her to present her relationship with a man as special and exclusive while the fact is that most of the time she is involved with several men simultaneously. Thus, the field of practice she engages in is generally associated with extremely low levels of trust. The issue of trust reappears as central in several of the other chapters as well. For instance, Willems describes in her chapter how mobile phones were made part of the business practices of the informal vendors in the Soweto Market. The vendors' various uses of the mobile phone strengthened their existing business networks as they made communication between customers and suppliers more efficient. This effect was, however, restricted to those relationships where mutual trust had already been established offline. Their uses of new media had not substantially helped to scale up their business networks for economic benefit. What was a concern for these vendors were the risks involved with trust in business relations. If they were to send goods to a customer or send money to a supplier, they had to be quite certain that they would receive the requested money or goods in return, otherwise they risked losing money rather than earning it. Thus, to be successful in using mobile communication in business, beyond just using it to inform or chase customers, trust was a necessary precondition. Many informal vendors therefore refrained from doing this unless they had first established mutual trust through face-to-face encounters. This is also why many of the informal vendors in the Soweto Market did not trust the opportunities offered on online platforms such as buy-and-sell Facebook groups, even though these in many ways mirrored the informality and lack of regulation of their local market. Despite the opportunities for finding customers more easily, for selling a particular item or finding goods otherwise difficult to obtain, their concern with relationships established through these platforms was that they were dealing with strangers, thus more risky relations. Their fears stretched from cybercrime to that of getting into trouble with the police for dubious origins of goods to that of transferring money to strangers. Thus, although the use of digital media had introduced a positive change, reducing travel and transactional costs for the vendors, their lack of trust in relations established through digital platforms constrained their use of these platforms to expand their business networks and improve economic outcomes.

Several of the book's chapters also illustrate that processes of building trust vary with the types of networks in question, who are connected and how. Some networks are open (buy-and-sell), some are closed to non-members (Facebook groups), and the digital competence of the given actor and digital divides among members in the networks are factors in how trust is dealt with and thus the outcomes of the network. The type of network Pype describes in her chapter is built by a private actor. Flavie uses the opportunities offered by digital media tools and networks as a private person to establish social contacts for her own concern, to better her chances of meeting men who can help support her family. Flavie's engagements here are time-consuming but it helps her to establish new particular relations to particular persons, and to establish a network that she can seek to activate to convert to economic capital in times of need. The maximum variation of this example in this book of a network of scale and scope is the one the South African state seeks to build through MomConnect (Schneidermann's chapter) or the Radio Frequency Identification (RFID)-based network of cattle and cattle owners in Botswana (Helle-Valle's chapter), and there are many other types of networks on this private–public continuum. Schneidermann describes for instance how the Muizenberg Notice Board on Facebook creates a novel kind of space for people with shared (political) concerns in a community, whereas Eriksen describes how blogs create spaces for negotiating cultural and national identity in Mauritius. The assemblages that are built in these different networks and the intended and actual outcomes of them are very different. In the MomConnect case, the motivation of the state is clearly linked to bio power (Foucault), to change the behaviour of expecting mothers for better child–mother health (and to reduce societal costs in this respect). The state has engaged developers to build a system for this purpose, a system to which expecting mothers are to subscribe to receive one-way SMS messages with what the state defines as relevant educational information (although there is a feedback loop).

The information that the mothers receive is controlled and mass communicated by the state as sender (unlike Flavie, who controls but customises), and it is also a system that allows the state to survey users and harvest data from them. Flavie is not able to connect to all the men she contacts, and far from all her contacts become a source of income for her, but some do, hence she is able to convert some of this social capital to economic capital, enough to send her children to school. In the case of MomConnect, the main problem is similar; not all women subscribe, and those who do and who receive the messages do not always find it useful. In fact, many do not find it useful at all, partly because they read the information through the voice of the person who made them subscribe (the care workers) and partly because the information does not connect to their main concerns with survival (cf. Callon, 1986). The intended conversion of the social capital collected through the network created by MomConnect to the expected socio-economic beneficial outcomes does not happen because the state has not managed to make their own concerns relevant to the mothers. Thus, the mothers are functionally unconnected (even though some data are harvested from them). This then highlights the fact that very different actors with different concerns, motivations and power to control others engage in activities to establish new connections with the help of rather similar digital technologies (i.e. messaging services). Whereas the connections are established by a shared interest/concern in the case of Flavie, it is less shared and disrupted by diverging interests in the case of MomConnect.

What we have done so far in this section is to point to important processes and dynamics that we find are in operation across sites and countries. This does not provide an overview in the sense that we can present clear, general answers to the question of the relationship between media and social change. However, we believe that this strategy points to some social mechanisms that are in operation and thus gives a better understanding of the issue, and provides explanations for the diverse and seemingly chaotic landscape of media practices. The cases are of course grossly simplified, as real life is extremely complicated. Let us therefore provide some suggestions for how these various mechanisms can be combined. Chapter 7 provides an example of composite media-related practices. Funeral processes in the Kalahari village have indeed been affected by new media, but in unpredictable ways. On the one hand, increased accessibility has reduced the time needed to gather relatives for the burial. This could have generated faster, cheaper funerals. However, changing expectations about what a proper funeral should be, partly triggered by the massive presence of social media, have had the opposite effect.[12] More expensive, almost lavish rituals are now the rule, and improved connectivity has led more people to attend. We find the same mechanisms at work in weddings. Today, getting 'properly' married puts many couples in debt, which can take many years to repay (van Dijk, 2017). Another example is the complicated assemblages around cattle in Botswana. This involves relationships that range from man vs. beast – which can be very close and emotional – via state-driven, new media-linked systems that include RFID-tagging and surveillance of vaccination, to global production networks involving the EU. The network of relationships can be described as a success, also because it includes the unanticipated effect that cattle thefts have been dramatically reduced.

To sum up so far: social capital is indeed central – all the chapters bear witness to that. However, it is not the only form relevant in relation to media. New media are highly relevant in relation to cultural capital – that is, various forms of formal and informal education. Most important is the fact that most young Africans get their introduction to and education in using new media through schools. To the extent the infrastructure is there, and working, ICT is an integral part of education in most African countries. Moreover, as Storm-Mathisen highlights in Chapter 5, access to social networks acquired from schooling is used in peer relationships, further improving their competence to exploit life opportunities, including those that are digital. In addition, it seems that such competence is highly valued among youth all over Africa. Thus, a premise for developing and realising the potential for a digital future is to be found in the young's cultural capital (education).

The chapters in this book have concentrated on the everyday, the nitty gritty of everyday life. This is what we can say something about with a degree of certainty. However, the topic of change and media in Africa also requires a look at the most important form of capital – the economic. Economic concerns are directly or indirectly a theme in all the chapters, simply because they are among the most pressing needs faced by many Africans. However, we find that the link between new media and economic concerns mostly goes through social capital, whereas education (cultural capital) most often serves as a premise for realising the connection between social and economic capital (cf., e.g., Chapter 5 in this book). Therefore, we also need to look at the economic sector in order to get the bigger picture. Are there signs of a developing ICT production sector? Or e-commerce? Simply stated: is the continent turning into a knowledge economy?

For this we need to turn to other researchers' work. Murphy and Carmody's book *Africa's Information Revolution* (2015) is in this respect a valuable source. They have studied small, medium and micro-scale enterprises (SMME) in Tanzania and South Africa. Their findings are not good news. They contend that, 'While the social implications of ICTs are arguably disruptive and transformational … their mere diffusion is not resulting in the creation of a knowledge economy in Africa. Instead, our findings indicate that sub-Saharan Africa is becoming an informationalized agrarian and resource-extractive economic region' (ibid., p. 210). According to them, the main reason for this is that the ICT revolution happens within a continued structural inequality that reproduces unequal global positions. The initiatives that institutions like ICT4D and the World Bank support do nothing to rectify the fundamental, structural impediments to sustainable development. Murphy and Carmody distinguish between imminent development – the intended policy-related measures taken by governments and NGOs – and immanent development, which refers to the structural inequalities generated by global production networks (i.e. world capitalism). 'All told, our analysis details how new ICTs do not obliterate the (immanent) structural constraints or factors accompanying a political economy of neoliberalism, but are instead absorbed into this context in ways that selectively rework extant economic regimes and patterns of uneven development' (ibid., p. xxviii). Their gloomy prediction for Africa's future is that 'the particular path [to modernity] being followed across Africa will not, it appears, lead it to the type and level of development of Europe or North America. This raises the key questions about who benefits from the celebratory "rising" discourse, and how mainstream ICT4D initiatives are implicated in the reproduction of these immanent [structural] conditions' (ibid., p. 208).

This perspective resonates well with our own experiences. The ordinary Zambian and South African, not to mention those living in DRC, see no visible effect on their own economic situation. Even Botswana, despite the state's wealth and its grand plans to initiate a turn towards a knowledge economy (Carmody, 2013), has not succeeded. As Storm-Mathisen and Helle-Valle's chapter demonstrates, Botswana shows no clear signs of changing its economy from depending on mineral resources to a diversified economy.

Lastly, we need also to consider the other big area of potential for the large institutions – namely the possibility for increased efficiency in bureaucratic institutions. It seems that within this area a lot more has happened. The ICT-ification of administration and politics seems to have come a long way, although there is uneven development and a huge gap between plans and reports on the one hand and reality on the other. These sectors are much more responsive to imminent initiatives as they depend to a lesser extent on global inequality structures. Still, as Storm-Mathisen and Helle-Valle in Chapter 2 and Scheidermann in Chapter 4 demonstrate, the implementation of digital systems, and their effects, often suffers from structural and competence-related hindrances (Botswana) and a class- and race-divided society (South Africa), which complicates the cooperation between state agencies and ordinary citizens.

To return to the initial research question about the relationship between new media and development in Africa: we cannot give a clear and simple answer. Not because we haven't done our job as researchers (although we would have been able to open up a lot more black boxes if we had more funding and more time). The reasons are many. For one, and most importantly, the field Africa + media + development is so immensely complex and heterogeneous that an answer simply cannot be given. What happens in Kenya is very different from what happens in DR Congo – for many reasons, linked to history, wealth, governance and so on – not to mention Egypt or Mauritius. Secondly, our theoretical perspective precludes from the very beginning the possibility of arriving at one answer. Different people live different lives in different ways, leading to media playing different roles in different socialities. In fact, media is not one thing. By that we do not mean that there are different ICTs and different devices and platforms, but that since media play such different roles in different settings it is highly questionable even to give these technology-linked practices a common term (see also Slater, 2013, p. 18).

Nonetheless, we believe that asking these impossible questions is the right thing to do. Although we have no possibility of giving definitive answers, we still do important things. First, we focus our research on an issue that no one doubts is extremely important. Although we cannot know exactly how new media and development in Africa are connected, we know that there is some connection – if for no other reason than the fact that new media (i.e. mobile phones) have become a ubiquitous part of almost all African sociality. Thus, it cannot be of no importance. Secondly, although we can never reach the finishing line in this race for understanding – also because the field itself is rapidly changing – it is the collective effort of researchers from different parts of the world, from different academic perspectives and with different research questions (related to media and development) that will give us an ever better understanding of this extremely important arena in which people, technologies and places meet and make new things happen.

This book is our contribution to this vast narrative.

Acknowledgements

The research was funded by the New Media Practices in a Changing Africa project, financed by the Research Council of Norway (grant no. FriPro 240714).

Jo Helle-Valle is a social anthropologist and Professor in the Development Studies Department at Oslo Metropolitan University. He has carried out fieldwork in Botswana, Uganda, Ethiopia and Norway. His main research areas are media practices, gender, local politics and economy, and theoretical issues related to the social sciences. Helle-Valle has served as a Visiting Scholar at Harvard, Oxford, Simon Fraser University, the University of Botswana and Makerere University. He has published in journals such as *Journal of African Media Studies, Africa, Ethnos, History and Anthropology* and *New Media & Society*.

Ardis Storm-Mathisen is Research Professor at Consumption Research Norway and Faculty of Education, Oslo Metropolitan University. Her research has focused on issues of gender, identity and vulnerability among children, youth and families in relation to their everyday, digital media-related practices, currently as Principal Investigator for Relink (Building resilient households through interdisciplinary and multi-level exploration and intervention), a project funded by the Research Council of Norway. She conducted fieldwork in Botswana between 2015 and 2018, giving special attention to gender relations and the lives of the young. During this research she was affiliated to the Centre for Gender Research, University of Oslo as a senior researcher and a visiting researcher at the University of Botswana.

Notes

1. Many claim, however, that this conclusion was at best a half-truth. As Morten Jerven writes, 'The marked improvement we see in the GDP time studies in the mid-1990s was driven by … adding the informal sector and the service sector to the old estimates' (Jerven, 2005, pp. 112–13). Still, most economists still claim that there has been a marked economic growth in most of Africa in the last two decades, a view that is expressed in numerous publications from the World Bank.
2. The IDI index is built from measures on variables in three sub-indexes: ICT access, ICT use and ICT skills, https://www.itu.int/en/ITU-D/Statistics/Pages/publications/misr2018.aspx (last accessed 7 October 2019).
3. The African average IDI value in 2017 was only 2.64 points, compared to the global average of 5.11. Mauritius was the only African country that ranked in

the upper half of the global IDI distribution (global rank 72, value 5.88), while the majority of African countries fell into the lowest. Among the countries we look at here, South Africa ranked third in the region (global rank 92), Botswana fifth (global rank 105), Zambia seventeenth (global rank 146) and DR Congo thirty-third (global rank 171). Furthermore, among these only Mauritius and Zambia have recently been climbing on the index. In more concrete terms, while 61 per cent of households in Mauritius have access to computers, the comparable figures are 28 per cent in Botswana, 24 per cent in South Africa, 8 per cent in Zambia and merely 2.7 per cent in DR Congo. And whereas more than half of the population in Mauritius and South Africa are internet users and 39 per cent in Botswana, only 25.5 per cent are so in Zambia and as few as 6 per cent in DRC.

4. The NRI index consists of variables in four sub-indexes: environment, readiness, usage and impact (economic and social). In terms of socio-economic impact of ICTs, Mauritius again performs best (rank 67, value 3.7) followed by South Africa (rank 93, value 3.4), Botswana (rank 108, value 3.1) and Zambia (rank 113, value 3.0), whereas there are no available data on DR Congo (WEF, 2016, p. 20).
5. A quick word on terminology. ICT, media, new media, social media, digital media, electronic media … . As we say in Norway: a loved child has many names. Our stance is that sticking to one term reflects a misconceived precision. Tendentially, ICT points to the material and technological aspect while media focus on content. However, they are sometimes used interchangeably (e.g. Vokes, 2018a) as one often has both the material and the content in mind. As to 'social', 'digital' and 'new', we use the terms that we find most relevant. Thus, in highlighting the dialogical quality of a mediated communication it is natural to use 'social media', and when pointing to the vastness and speed of communication 'digital' is a more fitting word. The 'new' prefix is used when the contrast between the media landscape before and after the advent of mobile phones and the internet is the main issue.
6. We here use ICT4D as a cover term for various media or communication for development approaches including M4D and ComDev.
7. However, even if placing people centre stage has been the conventional methodological strategy, the analytical approach varied a lot more (e.g. structuralism and functionalism that placed society, not persons, in the centre of attention). All this being said, the sensible approach should of course be to look at both artefacts and persons, and focus on the interactions between them. Bruno Latour (2005), who insists that the two – as actants and actors respectively – must be analytically symmetrical, brings this to its logical end-point.
8. '… The social has never explained anything: the social has to be explained instead' (Latour, 2005, p. 97); '… society is the consequence of associations and not their cause. … [The] social is not a place, a thing, a domain, or a kind of stuff but a provisional movement of new associations' (ibid., p. 238).
9. Comaroff and Comaroff (2012, pp. 12ff) highlight the productive aspect of the view 'from the South': that the position from the underbelly of capitalism and hegemony holds the potential for new, creative perspectives (cf. also Nyamnjoh and Brudvig, 2016). By letting the voices of ordinary Africans play a significant part in our research, we believe that other, new perspectives can emerge.

10. For the outcome of this process – which was crafted by web designer Niels Theissen – go to www.letlhakeng.com.
11. This fact well illustrates the problems associated with the tendency of some to essentialise 'indigenous knowledge' (cf., e.g., Denzin et al., 2008). As in all socialities, people are differently positioned, have different concerns and life trajectories, and hence also have different 'knowledges' – however local they are.
12. See Vokes (2018b) for similar, yet different mechanisms associated with funerals in Uganda.

References

Alasuutari, P. 1999. 'Introduction: Three Phases of Reception Studies', in P. Alasuutari (ed.), *Rethinking the Media Audience: The New Agenda.* London: Sage Publications, pp. 1–21.

Amankwah-Amoah, J. 2019. 'Technological Revolution, Sustainability, and Development in Africa: Overview, Emerging Issues, and Challenges', *Sustainable Development* 27(3): 1–13.

Appadurai, A. 1986. *The Social Life of Things.* Cambridge: Cambridge University Press.

Barth, F. 1981. *Process and Form in Social Life: Selected Essays of Fredrik Barth.* London: Routledge & Kegan Paul.

Borgerson, J., and D. Miller. 2016. 'Scalable Sociality and "How the World Changed Social Media": Conversation with Daniel Miller', *Consumption Markets & Culture* 19(6): 520–33.

Bourdieu, P. 1977. *Outline of a Theory of Practice.* Cambridge: Cambridge University Press.

———. 1986. 'The Forms of Capital', in J. Richardson (ed.), *Handbook of Theory and Research for the Sociology of Education.* Westport, CT: Greenwood, pp. 241–58.

Brinkman, I., and M. de Bruijne. 2018. 'Mobile Phones in Mobile Margins: Communication, Mobility and Social Hierarchies in/from Africa', in B. Mutsvairo (ed.), *Palgrave Handbook for Media and Communications Research in Africa.* Basingstoke: Palgrave Macmillan, pp. 225–41.

Bryant, L. 2011. 'A Logic of Multiplicities: Deleuze, Immanence, and Onticology', *Analecta Hermeneutica* 3: 1–20.

Callon, M. 1986. 'Some Elements of a Sociology of Translation: Domestication of the Scallops and the Fishermen of St Brieuc Bay', in J. Law (ed.), *Power, Action and Belief: A New Sociology of Knowledge?* London: Routledge, pp. 196–223.

Carmody, P. 2013. 'A Knowledge Economy or an Information Society in Africa? Thintegration and the Mobile Phone Revolution', *Information Technology for Development* 19(1): 24–39.

Cohen, A. 1969. *Custom & Politics in Urban Africa: A Study of Hausa Migrants in Yoruba Towns.* London: Routledge & Kegan Paul.

Comaroff, J., and J.L. Comaroff. 2012. *Theory from the South: Or, How Euro-America is Evolving toward Africa.* Boulder, CO: Paradigm Publishers.

Couldry, N., and A. Hepp. 2017. *The Mediated Construction of Reality.* Cambridge: Polity Press.

DeLanda, M. 2002. *Intensive Science and Virtual Philosophy.* London: Bloomsbury.

———. 2006. *A New Philosophy of Society: Assemblage Theory and Social Complexity.* London: Bloomsbury.

Denzin, N. 1989. *The Research Act: A Theoretical Introduction to Sociological Methods.* Englewood Cliffs, NJ: Prentice Hall.

Denzin, N., Y. Lincoln and L. Smith. 2008. *Handbook of Critical and Indigenous Methodologies.* Thousand Oaks, CA: Sage Publications.

DRC Health Survey. 2014. *Key Findings.* Rockville: MPSMRM, MSP and ICF International.

Elster, J. 2007. *Explaining Social Behaviour.* Cambridge: Cambridge University Press.

Flyvbjerg, B. 2006. 'Five Misunderstandings about Case-Study Research', *Qualitative Inquiry* 12(2): 219–45.

Geertz, C. 1984. '"From the Native's Point of View": On the Nature of Anthropological Understanding', in R.A. Schweder and R.A. Levine (eds), *Culture Theory: Essays on Mind, Self, and Emotions.* Cambridge: Cambridge University Press.

Gross, N. 2009. 'A Pragmatist Theory of Social Mechanisms', *American Sociological Review* 74(3): 358–79.

GSMA. 2012.. *Sub-Saharan Africa Mobile Observatory 2012.* London: Deloitte LLP, https://www.gsma.com/publicpolicy/wp-content/uploads/2013/01/gsma_ssamo_full_web_11_12-1.pdf (accessed 11 October 2019).

Hall, S. 1980. 'Encoding/Decoding', in *Culture, Media, Language: Working Papers in Cultural Studies.* London: Hutchinson, pp. 128–38.

Harré, R. 2009. 'Saving Critical Realism', *Journal for the Theory of Social Behaviour* 39(2): 129–43.

Hedström, P., and R. Swedberg. 1996. 'Social Mechanisms', *Acta Sociologica* 39(3): 281–308.

———. 1998. 'Social Mechanisms: An Introductory Essay', in P. Hedström and R. Swedberg (eds), *Social Mechanisms: An Analytical Approach to Social Theory.* Cambridge: Cambridge University Press, pp. 1–31.

Helle-Valle, J. 1997. *Change and Diversity in a Kgalagadi Village, Botswana.* Oslo: SUM, University of Oslo.

———. 1999. 'Sexual Mores, Promiscuity and "Prostitution" in Botswana', *Ethnos* 64(3–4): 372–96.

———. 2004. 'Understanding Sexuality in Africa: Diversity and Contextualised Dividuality', in S. Arnfred (ed.), *Re-thinking Sexualities in Africa.* Uppsala: NAI, pp. 195–207.

———. 2010. 'Language-Games, In/dividuals and Media Uses: What a Practice Perspective Should Imply for Media Studies', in B. Bräuchler and J. Postill (eds), *Theorising Media and Practice.* Oxford: Berghahn Books, pp. 191–211.

———. 2017. 'Media Culture in Africa? A Practice-Ethnographic Approach', in Wendy Willems and Winston Mano (eds), *Everyday Media Culture in Africa: Audiences and Users.* London: Routledge.

———. 2019. 'Advocating Causal Analyses of Media and Social Change by Way of Social Mechanisms'. *Journal of African Media Studies* 11(2): 143–161.

Hempel, C.G. 1966. *Philosophy of Natural Science.* Englewood Cliffs, NJ: Prentice-Hall.

ITU [International Telecommunications Union]. 2017. *Measuring the Information Society Report 2017 Vol. 1.* Geneva: International Telecommunications Union.

Jerven, M. 2005. *Africa Growing? Past, Present and Future.* European Union Institute for Security Studies (EUISS) no. 13, April 2017, https://www.iss.europa.eu/sites/default/files/EUISSFiles/Brief_13_African_economies.pdf (accessed 21 April 2017).

———. 2015. *Africa: Why Economists Get It Wrong.* London: Zed Books.

Latour, B. 2005. *Reassembling the Social: An Introduction to Actor-Network-Theory.* Oxford: Oxford University Press.

Malinowski, B. 1974 [1923]. 'The Problem of Meaning in Primitive Languages. Supplement 1', in C.K. Ogden and I.A. Richards: *The Meaning of Meaning: A Study of the Influence of Language upon Thought and of the Science of Symbolism. (With Supplementary Essays by B. Malinowski and F.G. Crookshank).* 8th edn. New York: Harcourt, Brace & World.

Marx, K. 1954. *The Eighteenth Brumaire of Louis Bonaparte.* 3rd rev. ed. London: Lawrence & Wishart.

Miller, D., E. Costa, N. Haynes, T. McDonald, R. Nicolescu, J. Sinanan, J. Spyer, S. Venkatraman and W. Wang. 2016. *How the World Changed Social Media.* London: UCL Press.

Moores, S. 2018. *Digital Orientations: Non-Media-Centric Media Studies and Non-Representational Theories of Practice.* New York: Peter Lang.

Morley, D. 2009. 'For a Materialist, Non-Media-Centric Media Studies', *Television & New Media* 10(1): 114–16.

Murphy, J.T. and P. Carmody. 2015. *Africa's Information Revolution: Technical Regimes and Production Networks in South Africa and Tanzania.* Chichester: Wiley Blackwell.

Needham, R. 1975. 'Polythetic Classification: Convergence and Consequences', *Man* 10(3): 349–69.

Nyamnjoh, F., and I. Brudvig. 2016. 'Mobilities, ICTs and Marginality in Africa: South Africa in Comparative Perspective', in F. Nyamnjoh (ed.), *Mobilities, ICTs and Marginality in Africa.* Cape Town: HSRC Press, pp. 1–18.

Ojo, T. 2018. 'Political Economy of ICT4D and Africa', in J. Cervaes (ed.), *Handbook of Communication for Development and Social Change.* Singapore: Springer Nature Singapore, pp. 1–13.

Postill, J. 2010. 'Introduction: Theorising Media and Practice', in B. Bräuchler and J. Postill (eds), *Theorising Media and Practice.* Oxford: Berghahn Books, pp. 191–211.

Reckwitz, A. 2002. 'Toward a Theory of Social Practices: A Development in Culturalist Theorizing', *European Journal of Social Theory* 5(2): 243–63.

Schatzki, T. 2002. *The Site of the Social: A Philosophical Account of the Constitution of Social Life and Change.* University Park: Pennsylvania State University Press.

Silverstone, R., and D. Hirsch (eds). 1992. *Consuming Technologies: Media and Information in Domestic Spaces.* London: Routledge.

Slater, D. 2013. *New Media, Development & Globalisation.* Cambridge: Polity Press.

Statistics Botswana. 2018. *Botswana Multi-Topic Household Survey 2015/16.* Gaborone: Government Printer.

Storm-Mathisen, A. 2018. 'Visual Methods in Ethnographic Fieldwork: On Learning from Participants through their Video-Accounts', *Forum for Development Studies* 45(2): 261–86.

———. 2019. 'New Media Use among Young Batswana: On Concerns, Consequences and the Educational Factor', *Journal of African Media Studies* 11(2): 163–182.

Taylor, I. 2016. 'Dependency Redux: Why Africa Is Not Rising', *Review of African Political Economy* 43(147): 8–25.

Thrift, N. 1996. *Spatial Formations.* London: Sage.

Tomaselli, K. 2005. *Where Global Contradictions Are Sharpest: Research Stories from the Kalahari.* Amsterdam: Rozenberg Publishers.

Tufte, T. 2016. *Communication and Social Change.* Cambridge: Polity Press.

Van Dijk, R. 2017. 'The Tent versus *Lobola*: Marriage, Monetary Intimacies and the New Face of Responsibility in Botswana', *Anthropology Southern Africa* 40(1): 29–41.

Vokes, R. 2018a. *Media and Development.* London: Routledge.

———. 2018b. 'Before the Call: Mobile Phones, Exchange Relations, and Social Change in South-western Uganda', *Ethnos* 83(2): 274–90.

Wikan, U. 1992. 'Beyond Words: The Power of Resonance'. *American Ethnologist* 19(3): 460–82.

Willems, W., and W. Mano (eds). 2017. *Everyday Media Culture in Africa: Audiences and Users.* London: Routledge.

Wittgenstein, L. 1968. *Philosophical Investigations.* Oxford: Basil Blackwell.

World Economic Forum (WEF). 2016. *The Global Information Technology Report 2016: Innovating in the Digital Economy.* Geneva: World Economic Forum. http://online.wsj.com/public/resources/documents/GITR2016.pdf (accessed 27 April 2017).

PART I

Economy

CHAPTER 1

Digital Development Imaginaries, Informal Business Practices and the Platformisation of Digital Technology in Zambia

Wendy Willems

While Zambia was declared a middle-income country by the World Bank in 2011, the country's economic performance has slowed down in recent years, exacerbated by the low copper price (caused by decreasing demand from China) and frequent electricity cuts. Coinciding with these changes, hopes are being vested in the ability of digital technology to contribute to economic growth. The Government of Zambia's *Sixth National Development Plan, 2011–2015* (2011, p. 153) and the *Seventh National Development Plan, 2017–2021* (2017, p. 75) both identify information and communications technology (ICT) as crucial in the country's socio-economic development, and consider the improvement of ICT infrastructure as a key policy priority. This echoes a wider belief in the ability of digital technology to transform economies in the Global South, as reiterated for example by the World Bank's 2016 World Development Report *Digital Dividends* and by scholars in the subfields of ICT4D, Mobile for Development (M4D) or Social Media for Development (SM4D). Tech hubs and start-ups are considered key to promoting innovation, investment and wider economic growth on the African continent, reflected by terms such as Kenya's 'Silicon Savannah', Nigeria's 'Silicon Lagoon' and Cameroon's 'Silicon Mountain'. Similarly, Zambia's capital Lusaka has in recent years seen a growth in start-up initiatives, network events and ICT hubs, which have received increasing government support. For example, the Zambia Information and Communications Technology Authority (ZICTA) intends to launch a programme aimed at 'unlocking the potential of ICT-related innovators, entrepreneurs, Micro, Small and Medium Enterprises (MSMEs) and start-ups in contributing to the growth and development of the ICT sector' (ZICTA, 2015, p. 2).

Digital technology is not only treated as a crucial growth sector in its own right but is also seen as a means to transform existing businesses, entrepreneurs and economic practices (Aker and Mbiti, 2010; Obijiofor, 2009; Porter, 2012; World Bank, 2016). Mobile phones are considered to be vital in the business practices of farmers, small-scale traders and market vendors. For some, they have enabled small businesses to communicate more effectively with customers or suppliers or made it possible for farmers to access market price information on livestock or agricultural commodities. However, in focusing attention on the contribution of digital technology to economic change, scholars – and particularly those associated with the ICT4D field – often fail to examine the way in which the internet itself is changing, slowly giving way to a space that is largely controlled by global social media platforms and marginalising local technology firms in the process. Hence, it is crucial to analytically situate digital media practices within the 'platformisation' of the global mobile internet which not only violates net neutrality but also raises concerns about the growing datafication of the Global South and threats to privacy (Helmond, 2015; Sambuli, 2016; Taylor and Broeders, 2015).

Against this background of global power relations which increasingly shape the nature of the internet, this chapter examines how informal traders and vendors in New Soweto Market in Lusaka, Zambia make use of digital technology in their working lives and the extent to which smartphones have transformed their business practices. Informal employment constitutes a substantial part of the labour force in Zambia, with a small minority of people employed in formal jobs (primarily in the mines in the northern part of the country and in the public sector). Only 28 per cent of those employed in Lusaka in 2014 held formal employment, and the majority (72 per cent) had informal jobs (Ministry of Labour, 2014, p. 53). Drawing on semi-structured interviews with informal traders and vendors, the chapter argues that smartphones, mobile internet and social media offer a number of opportunities to small-scale informal businesses, such as the ability to efficiently communicate with customers, to cheaply and instantly share information (e.g. images of goods) with traders in neighbouring countries, or to quickly transfer money to suppliers. However, technology does not radically transform informal businesses as face-to-face contact as well as building trust remain important preconditions for the scaling up of informal business networks. Furthermore, the growing 'platformisation' of Zambia's mobile internet marginalises local technology firms, is likely to reinforce user dependency on global corporate platforms and poses risks to traders' and vendors' privacy.

The first section of this chapter examines the way in which policy documents, media discourses and academic accounts have imagined the role of digital technology in economic development. This is followed by a discussion of four critical approaches to digital development imaginaries: (1) technological solutionism; (2) technological determinism; (3) dependency between Global North and South; and (4) ethical concerns around data extraction. The third and fourth sections offer background and context on digital technology, economic development and informal trading in Zambia. The final section discusses how informal traders and vendors in New Soweto Market in Lusaka, Zambia make use of digital technology in their working lives and examines the extent to which smartphones have transformed their business practices.

Digital Imaginaries and Economic Development

A social imaginary refers to a 'common understanding that makes possible common practices and a widely shared sense of legitimacy' (Taylor, 2004, p. 23). Contemporary social imaginaries on economic development often revolve around digital technology. Government policy documents, reports of international financial institutions, news articles and academic research are all involved in 'doing' this imagining. In the process, they construct narratives and discourses about the way in which digital technology transforms the economy. Hence, development imaginaries are increasingly also digital imaginaries which participate in reflecting on how digital tools and technologies such as mobile phones, mobile internet and social media platforms can potentially contribute to economic development. This is demonstrated by the following quotation from a November 2017 article in *The Economist*:

> As mobile phones spread, they speed economic growth and help boost productivity. Fast cable internet may be even better at creating well-paid jobs, boosting the number of startups and stimulating exports. Although data are still scarce, there is every reason to think that phones, the internet and the technologies that they enable may together provide Africa with the most powerful tools yet to alleviate poverty, boost growth and ultimately catch up with the rich world.[1]

Similarly, the World Bank's *Digital Dividends* report highlights that the internet has lowered the costs of 'acquiring and using information, which in turn has lowered transaction costs – and often as a consequence, production costs' (World Bank, 2016, p. 42). According to the report, digital technology has created new markets for small producers and has made transactions faster and cheaper, thereby increasing economic productivity. Similarly optimistic narratives can be found in other policy documents and reports on the role of information and communication technologies on the African continent which often 'propose Grand Visions of connectivity, attributing a self-evident positive, widespread, and transformational impact to the Internet' (Friederici et al., 2017, p. 1).

In examining the impact of technology on economic development, academic accounts often make a distinction between benefits at the macro-economic and micro-economic levels. At the level of nations, digital technology is considered to contribute to development 'by improving communication, opening new investment opportunities, incorporating the African diaspora in development, and integrating the continent into the global economy' (Otiso and Moseley, 2009, p. 99). Hopes are vested in the ability of technology to promote economic growth, and for some, 'there is a strong link between uptake of new technologies and the socioeconomic growth and development of different countries and communities' (Obijiofor, 2009, p. 32). At the level of individuals and households, the focus is frequently on the economic benefits of mobile phones, whose rapid growth on the African continent has been described as a 'revolution' (Etzo and Collender, 2010). For some, there is evidence that mobile phones 'can enable the poor to build livelihood assets and take up employment opportunities, not only through direct employment or job-search benefits, but also through the critical support they can bring to small businesses in terms of expanded profit margins' (Porter, 2012, p. 253). Studies often focus on the way in which micro-enterprises, market traders, street vendors or small-scale farmers have managed to reduce their communication costs and facilitated their search for information through mobile phones, which ultimately is also considered to translate into growth and benefits at the macro-economic level (Aker and Mbiti, 2010).

Mobile phones have been central in digital imaginaries of economic development. For example, basic phones were assumed to enable small-scale enterprises and farmers to improve the efficiency of their communication with both customers and suppliers, to assist them in accessing market prices of key commodities via short-message service market information systems, and to carry out money transfers through, for example, M-Pesa. With the emergence of smartphones, mobile technology gained additional functionalities, including the capacity to access the internet. As compared to fixed line internet access, mobile internet required 'fewer ICT skills, less financial resources and does not rely on electricity at home, compared to computers or laptops' (Stork et al., 2013, p. 34). Because of the relatively low costs of smartphones, the mobile internet is considered to have the potential to close the digital divide. The emergence of the mobile internet has coincided with the rise of social media, which are increasingly dominating smartphone use and for many users equal their experience of the internet. In the context of the so-called 'Arab Spring', social media were considered crucial in mobilising resistance and democratising authoritarian contexts. Following the protests, a number of development agencies similarly began to put their faith in the ability of social media to provoke social change and to promote good governance by providing aid packages to digital activists (Christensen, 2011). However, apart from vesting hope in the political transformation that social media could bring about, the development sector is also increasingly recognising the potential of social media in economic development. For example, several reports and handbooks emphasise the opportunities offered by social media in agricultural development, enabling farmers to extend their networks and market their products more effectively (Andres and Woodard, 2013; Pedrick, 2015).

The focus on technology in contemporary development policy, discourses and practices is inextricably linked to the idea that business and entrepreneurship are key to Africa's development and to 'bottom-of-the-pyramid' (BoP) approaches which are gaining ground on the continent. These approaches encourage large multinational corporations to take advantage of the vast, underserved potential consumer base represented by 'the global poor' (Prahalad, 2004). Instead of treating them as victims in need of development aid, the 'bottom-of-the-pyramid' argument considers the poor as a crucial, profitable market. Furthermore, connecting the poor with multinational corporations (MNCs) via the internet is expected to enable them to develop business opportunities. As Dolan and Rajak (2016, p. 515) argue, 'from national governments to international financial institutions, donor agencies and NGOs, from big business to start-ups, diverse actors with varying interests are rallying behind the potential of BoP enterprise to discipline, and at the same time unleash, a new generation of African microentrepreneurs'.

For example, under the developmental banner of 'connecting the unconnected', corporate social media platforms such as Facebook have increasingly shifted their attention to emerging economies in the Global South in the face of saturating Global North markets. Since 2009, Facebook has developed a number of products and projects to target mobile internet users in low-income or low-bandwidth contexts such as Facebook Lite, Facebook Zero, Internet.org and Free Basics (Goggin, 2014, pp. 1071–72). By July 2017, Facebook's Free Basics app had been launched in twenty-four African countries. The app enables mobile phone users to access a text-based version of Facebook free of charge while Facebook Lite allows users to run the application with less consumption of mobile data.[2] These strategies have enabled Facebook to increase the number of African users to 170 million in 2017, representing significant growth of 42 per cent since 2015 (Shapshak, 2017).

Critical Approaches to Digital Development Imaginaries

Large social media corporations such as Facebook are thus increasingly part of an economic development paradigm that places technology at the heart of economic growth. However, critics have raised a number of concerns about the optimistic utopianism that is often part of these digital imaginaries on development (Friederici et al., 2017; Kleine and Unwin, 2009; Murphy and Carmody, 2015). First of all, they could be seen to reproduce a form of 'technological solutionism' (Morozov, 2013). Echoing modernisation theory of the 1950s and 1960s, economic development here continues to be framed as a problem that can be solved with technology, thereby ignoring or neglecting other key structural inequalities between Global North and South. For example, the focus on the role of ICTs in economic development can 'distort development priorities away from core issues like debt and poverty alleviation towards the pursuit of a "virtual panacea" for Africa's deep-rooted problems' (Alden, 2003, p. 457), or it can present 'the mobile phone as a technical fix for what are primarily problems of power maldistribution' (Carmody, 2012, p. 1).

Secondly, utopian digital imaginaries convey a sense of technological determinism which presupposes that technology has the potential to transform economic practices and 'accords no importance to existing social conditions, assuming that equipping people with computers will suffice to leapfrog them into the technological world of economic opportunities' (Alzouma, 2005, p. 228). Technology is not always used in the way it is intended by those designing it, and its use is strongly shaped by a range of social factors, including class, gender, race, ethnicity, age and so on, as social constructivists have reminded us (Bijker et al., 1987). Some scholars have emphasised the 'othering' of Global South digital media users in ICT4D discourses, who are often presented as using digital media purely for instrumental or utilitarian purposes, while much of their digital media use is in fact leisure-oriented (Arora, 2012; Arora and Rangaswamy, 2014).

A third critique reiterates the structuralist position of 1970s dependency theorists such as Andre Gunder Frank and Immanuel Wallerstein, who argued that the transfer of technology from the Global North to the Global South perpetuates dependencies and hampers the advancement of home-grown technology in developing countries. For example, Murphy et al. (2014, p. 264) have argued that 'ICTs are enabling new forms of outside intervention and intermediation into African markets, often further marginalising local firms and industries'. They contend that information and communication technologies on the continent are primarily used for the purpose of communication rather than more intensive uses such as information processing and management. This is echoed by Carmody (2013, p. 24), who points out that, 'while Africa may be an information society, it is not, as yet, developing a knowledge economy. Mobile phone usage then represents a form of thin, rather than thick, integration ("thintegration") in the global economy, which, because it does not lead to high value-added exports, does not fundamentally alter the continent's dependent position'. Hence, the advent of information and communication technologies on the continent has not transformed Africa's position within the larger global economy in any significant way, but instead the adoption of digital technology continues to reinforce dependency and global inequalities. For others, the prevalence of mobile-only or mobile-centric internet access has produced an emerging underclass as compared to fixed internet access. The mobile internet 'offers lower levels of functionality and content availability; operates on less open and flexible platforms; and contributes to diminished levels of user engagement, content creation, and information seeking' (Napoli and Obar, 2014, p. 323). Similarly, Donner (2015) points to the limitations of smartphones, arguing that these do not offer users the same opportunities as desktop computers.

Finally, for some, the expansion and growing power of global social media corporations in the Global South raises fundamental ethical concerns. Through the selling of adverts and (extracted) personal data to third parties, social media corporations have transformed themselves into highly profitable enterprises. Data are increasingly seen as 'the fuel of the future'[3] or 'the world's most valuable resource'.[4] Ekbia and Nardi (2017, p. 1) use the term 'heteromation' to refer to the 'extraction of economic value from low-cost or free labor in computer-mediated networks', and argue that data are essential to contemporary processes of capital accumulation. The expansion and growing power of global social media corporations in the Global South has to a large extent been made possible by the more relaxed privacy, corporate and investment regulations in the Global South as compared to the Global North, which leaves them freer to go about their business. Furthermore, the highly invisible nature of data mining and general lack of consumer awareness on the process further facilitates the expansion of these corporations.

Utopian debates on the role of ICT in economic development often emphasise how digital technology is changing business practices. However, in that way, they have failed to take into account how the internet itself is changing. Particularly in the context of Global South countries, internet access and use are increasingly shaped by global social media platforms such as Facebook and WhatsApp. For Helmond (2015, p. 1), this has resulted in the 'platformisation' of the internet, which refers to 'the rise of the platform as the dominant infrastructural and economic model of the social web and its consequences'. The growing level of control wielded by powerful global platforms reduces opportunities for local software developers to grow and contribute to the economy, while the extraction of personal data raises concerns about the datafication of the Global South and threats to privacy (Taylor and Broeders, 2015). Furthermore, the subsidisation or zero-rating of social media data violates (mobile) net neutrality (Sambuli, 2016). Ultimately, this provokes critical questions about the role of digital technology in development and change. It problematises the frequently assumed liberating and empowering aspects of digital technology and reveals the way in which it is caught up in older, unequal North-South relations of unfair competition, exploitation and extraction.

Some anthropologists have advocated for studying social media primarily through the lens of user practices. They have focused their analysis on 'what people post and communicate through platforms, … why we post and the consequences of those postings' (Miller et al., 2016, p. 1). They have argued that 'although social media platforms are themselves owned by private companies, social media does not necessarily favour the interests of commerce' (ibid., p. xiii). This section has avoided uncritically celebrating the agency of users of technology but instead highlighted the importance of analytically situating digital media practices within the constraints imposed by the growing power of global social media platforms. The next section examines the changing nature of digital media in Zambia against the background of recent economic developments.

Digital Technology and Economic Development in Zambia

In 2015, the Zambian kwacha lost 51 per cent of its value against the US dollar, which resulted in accelerating inflation rates and higher prices of imported goods (see, e.g., Hill, 2015; York, 2015). The country's economic performance suffered further from a reduced demand for copper from China, which lowered the price of copper. Subsequently, the mining industry experienced a slowdown, which provoked a number of job losses. Against the background of this economic slump, the Government of Zambia vested hope in the ability of digital technology to contribute to economic growth, as reflected in its last two development plans, which attributed an important role to digital technology (Government of Zambia, 2011, p. 153; 2017, p. 75). However, as compared to other African economies, such as Kenya, which has increasingly profiled itself as 'digital Kenya', spearheading a number of ICT innovations on the continent (Ndemo and Weiss, 2017), digital technologies in Zambia are more likely to be treated as means towards other ends instead of as a growth sector on its own.

Agriculture and mining continue to be imagined as the most crucial economic sectors. In terms of employment, most Zambians earn a living through self-employment in the informal economy. Since the implementation of economic deregulation and structural adjustment policies in the 1990s, formal employment has shrunk, and many Zambians in urban areas engage in street trading or market vending to sustain themselves. The increased number of street vendors has put growing pressure on urban space, with frequent attempts by local government to 'clean up' the streets and evict street traders or to confine them in so-called 'modern markets' (Hansen, 2008). Hence, small-scale entrepreneurship has become a dominant way of life for many urban residents of Lusaka, who are increasingly seen as entrepreneurial selves responsible for their own welfare, concomitant with neoliberal ideas on subjectivity and citizenship (Freeman, 2014).

Economic liberalisation did not only result in a growing informalisation and casualisation of employment and a substantive class of self-employed traders and vendors but also enabled the deregulation of economic sectors, including telecommunications. Since the 1990s, a number of privately owned mobile phone networks have been allowed to operate in Zambia, and mobile phones have become widely available in the last decade. While in 2000 just under ninety-nine thousand Zambians had access to a mobile phone (equal to less than 1 per cent of the population), this had grown spectacularly to a total of twelve million active mobile phone subscribers in 2016, which translates to 79.4 per cent of the population.[5] Moreover, smartphones have recently contributed to an increase in internet access, which is now largely accessed via mobile devices. In 2016, 5.2 million people were using mobile broadband, equal to 32.2 per cent of the population.[6] While network access has improved and the costs of mobile devices (including smartphones) have decreased in the last decade, it seems probable that urban, middle-class residents are more likely to use mobile internet services than less well-off, rural residents, although survey data are currently lacking to substantiate this further. However, the costs of mobile internet access have been reduced in recent years, and this has made the service more accessible to younger, less well-off users.

The growth in mobile internet use has to a large extent been driven by social media, enabled by subsidised access to platforms such as Facebook and WhatsApp via 'data bundles' or 'social bundles', which are provided by most Zambian mobile phone operators. For example, Airtel offers combined bundles of voice, data and SMS messages.[7] For ZMW1.5 (£0.11), customers receive six minutes and five hundred SMS messages per day; for ZMW3 (£0.23), customers receive twelve minutes, 20MB data and one thousand SMS messages per day; and for ZMW5 (£0.38), customers receive twenty-one minutes, 20MB data and one thousand SMS messages. MTN Zambia, which is often credited with higher mobile internet speeds, offers a daily bundle of 20MB data and free WhatsApp for ZMW3.15 (£0.24).[8] The prevalence of 'social bundles' has made mobile internet access more affordable but it also means that for many Zambians the internet increasingly equals social media, pointing to the growing 'platformisation' of the Zambian web. In the last few years, the number of Facebook subscribers has grown from an estimated 117,520 users in 2011 to 1.4 million users in 2016, which is equal to 9 per cent of the population.[9]

Hence, while access to the internet was previously largely via desktop computers in public spaces such as internet cafes or libraries during specified office hours, the growing availability of mobile internet access has made possible on-the-go internet access *anywhere, anytime* – whether on public transport or at home. This has not only decoupled internet access from physical travel as browsing the web no longer requires one to move, it has also made available the internet at any point of the day, unconstrained by the opening hours of public access points. Furthermore, it has reduced the urban spatial divide in internet access. For example, in Lusaka, internet cafes were more likely to be available in formal, busy shopping areas such as around Cairo Road or in upmarket shopping malls such as Arcades rather than in informal market areas such as Soweto Market which lacked security. However, smartphones have now made access possible in areas that previously did not have public access points. In the following section, I discuss how market vendors based in New Soweto Market, which is part of the larger Soweto Market at the edge of Lusaka's city centre, have appropriated these new forms of technology.

New Soweto Market, Informal Trading and Uses of Mobile Digital Technology

New Soweto Market was constructed in the mid-2000s as part of the Urban Markets Development Programme, which was funded by the European Union and sought to construct eleven 'modern markets' in different parts of Zambia. The market is surrounded by a gate, which separates it from the remainder of Soweto Market. It has an estimated three thousand stalls (Bzrozowski, 2015, p. 20) and hosts a range of vendors – old and young, male and female, low-income and relatively well-off – trading in food, clothes, fabrics, homeware, electronic equipment, mobile phones, phone accessories and credit. The market has designated, small lock-up shops for high-value goods such as clothes, electronics or agricultural implements; larger warehouse-style shops for agricultural commodities such as grains; larger spaces for restaurants; and covered rows of shared, long table-style displays for the selling of vegetables and dried fish. Apart from the formal structures of the market, vendors have also erected their own structures within the market, such as covered stalls (made of wood and fabric), container shops, or they simply display their goods on the ground on the outer edges of the walkways inside the market.

As part of my fieldwork in this market in July–August 2016, I spent time in New Soweto Market chatting to vendors about their work, getting to know a range of different businesses and observing both business practices and uses of digital technology. I interviewed a total of thirty-seven market vendors (twenty-three male and fourteen female), mostly through individual interviews and via a small number of focus groups. Interviewees broadly represented the wide range of vendors described above. They included vendors trading basic food items such as grains, beans and dried fish; traders selling wholesale agricultural supplies and pesticides; stall holders offering clothes, curtains, second-hand shoes and fabrics; shop owners providing new clothes or electronic goods like digital music, memory cards, mobile phones and phone accessories; as well as restaurant employees and security guards.

At the time of my research, there was a general perception that trading opportunities had deteriorated because of higher inflation and the general slowdown of the economy. As a female restaurant employee shared, 'it has become difficult to earn money. Business is hard and money is scarce .... It was better the way it was back then but now it has become harder. Everything is now expensive and money is even harder to find'.[10] Traders used a range of phones, from branded Samsung or Huawei smartphones to low-cost imported internet-enabled phones from China. Most had dual- or triple-SIM phones which allowed vendors to use SIM cards from different mobile phone networks such as Airtel or MTN. This enabled them to take advantage of attractive special offers on 'talk time' or mobile data, or to benefit from the good coverage of a particular network in a certain area. Those vendors who owned a smartphone tended to be younger, or relatively educated, or were trading in higher-value goods (e.g. new clothes or electronic goods). Interviewees described more expensive, branded smartphones as 'original phones' (common brands included Samsung, Huawei, LG and Nokia) and low-cost smartphones as 'Chinese phones' (common brands included TECNO, KGTel and ZTE), which typically had a shorter battery life.

The focus in this chapter is on business uses of mobile and social media. This is not to suggest that vendors primarily or exclusively use their phone for their businesses. As other scholars have pointed out, digital media use in the Global South is not strictly motivated by instrumental or utilitarian reasons but is in fact often driven by leisure and play (Arora, 2012; Arora and Rangaswamy, 2014). However, my main interest in this chapter is to gain an understanding of the role of digital technology in economic life. While most interviewees used mobile call or SMS services in their trading practices, not all could see the relevance of mobile internet or social media in their business. Some perceived social media as primarily suitable for private communication and less appropriate for business communication. As a female soft drink seller intimated, 'Social media? Ah, it doesn't help. Because you get to, right here we just get to chat like, "Hey, how are you?", "How was your day?", "How is your family?". Things like that. Not really for business'.[11] Others associated the (mobile) internet or SMS with a more well-off, well-educated and younger group of users. A middle-aged wholesale trader put it as follows:

> If you want to go on the internet you need to be educated, like you must have at least an idea. Because you can't even do business where even I haven't done it if I can say .... Most of us are used to doing business hand-to-mouth. So if you think of going to a café you may feel that you are

> wasting a lot of time .... Because within our class, we mainly use calling. Just buy talk time and call someone. We don't mainly depend on messages and internet. So, it's calling, you see, but we do know that it's more expensive than using a message, or going on the net which is cheaper. We know that. We know that.[12]

Older, middle-aged traders, low-income vendors or those with little education attributed less importance to smartphones as compared to younger, relatively educated or better-off traders for whom the smartphone opened up a number of opportunities, including communicating with suppliers or customers, browsing social media, listening to music or playing games. This was a welcome distraction during the ample time spent waiting for business in the market.

Apart from lack of digital literacy, other constraints in using smartphones during the period of research included the frequent electricity cuts (particularly common in 2016 due to serious shortages at the time) which hampered effective phone use. Interviewees indicated that smartphones required more frequent charging than older basic phone models, and this was challenging during a time when the electricity supply in New Soweto Market was rather erratic, or because not all vendors had access to electricity from their stall or workplace. Traders deployed a number of strategies to overcome these limitations. Some used an older phone model for basic communication such as calling and SMS messages in combination with a smartphone for internet browsing and social media use. Those vendors not intensively making use of mobile internet (and therefore not quickly draining battery life) would just use a smartphone only, and those not using the mobile internet at all for various reasons would merely use a basic phone. In response to lower electricity supply (as a result of frequent power cuts in 2016) and higher electricity demand (because of higher smartphone use which required more frequent charging), innovative traders with access to mains electricity or generators (during power cuts) offered mobile phone charging services to fellow vendors or customers against a small payment.

Mobile Digital Technology, Economic Practices and Business Networks

For most vendors, digital technology offered a range of opportunities for use in their businesses, that is, to communicate easily and cheaply with existing customers and suppliers both within and outside Zambia; to strengthen existing and to develop new business networks;

to coordinate management of the business; to entertain during quiet hours through listening to music or religious sermons; to easily transfer money to suppliers or receive money from customers; or to calculate invoices.

As several scholars have argued, the mobile phone is often primarily used to strengthen existing 'strong ties' with family and friends (Ling and Campbell, 2011, p. 8). However, it can also be a tool 'to build a network of strong and weak ties that potentially could be called upon in the future' (Wallis, 2017, p. 72). Vendors in New Soweto Market confirmed that the mobile phone was indispensable in communicating with existing customers and suppliers. Informal businesses often strongly rely on personal networks, and the mobile phone was perceived as an important tool in cultivating these and maintaining social networks more efficiently. Having access to a mobile phone enabled traders to inform their customers when certain products were in stock, as pointed out by a second-hand clothes seller: 'When I am ordering new stock, I call the customers and tell them. They will come and buy'.[13] If customers are not forthcoming or fail to visit, traders report using mobile phones to chase them: '[clients] usually call me notifying when they will come next and sometimes I usually call them telling them that they are taking long'.[14] Social media networks such as Facebook enable traders to bring customers together within an online space that can potentially be used to market their stock or cultivate customers. For example, as a young male seller of agricultural supplies suggested, 'if your customer has already given you their name, you could say maybe Wisdom. Then you can go to Facebook and find that person through Facebook. If you find that one, maybe they can accept it or not (friend request). So if they accept, you can start chatting with them'.[15] Conversely, it has allowed customers to double check on the availability of certain items, thereby potentially avoiding costly physical travel if the goods were not available.

Visual social media platforms such as WhatsApp facilitate communication further as they enable the exchange of images. Hence, traders can take images of certain goods and share these cheaply with customers because of their subsidised access to social media via data bundles. As a young female clothes seller told me, 'I can capture pictures of things I am selling here. Then send them on WhatsApp and people who are interested would call me'.[16] Vendors mostly used WhatsApp for the sharing of images with customers as compared to Facebook Messenger because WhatsApp's interface was more user-friendly to carry out this task. If they wanted to share images with other users who were in close physical proximity, they would use Bluetooth. Mobile phones have also made communication between traders and suppliers easier. Traders can check with suppliers whether they have certain items in stock, either by phone or by sharing an image of the item they would like to source via WhatsApp, or they can order goods without having to travel to their suppliers. This is particularly important because suppliers are highly mobile and travel frequently. Clothes, in particular, are often sourced by Zambian cross-border traders from South Africa and Tanzania. Because they tend to be on the move, the mobile phone has become an important tool that can literally 'locate' them: '[cross-border traders] usually move about so when they call you, you quickly go get the merchandise before they make another move'.[17]

Mobile phones have enabled vendors to extend their customer base beyond the immediate vicinity of New Soweto Market and to maintain customer networks in other parts of the country. Assuming a certain level of trust is present between traders and customers, vendors mentioned doing business over the phone without the need to physically meet the customer: 'Sometimes I receive calls from my customers to prepare for them some products. I am able to send trade items as far as Kasama. In such a case I usually send products by bus'.[18] Relatedly, a male fish and grain seller reported having customers located far from Lusaka: 'Because we have got customers, maybe who stay in Copperbelt, Western Province, they will phone you: "Do you have this type of fish which I want? How much is the price?" Then we can communicate. "Send me so many bags"'.[19] Social media access via smartphones has further scaled up and facilitated international networks beyond Zambia. Both the low costs of contacting suppliers based abroad and the opportunity to exchange images of commodities via WhatsApp have enabled traders to easily do business with suppliers located abroad, as demonstrated in the following quote from a female curtain and clothes seller:

> Like this time, I would like some supplies from South Africa so what I do these days is that I just take pics of the things I want from South Africa and then I send them on WhatsApp. Sometimes when I don't want to travel, I just do the same and the suppliers in South Africa will send the items I want then I send the money .... I do travel but when I don't want to travel or when I have run out of stock very fast that's when I normally send the pics on WhatsApp to South Africa and then those guys there would buy for me.[20]

Purchasing stock from international suppliers or selling to international customers has also been enhanced by mobile money services that have increasingly been offered by a number of mobile network operators in Zambia. Mobile money transfers suit vendors because formal banks may not have a strong presence in informal markets, making it more time-consuming to access banking services and once again requiring more physical travel. For low-income vendors who may not have access to formal bank accounts, mobile money transfers make it possible to effect electronic transactions. However, again, mobile money transactions strongly rely on mutual trust and existing strong ties between traders and suppliers.

So far, this section has summed up a number of ways in which the various uses of mobile phone technology have strengthened existing networks or enabled communication between customers and suppliers with a prior business relationship. However, a key distinguishing feature of social media platforms such as Facebook and Twitter is that they make it possible for strangers to meet and interact. While most appropriations of social media for business uses appear to reinforce existing networks, there are a few opportunities which traders in New Soweto Market highlighted that have enabled them to scale up and to take advantage of the opportunity to develop new business networks with strangers. In this regard, Facebook has been more frequently used than Twitter, for two reasons. First of all, the platform's specific affordances lend themselves better to small businesses. While Twitter is associated with sharing commentary on political or other affairs, Facebook orients itself more to small businesses through its buy-and-sell groups.[21] Secondly, at the time, Zambia had relatively low numbers of Twitter users given that Facebook was typically included in data bundles and Twitter tended not to be, which made it rather pricey to access this particular platform.

Although some vendors reported using their Facebook profile to market goods to their contacts, most referred to Zambian Facebook buy-and-sell groups such as 'Amasampo mu Lusaka' or 'Ama Sampo'.[22] Both groups are closed and bring together nearly two hundred thousand members. For some, this was a convenient way to sell an unwanted item or to source a particular commodity such as a mobile phone. As a young male curtain seller illustrated, 'Maybe say, you want to sell your phone, you post it there then you sell it .... Maybe there is someone who has whatever you want. He can simply respond, then make communication, then you have your thing. You can be done without you worrying going around looking for something. You just post it'.[23] However, others were uncomfortable using online shopping platforms or Facebook groups as they feared becoming a victim of crime:

> Though I fear there is a risk. I was thinking that maybe there is a risk. That's why I have not used it. The internet thing when buying something

> that I want from outside the country. I was thinking that maybe there is cybercrime.[24]

> There are Amasampo groups. Those where, if you have a phone, you can just go there and say: 'Ah, I have got this phone'. Then maybe you find that a person just stole that phone, then they bring it onto Facebook, selling it. Then you like it and you are like let me buy that phone. Then after you take it, you may find yourself in deep trouble. The police will start following you.[25]

In many ways, online platforms such as buy-and-sell Facebook groups mirror the informality and lack of regulation of spaces such as New Soweto Market but the fact that they do not involve immediate face-to-face contact ensures that many Zambians do not trust them. Unlike 'Amasampo mu Lusaka', 'Ama Sampo' has made attempts to formalise its page and enhance trust and legitimacy (Chimpala, 2014). However, they do not take responsibility for protecting transactions and recommend their members to 'NEVER send any random member money remotely, only do this with people you know and trust – otherwise consult with the administration of the group'. Hence, arguably, a more effective use of social media platforms for business purposes would depend – among other factors – on stronger forms of customer protection, currently offered by ecommerce platforms such as eBay.[26]

There have been other attempts in Zambia to formalise and develop local ecommerce platforms. For example, Dot Com Zambia launched a donor-funded project in May 2017 aimed at providing Zambian micro, small and medium enterprises with access to an online business platform, enabling them to access new markets locally and globally.[27] It is uncertain at present whether these platforms will be able to compete with global social media platforms in the future, which may choose to invest in incorporating business features in their networks and platform architecture. While at present Facebook Business and Facebook Marketplace address businesses as well as traders, there are indications that the platform envisages further engagement with the small and medium enterprise (SME) sector, including on the African continent.[28] In October 2017, the company set up an SME council in Nigeria, the first one on the African continent. At the launch of the council, a Facebook representative reiterated that business was key to development on the continent. As he pointed out, 'small businesses form the backbone of most of the thriving economies in the world, driving sustainable growth and creating jobs, and those in Nigeria are no different. Facebook is strategically positioned to help SMEs grow their businesses' (Osuagwu, 2017).

These developments could potentially further reinforce the 'platformisation' of Zambia's internet. As indicated earlier in this chapter, platformisation refers to the growing infrastructural and economic power of social media platforms on the internet (Helmond, 2015). In the Zambian context, internet access increasingly equals mobile access to social media as a result of data bundles which effectively subsidise users' access to social media. The mobile internet experience of most of my interviewees was dominated by Facebook and WhatsApp given that these were part of data bundles and therefore much cheaper to access than regular websites, other platforms or search engines such as Google. When users leave Facebook, they receive a warning, 'You are about to leave Facebook. Standard data charges may apply', thereby encouraging users to remain within the platform. The reliance of digital technology users on platforms has encouraged Zambian businesses to offer their services on these spaces rather than on regular websites (expensive for users to access), which has further reinforced platformisation. Ultimately, this challenges the principle of net neutrality which maintains that users should be able to access all areas of the internet equally without price discrimination or differentiation (Sambuli, 2016). The concentration of power into a handful of platforms not only raises concerns about net neutrality but also threatens users' privacy. Personal data are continuously extracted in internet user experiences that are dominated by platforms (Taylor and Broeders, 2015).

While the zero-rating of Facebook via the introduction of Free Basics in India provoked resistance from activists linked to the #SaveTheInternet campaign (and ultimately led the Telecom Regulatory Authority of India [TRAI] to block the initiative [see Mukerjee, 2016]), there has been little critical debate in the Zambian context on zero- or subsidised rating of social media data. None of my interviewees raised concern about the way in which their mobile internet experience was shaped by social media platforms, and there has not been an extensive public debate on the issue to my knowledge. However, it is crucial to situate digital user practices within the wider constraints of global power relations so as to avoid an uncritical celebration of the potential role of technology – whether mobile phones, mobile internet or big data – in economic growth in the Global South. Clearly, technology is not always taken up as expected and the concentration of power in a handful of global social media platforms could in the future inhibit local actors from taking advantage of the economic opportunities offered by digital technology.

Conclusion

To sum up, it could be argued that key to the relevance, or 'success', of mobile digital technology for informal traders was the convergent nature of the smartphone, and its ability to combine a range of services in a portable, mobile, compact device. Smartphones bring together call and SMS services, internet access, social media use, MP3 playback, mobile money transfer options, and phone functions such as a calculator, camera and torch. Hence, those vendors who were able to afford and use smartphones (typically younger, better-off and relatively educated users) could employ the phone to complete a number of different tasks in relation to their businesses. Furthermore, given that informal trading is associated with a high level of physical mobility on the part of traders, customers and suppliers, mobile phones have succeeded in speeding up and facilitating communication. Because vendors were able to do business 'on the phone', they had less of a need to visit suppliers, thereby minimising physical travel, reducing transport costs and saving time.

While much hope has been vested in the ability of digital technology to bring about economic growth and to enhance the livelihoods of farmers, small-scale traders and market vendors, this chapter has highlighted a number of limitations which challenge these utopian assumptions. First, while the literature has celebrated the potential of commodity price information systems to make economic transactions more profitable and efficient, my research has emphasised the importance of trust and personal networks between traders and customers in the exchange of information on prices. Mobile phones tend to primarily facilitate communication between existing business networks during which information on prices is exchanged. Lack of trust in dealing with 'anonymous', unregulated business spaces such as Facebook buy-and-sell groups arguably hampers a 'scaling up' of business networks.

Unlike informal traders and businesses, it could be argued that Zambia's formal sector has more intensively exploited social media platforms to maintain customer relations and to market products. Many medium-sized businesses no longer use websites but instead rely on the infrastructure provided by corporate social media platforms. The technical affordances of Facebook's platform provide small- to medium-sized businesses with a cheap and easy-to-manage digital interface which avoids the higher design, hosting and maintenance costs and skillset required to set up a formal website. Combined with the fact that most mobile internet users regularly visit social media platforms because of their subsidised nature, businesses tend to avoid setting up websites and limit their digital presence to Facebook pages.

Conventional studies on the role of digital media in economic life in the Global South often reproduce a simplistic causality between technology and economic growth and development. This chapter has advocated for a more nuanced and critical approach, acknowledging both the changes and continuities associated with the incorporation of technology by informal traders and vendors. Trust and social capital remain crucial in informal business practices, and are essential preconditions to the potential scaling up of business networks enabled by social media. Secondly, the chapter has argued that the strong focus on the role of digital technology in economic change in ICT4D discourses and digital development imaginaries has prevented us from fully appreciating the way in which technology itself is changing over time. Particularly in the context of Global South countries, internet access and use are increasingly shaped by global social media platforms such as Facebook and WhatsApp. The 'platformisation' of the internet and the growing level of control wielded by these powerful players reduces opportunities for local software developers to grow and contribute to the economy, while the extraction of personal data raises concerns about the datafication of the Global South and threats to privacy. Finally, the subsidisation or zero-rating of social media data violates (mobile) net neutrality. Ultimately, this provokes critical questions about the role of digital technology in development and change. It problematises the frequently assumed liberating and empowering aspects of digital technology and demonstrates the importance of analytically situating user practices within older, unequal North-South power relations of unfair competition, exploitation and extraction.

Wendy Willems is Associate Professor in the Department of Media and Communications at the London School of Economics and Political Science. Her research interests include global digital culture; postcolonial/decolonial approaches to media and communications; media culture and neoliberalism in the Global South; and popular culture, performance and politics in Africa. Her research has been published in journals such as *Communication Theory*, *Popular Communication*, *Telematics and Informatics*, *World Development* and *Africa Development*. She is co-editor of *Civic Agency in Africa: Arts of Resistance in the Twenty-First Century* (James Currey, 2014) and *Everyday Media Culture in Africa: Audiences and Users* (Routledge, 2016).

Notes

1. 'Mobile Phones and Development: How the Taxman Slows the Spread of Technology in Africa', *The Economist*, 9 November 2017, https://www.economist.com/news/middle-east-and-africa/21731206-if-you-want-less-something-tax-it (accessed 10 November 2017).
2. Facebook Free Basics, 'Where We've Launched', https://info.internet.org/en/story/where-weve-launched (accessed 20 July 2017).
3. 'Fuel of the Future: Data is Giving Rise to a New Economy', *The Economist*, 6 May 2017, https://www.economist.com/news/briefing/21721634-how-it-shaping-up-data-giving-rise-new-economy (accessed 23 July 2017).
4. 'The World's Most Valuable Resource is No Longer Oil, But Data', *The Economist*, 6 May 2017, https://www.economist.com/news/leaders/21721656-data-economy-demands-new-approach-antitrust-rules-worlds-most-valuable-resource (accessed 23 July 2017).
5. Zambia Information and Communications Technology Authority (ZICTA), ICT Indicators, http://onlinesystems.zicta.zm:8585/statsfinal/ICT%20Indicators.html (accessed 11 December 2017).
6. Zambia Information and Communications Technology Authority (ZICTA), ICT Indicators, http://onlinesystems.zicta.zm:8585/statsfinal/ICT%20Indicators.html (accessed 11 December 2017).
7. Retrieved 24 August 2016 from http://www.africa.airtel.com/wps/wcm/connect/africarevamp/zambia/home/personal/so-che. Exchange rate as on 24 August 2016 retrieved from http://www.xe.com.
8. Retrieved 24 August 2016 from http://www.mtnzambia.com/personal/internet/colum-1/data-bundles.html. Exchange rate retrieved on 24 August 2016 from http://www.xe.com.
9. Retrieved 24 August 2016 from http://www.internetworldstats.com/africa.htm#zm.
10. Interview with female restaurant employee, New Soweto Market, Lusaka, Zambia, 27 July 2016.
11. Interview with young female soft drink seller, New Soweto Market, Lusaka, Zambia, 28 July 2016.
12. Interview with middle-aged wholesale trader, New Soweto Market, Lusaka, Zambia, 28 July 2016.
13. Interview with female second-hand clothes seller, New Soweto Market, Lusaka, Zambia, 1 August 2016.
14. Interview with young female dried fish seller, New Soweto Market, Lusaka, Zambia, 3 August 2016.
15. Interview with young male seller in agricultural supply store, New Soweto Market, Lusaka, Zambia, 27 July 2016.
16. Interview with young female clothes seller, New Soweto Market, Lusaka, Zambia, 2 August 2016.
17. Interview with young male stall holder, New Soweto Market, Lusaka, Zambia, 2 August 2016.
18. Interview with middle-aged female fish and beans seller, New Soweto Market, Lusaka, Zambia, 3 August 2016.
19. Interview with male fish and grain seller, New Soweto Market, Lusaka, Zambia, 3 August 2016.

20. Interview with female curtain and clothes seller, New Soweto Market, Lusaka, Zambia, 2 August 2016.
21. Just after my fieldwork in October 2016, Facebook introduced another functionality, Facebook Marketplace, which operated like a giant buy-and-sell group that could be accessed by any Facebook user. See also https://newsroom.fb.com/news/2016/10/introducing-marketplace-buy-and-sell-with-your-local-community/.
22. Amasampo mu Lusaka, closed group, 194,065 members on 3 November 2017, https://www.facebook.com/groups/369329713102271 (accessed 3 November 2017). Ama Sampo, closed group, 183,037 members on 3 November 2017, https://www.facebook.com/groups/amasampo (accessed 3 November 2017).
23. Interview with young male seller in curtain shop, New Soweto Market, Lusaka, Zambia, 2 August 2018.
24. Interview with young female second-hand clothes seller, New Soweto Market, Lusaka, Zambia, 1 August 2016.
25. Interview with young male seller in mobile phone tuckshop, New Soweto Market, Lusaka, Zambia, 4 August 2016.
26. eBay currently does not operate a specific country website in Zambia, nor does it work with Zambian traders. Zambian consumers can, however, purchase goods from eBay and have these shipped to Zambia via services offered by shipping companies such as Import Zambia (http://www.importzambia.com/services.html).
27. 'Dot Com Zambia to Launch Global e-Commerce Platform for Zambian Companies', 22 May 2017, http://www.techtrends.co.zm/dot-com-zambia-launch-global-e-commerce-platform-zambian-companies (accessed 9 April 2018).
28. See https://www.facebook.com/business and https://www.facebook.com/marketplace.

References

Aker, J.C., and I.M. Mbiti. 2010. 'Mobile Phones and Economic Development in Africa', *Journal of Economic Perspectives* 24(3): 207–32. doi:10.1257/jep.24.3.207.

Alden, C. 2003. 'Let Them Eat Cyberspace: Africa, the G8 and the Digital Divide', *Millennium – Journal of International Studies* 32(3): 457–76. doi:10.1177/03058298030320030601.

Alzouma, G. 2005. 'Myths of Digital Technology in Africa', *Global Media & Communication* 1(3): 228–56. doi:10.1177/1742766505058128.

Andres, D., and J. Woodard. 2013. *Social Media Handbook for Agricultural Development Practitioners.* Washington, DC: USAID. http://ictforag.org/toolkits/social/SocialMedia4AgHandbook.pdf (accessed 10 November 2017).

Arora, P. 2012. 'The Leisure Divide: Can the "Third World" Come Out to Play?', *Information Development* 28(2): 93–101. doi:10.1177/0266666911433607.

Arora, P., and N. Rangaswamy. 2014. 'ICTs for Leisure in Development: A Case for Motivation, Exploration, and Play in the Global South', *Information Technologies & International Development* 10(3): v–vii.

Bijker, W.E., T.P. Hughes and T. Pinch. 1987. *The Social Construction of Technological Systems: New Directions in the Sociology and History of Technology.* Cambridge, MA: MIT Press.

Bzrozowski, T. 2015. *Programmes Managed by EU Delegation & Government of Republic of Zambia.* https://eeas.europa.eu/sites/eeas/files/compendium_2000to2014.pdf (accessed 11 December 2017).

Carmody, P. 2012. 'The Informationalization of Poverty in Africa? Mobile Phones and Economic Structure', *Information Technologies & International Development* 8(3): 1–17.

———. 2013. 'A Knowledge Economy or an Information Society in Africa? Thintegration and the Mobile Phone Revolution', *Information Technology for Development* 19(1): 24–39. doi:10.1080/02681102.2012.719859.

Chimpala, S. 2014. 'Wanna Sell Something on Facebook? Let's Talk Ama Sampo', *Techtrends Zambia,* 16 April 2014. http://www.techtrends.co.zm/wanna-sell-something-facebook-lets-talk-ama-sampo (accessed 15 December 2017).

Christensen, C. 2011. 'Discourses of Technology and Liberation: State Aid to Net Activists in an Era of "Twitter Revolutions"', *The Communication Review* 14(3): 233–53. doi:10.1080/10714421.2011.597263.

Dolan, C., and D. Rajak. 2016. 'Remaking Africa's Informal Economies: Youth, Entrepreneurship and the Promise of Inclusion at the Bottom of the Pyramid', *The Journal of Development Studies* 52(4): 514–29. doi:10.1080/00220388.2015.1126249.

Donner, J. 2015. *After Access: Inclusion, Development, and a More Mobile Internet.* Cambridge, MA: MIT Press.

Ekbia, H.R. and B.A. Nardi. 2017. *Heteromation, and Other Stories of Computing and Capitalism.* Cambridge, MA: MIT Press.

Etzo, S., and G. Collender. 2010. 'The Mobile Phone "Revolution" in Africa: Rhetoric or Reality', *African Affairs* 109(437): 659–68. doi:10.1093/afraf/adq045.

Freeman, C. 2014. *Entrepreneurial Selves: Neoliberal Respectability and the Making of a Caribbean Middle Class.* Durham, NC: Duke University Press.

Friederici, N., S. Ojanperä and M. Graham. 2017. 'The Impact of Connectivity in Africa: Grand Visions and the Mirage of Inclusive Digital Development', *The Electronic Journal of Information Systems in Developing Countries* 79(2): 1–20. doi:10.1002/j.1681-4835.2017.tb00578.x.

Goggin, G. 2014. 'Facebook's Mobile Career', *New Media & Society* 16(7): 1068–86. doi:10.1177/1461444814543996.

Government of Zambia. 2011. *Sixth National Development Plan, 2011–2015.* Lusaka: Government of Zambia.

———. 2017. *Seventh National Development Plan, 2017–2021.* Lusaka: Government of Zambia.

Hansen, K.T. 2008. 'The Informalization of Lusaka's Economy: Regime Change, Ultra-Modern Markets, and Street Vending, 1972–2004', in J.-B. Gewald, M. Hinfelaar and G. Macola (eds), *One Zambia, Many Histories: Towards a History of Post-colonial Zambia*. Leiden: Brill, pp. 213–42.

Helmond, A. 2015. 'The Platformization of the Web: Making Web Data Platform Ready', *Social Media + Society* 1(2): 1–11. doi:10.1177/2056305115603080.

Hill, M. 2015. 'Zambia Debt Ratio Soaring as Kwacha Loses 51% of Its Value against the Dollar, World Bank Says', *Mail and Guardian*, 6 November 2015. http://mgafrica.com/article/2015-11-06-zambia-debt-ratio-soaring-as-currency-plunges-world-bank-says (accessed 13 December 2017).

Kleine, D., and T. Unwin. 2009. 'Technological Revolution, Evolution and New Dependencies: What's New about ICT4D?', *Third World Quarterly* 30(5): 1045–67. doi:10.1080/01436590902959339.

Ling, R., and S. Campbell (eds). 2011. *Mobile Communication: Bringing Us Together or Tearing Us Apart*. New Brunswick, NJ: Transaction Publishers.

Miller, D., E. Costa, N. Haynes, T. McDonald, R. Nicolescu, J. Sinanan, J. Spyer, S. Venkatraman and X. Wang. 2016. *How the World Changed Social Media*. London: UCL Press.

Ministry of Labour. 2014. *Zambia Labour Force Survey Report 2014*. Lusaka, Zambia: Central Statistical Office. http://www.mlss.gov.zm/upload/Labour_Force_2014/2014_LFS_FULL_FINAL_Report.pdf (accessed 4 April 2018).

Morozov, E. 2013. *To Save Everything, Click Here: The Folly of Technological Solutionism*. New York: PublicAffairs.

Mukerjee, S. 2016. 'Net Neutrality, Facebook, and India's Battle to #SaveTheInternet', *Communication and the Public* 1(3): 356–61. doi:10.1177/2057047316665850.

Murphy, J.T., and P. Carmody. 2015. *Africa's Information Revolution: Technical Regimes and Production Networks in South Africa and Tanzania*. Oxford: Wiley-Blackwell.

Murphy, J.T., P. Carmody and B. Surborg. 2014. 'Industrial Transformation or Business as Usual? Information and Communication Technologies and Africa's Place in the Global Information Economy', *Review of African Political Economy* 41(140): 264–83. doi:10.1080/03056244.2013.873024.

Napoli, P.M., and J.A. Obar. 2014. 'The Emerging Mobile Internet Underclass: A Critique of Mobile Internet Access', *The Information Society* 30(5): 323–34. doi:10.1080/01972243.2014.944726.

Ndemo, B., and T. Weiss. 2017. *Digital Kenya: An Entrepreneurial Revolution in the Making*. Houndmills, Basingstoke: Palgrave Macmillan.

Obijiofor, L. 2009. 'Mapping Theoretical and Practical Issues in the Relationship between ICTs and Africa's Socioeconomic Development', *Telematics & Informatics* 26(1): 32–43. doi:10.1016/j.tele.2007.12.002.

Osuagwu, P. 2017. 'Why Facebook Sited Africa's First SME Council in Nigeria', *Vanguard*, 8 November 2017. https://www.vanguardngr.com/2017/11/facebook-sited-africas-first-sme-council-nigeria (accessed 13 December 2017).

Otiso, K., and W.G. Moseley. 2009. 'Examining Claims for Information and Communication Technology-Led Development in Africa', *African Geographical Review* 28: 99–116. doi:10.1080/19376812.2009.9756219.

Pedrick, C. 2015. *Embracing Web 2.0 and Social Media: A Life-Changing Pathway for Agricultural Development Actors.* Wageningen: Technical Centre for Agricultural and Rural Cooperation ACP-EU (CTA). https://publications.cta.int/en/publications/publication/1816 (accessed 10 November 2017).

Porter, G. 2012. 'Mobile Phones, Livelihoods and the Poor in Sub-Saharan Africa: Review and Prospect', *Geography Compass* 6(5): 241–59. doi:10.1111/j.1749-8198.2012.00484.x.

Prahalad, C.K. 2004. *The Fortune at the Bottom of the Pyramid: Eradicating Poverty through Profits.* Upper Saddle River, NJ: Wharton School Publishing.

Sambuli, N. 2016. 'Challenges and Opportunities for Advancing Internet Access in Developing Countries while Upholding Net Neutrality', *Journal of Cyber Policy* 1(1): 61–74. doi:10.1080/23738871.2016.1165715.

Shapshak, T. 2017. 'Facebook Has 170 million African Users, Mostly on Mobile', *Forbes Magazine,* 5 April 2017. https://www.forbes.com/sites/tobyshapshak/2017/04/05/facebook-has-170m-african-users-mostly-on-mobile/#4346e7db53dc (accessed 20 July 2017).

Stork, C., E. Calandro and A. Gillwald. 2013. 'Internet Going Mobile: Internet Access and Use in 11 African Countries', *Info: The Journal of Policy, Regulation and Strategy for Telecommunications, Information and Media* 15(5): 34–51. doi:10.1108/info-05-2013-0026.

Taylor, C. 2004. *Modern Social Imaginaries.* Durham, NC: Duke University Press.

Taylor, L., and D. Broeders. 2015. 'In the Name of Development: Power, Profit and the Datafication of the Global South', *Geoforum* 64: 229–37. doi:10.1016/j.geoforum.2015.07.002.

Wallis, C. 2017. '(Im)mobile Mobility: Marginal Youth and Mobile Phones in Beijing', in S. Campbell (ed.), *Mobile Communication: Bringing Us Together and Tearing Us Apart.* London: Routledge, pp. 71–92.

World Bank. 2016. *World Development Report 2016: Digital Dividends.* Washington, DC: World Bank.

York, G. 2015. 'Declining Copper Prices a Large Factor in Zambia's Economic Tumble', *Globe and Mail,* 26 October 2015. https://www.theglobeandmail.com/report-on-business/international-business/african-and-mideast-business/declining-copper-prices-send-zambia-into-economic-crisis/article26995466 (accessed 13 December 2017).

Zambia Information and Communications Technology Authority (ZICTA). 2015. *Support to Innovation and Entrepreneurship in the Information and Communication Technology Sector in Zambia: Financing and Implementation Proposal.* Lusaka: ZICTA.

CHAPTER 2

Botswana's Digital Revolution

What's in It?

Ardis Storm-Mathisen and Jo Helle-Valle

Introduction

> Botswana will be a globally competitive, knowledge and information society where lasting improvements in social, economic and cultural development is achieved through effective use of ICT.
>
> —Ministry of Communications Science and Technology, 2007

That information and communication technology (ICT) will be the Global South's way out of poverty has been a strong discourse for more than two decades. So far, this has not happened. An ICT revolution has undoubtedly taken place but the socio-economic outcomes so far are meagre – and hard to comprehend. Botswana is no exception. This chapter discusses the relationship (which is sometimes a gap) between the Botswana government's plans and policies for ICT and development, and the reality of the situation 'on the ground'. It thus raises a central theme for all states, as it seeks to describe and analyse the various mechanisms and dynamics that take place in the vastly complex process of trying – sometimes with success but often not – to turn the potential of ICT into sustainable development.

The quote that starts this chapter is from Botswana's first ICT policy document (Ministry of Communications Science and Technology, 2007, p. 5). It articulates the government's high hopes and ambitions for a digital revolution to become a driver for positive social, economic and cultural changes in the country. ICT as the means to propel such a development has been repeated in consecutive national plans, strategies and budgets (e.g. Ministry of Finance and Planning Development, 2009, 2016; Mutula et al., 2010). However, many of these plans have not turned into reality and goals have had to be adjusted. This is not to say that Botswana's ICT policy is a fiasco; it might be that it simply requires more time and that turning ICT into development is more complex than optimists envisioned. Thus, our question is in what ways and how has ICT come into use with implications for development in the country? What is in Botswana's digital revolution?

For us, the key point is that in order to understand this we need to study both plans and everyday practices. Plans are not neutral foresights; they are a part of the field of practice in which people act. Thus, plans affect people and people affects plans. All belong to the field of practice; the difference lies in the reach and power the different actors represent and the impact they have. It is the meeting of these 'big' and 'small' actors that concerns us here. We approach the phenomenon through the lens of 'scaling'. 'Scaling' – understood as the ways in which actors 'identify, classify construct and act upon connections at different degrees of proximity and distance [of connections]' (Slater, 2013, p. 139) and closely connected to the perspectives of Latour (2005) and Moores (2012) – is useful for several reasons. First, the concept allows us to approach practices with an open mind 'without making any *a priori* assumptions about the shape of the connections or how they are represented' (Slater, 2013, p. 139). Second, 'scaling' highlights that people's practices in making connections entail more than using representations and discourse and more than using or relating to media (ibid., p. 26). To understand what is in Botswana's digital revolution thus requires a perspective that allows for a wide, non-media-centric and not only representational approach (Moores, 2018; Morley, 2009) to actors' 'understandings and calculations of the future' within their wider setting and with an eye to the extent and ways in which these practices are 'mediated through ... new media' (Slater, 2013, p. 99). Third, the concept of 'scaling' is useful because it reminds us to treat the scaling practices and devices used by 'big' and 'small' actors in analytically symmetrical ways (ibid., p. 153). What is in Botswana's digital revolution is much defined by what powerful actors (international bodies, governments, global providers) say and do. Apart from the fact that the 'big actors' have power to roll out infrastructure, define the economic framework and so on, one important role they play is in producing planning documents that portray the way forward. Plans are scaling devices; they are partly attempting to look into the future, but they are also defining practices in the sense that they set the agenda for what is considered good and desirable action (see Abram and Weszkalnys, 2011). Producing and presenting numbers of a statistical kind is used to lay claims to what connections reality consist of and to force other actors to play the game defined by such numbers (Comaroff and Comaroff, 2006). However, although statistical data are scaling devices that can provide authoritative and politically relevant information on an aggregate level, they can be imprecise (even misleading) on the national and regional levels (Jerven, 2018). Moreover, they often provide few clues to what is going on and what is experienced locally (ibid.).

In order to understand what Botswana's digital revolution entails, therefore, in what follows we include the perspectives and actions of both small and big actors. The big ones, the national and global institutions, seek to steer the actions of the small through developing infrastructure, and by making plans and policies that have the dual role of defining how the world is and how it should develop. However, the analysis requires an empirically informed understanding of how citizens actually react to this framework. As planners and assessors have identified young entrepreneurs as key to sustainable new media-assisted development in Botswana (e.g. Ministry of Communications Science and Technology, 2007; World Bank, 2015a), we have chosen three such strategic cases (cf. Flyvbjerg, 2006) that we believe illuminate the challenges and opportunities that face those with the competence and orientation to make use of new media in their efforts to make a living for themselves. The presentation is based on qualitative and quantitative data produced and gathered by the two authors during fieldwork in the capital and a semi-urban village in 2012, 2015, 2016, 2017 and 2018.[1] Our argument consists of four steps. First, all connections have a trajectory, come from somewhere, and are situated. So does the narrative of ICT in Botswana. We therefore start by briefly describing some major changes that have taken place in Botswana since independence in which the recent ICT development is situated. Then we look at how the present situation of ICT in Botswana is described by 'big actors' (international and national) and the 'scaling devices' (in the form of plans, national statistics and international indexes) that orient these descriptions. Third, we turn our attention to 'small actors'. We delimit this focus to those actors who have the best opportunities to use ICT and particularly those the government imagines to be vanguards for ICT development and future improvements in the country – namely the young entrepreneurs with tertiary education.[2] Finally, we discuss the dynamics whereby the different ways of 'scaling' used by these different actors connect and link to other ongoing processes and what this may teach us about what is in Botswana's digital revolution.

ICT in Trajectories of Botswana's Recent Development

When Botswana gained independence in 1966 it established a modern constitution with freedom of expression for all citizens and started developing Gaborone as its capital. The country was then predominantly a patriarchal tribal Tswana society and among the ten poorest in the world. Ninety-eight per cent of the population of around one million lived in rural areas, most were unskilled and survived through subsistence farming and animal husbandry. A third of the men between the ages of twenty and forty were migrant workers in South Africa (Christian Michelsens Institutt [CMI], 1988, p. 9).

A fortunate combination of the discovery of large diamond and mineral deposits, stable political governance and low levels of corruption spurred a rapid growth in gross domestic product (GDP) and the state's wealth grew remarkably over the next thirty years. This made it possible for Botswana to invest in and gradually improve infrastructure and public education – something that was also supported by an open migration policy that allowed the import of skilled labour from abroad (Lefko-Everett, 2004). In the 1970s there was also a large influx of foreign aid and private investments and the country was supported by loans from multilateral sources (Rakner, 1996). Many of these sources dried up by the late 1990s when Botswana reached the status of a middle-income country. A long-term vision, with the goal to transform Botswana into an after-diamond-dependent economy where digital connection to world markets, education and social life were to ensure sound development for the country, was therefore initiated (Presidential Task Group, 1997). The aforementioned ICT policy (commonly called Maitlamo), was later based on this vision and instituted in 2007 (Ministry of Communications Science and Technology, 2007; Mutula et al., 2010). One effect of this was that Botswana's mass media, which until 1998 had consisted of one state-controlled newspaper and one radio station (the national TV station started in 2000), was liberalised, also allowing internet service providers to build their own infrastructures, and that competition for international voice gateways was opened in 2006 (Esselaar and Sebusang, 2013; UNESCO/IFAP, 2016). The government has since, in collaboration with private actors (not least the three mobile operators Orange, Mascom and beMobile), invested heavily in infrastructure and set up plans to build up e-services in health, education, government and business (Ministry of Finance and Development Planning, 2009, 2016).

Botswana today can be described as a country of large contrasts. It is on the one hand a country where much has been invested to build infrastructure, provide public health care, social welfare and education, and the country has the highest human development index score in sub-Saharan Africa (UNDP, 2015). Botswana's educational expenditure is especially impressive – in fact among the highest in the world, around 9 per cent of GDP – and includes the provision of nearly universal free primary education (World Bank, 2015b). Ninety-eight per cent of children complete primary education, 78 per cent continue to secondary level and 20 per cent enter tertiary education based on grades (ibid.). Uptake of mobile phones has been rapid and practically every adult Batswana has one. Despite high state expenditure on infrastructure, education, social welfare and poverty eradication schemes, Botswana is still among the world's economically most unequal countries (Gini 60.4). The growth rate of GDP and revenues from mining and agriculture is slowing down (Ministry of Finance and Development Planning, 2016). Levels of unemployment (17 per cent), poverty (18 per cent) and HIV/AIDS (18.5 per cent) remain high, not least among young people, and the quality of education too low to create a workforce sufficiently skilled for the knowledge economy (World Bank, 2015a).

Botswana is a large country with a small population. Although the improvements of roads and the rollout of cellular connection have made it easier for Botswana's highly mobile population to move around in pursuit of work and education (Hope, 2001), the fundamental infrastructure does not yet reach everywhere. Recent numbers suggest that 5 per cent of Botswana's 2.2 million people presently live in urban areas, with 10 per cent – predominantly young – in the capital (World Bank, 2015b). The complex consumer-oriented new media market is most visible and available in Gaborone and the other larger cities, although connections by now reach most larger villages. However, even if ICT infrastructures, devices and services in principle are in place, residents may not have the necessary means to access and make use of them. How to investigate the extent to which they do, why and with what outcomes is, in Botswana as elsewhere, a complex question. There are many methods and ways of reasoning around the current ICT situation and what it implies, each with its blind spots. However, since different actors use different scales and devices for measurement, we need to address several of them. We start below by taking a closer look at how the ICT situation in Botswana is judged through the 'scaling devices' of large global actors.

Global Actors on the State of Botswana's Digital Revolution: Two ICT Indexes

The collection of statistical data for purposes of nation state governance has long been central to Euromodern conceptions of society (Hacking, 1990). Today there is also increasing engagement from an international machinery of global actors to monitor, evaluate and construct knowledge for purposes of governance towards progress (Slater, 2013, p. 166). The World Bank is one such powerful actor. They state in their World Development Report 2016, *Digital Dividends*, that 'countries that complement technology investments with broader economic reforms reap digital dividends in the form of faster growth, more jobs and better services' (World Bank, 2016, p. xiii). Botswana is complemented in this report for having maintained 'a unique ID and trace-back systems for livestock that fulfill requirements for beef exports to the EU, while making the production process more efficient' (ibid., p. 13). However, the outcomes of Botswana's investments have, in all, not met expectations, according to the report *Botswana: Systematic Country Diagnostic*:

> While Botswana is rightly praised for its management of resource wealth, it is apparent that the high levels of investment by government (in health, education, and infrastructure) are not delivering quality outcomes, making it increasingly difficult to meet the objectives of growth, diversification, and poverty elimination. Indeed, some of the foundations which drove the development success of Botswana over the past half century are being eroded or face risks. (World Bank, 2015b, p. vi)

Knowledge constructions like those above are based on many sources of available evidence, much of which is derived from international and national statistical data. Such data feed into global indexes constructed and designed as tools to measure stages of development through time-space comparisons. The outcome is a type of facts that 'originate from, and are embedded in, social and political structures', but go beyond the confined structures of a single state (Jerven, 2018, p. 468). Of interest here is how such international data and global indexes – as a type of 'scaling devices' for 'mapping, representing and constructing different kinds of distance and proximity of connections' (Slater, 2013, p. 25) – have been constructed and are put to use by different kinds of actors.

One such actor is the World Economic Forum (WEF). Since the early 2000s the WEF has published the *Global Information Technology Report* (GIT report) to raise awareness among governments, businesses and society of how ICT impacts competitive economies and sustainable growth by assessing 'countries' ability to capitalize on the digital revolution' (WEF, 2016, pp. 5, 35). Central to this assessment is the Network Readiness Index (NRI), which is constructed from four sub-indexes: *environment* (eighteen indicators), *readiness* (eleven indicators), *usage* (sixteen indicators) and *impact* (eight indicators) (ibid., p. 5). Sub-Saharan Africa is, according to the latest GIT report, the region with the lowest NRI scores (with the exception of political and regulatory environment) and a region where 'affordability remains a barrier to ICT adoption and use' (ibid., p. 21). Botswana is at the lower end of the measured countries (ranked 101 of 139), with an overall score of 3.5 out of 7. This NRI score places Botswana in a middle position in comparison to the other countries looked at in this book: behind Mauritius (world rank 49, score 4.4) and South Africa (world rank up from 75 to 65, score 4.3), but ahead of Zambia (world rank 116, score 3.2) and probably also DR Congo, where data are lacking. Botswana is presently doing best on the NRI sub-index for political, regulatory and business innovation environment (rank 59, score 4.1) and worst on the sub-index for economic and social impact (rank 108, score 3.1), whereas it is mediocre on individual, business and government usage, readiness of infrastructure, affordability and skills. Although Botswana's NRI score has slightly improved from previous years, it scores in a way that suggests the digital revolution is moving slowly and with limited effects on the economy and growth in the nation.

Another internationally agreed upon standardised tool in use since the late 2000s is the ICT Development Index (IDI) published yearly in the *Measuring the Information Society Report* (MIS report) by the International Telecommunications Union (ITU, 2017b), the UN specialist agency for global ICT statistics. IDI measures the digital divide and compares ICT performance within and across countries as the outcome of eleven indicators in three sub-indexes: *access* (five indicators), *use* (three indicators) and *skills* (three indicators).[3] The latest MIS report (ITU, 2017a) shows that Africa continues to have much lower averages in IDI performance than any other region. Botswana is – if judged by the IDI index – barely above the average value for developing countries and in a middle position in Africa in terms of being an information society (rank 105 of 176 ITU member states). It is – compared to the other countries discussed in this book – behind Mauritius (global rank 72) and South Africa (global rank 92), but has much better scores than Zambia (global rank 146) and DR Congo (global rank 171).

Botswana's performance in the sub-index for *skills* is relatively good (score 5.67), but lower on the sub-indexes for *access* (score 4.9) and *use* (score 3.73). The interpretation of these data in the latest MIT report is that 'Botswana has an advanced ICT market and regulatory framework. The Government has opted for a wholesale backbone model to facilitate open access and cost-based pricing in order to lower prices' (ITU, 2017b, p. 156) and that a falling score in the sub-index for *use* in part can be attributed to changes in methodology (ITU, 2017a). So, although mobile cellular subscriptions per 100 inhabitants are high (159 per cent), the rather low access to computers in households (29 per cent), the very low percentages of the population that have access to a fixed line telephone (7 per cent) and fixed broadband subscription (3 per cent), still means that few individuals use the internet (39 per cent). The indicators can also speak to how Botswana's digital revolution is different to that of the other countries discussed in this book. For instance, access to computers is much higher among households in Mauritius (61 per cent) than in Botswana (29 per cent), but higher in Botswana than in South Africa (24 per cent), Zambia (8 per cent) and in DR Congo (3 per cent). And even if the percentage of the population that uses the internet is lower in Botswana than in Mauritius and South Africa (where it is above 50 per cent), it is much higher in Botswana than in Zambia (26 per cent) and in DR Congo (6 per cent).

Botswana's digital revolution can thus, according to the NRI and IDI as international index measurements, be summed up as something like upper-medium in the sub-Saharan region. The country has infrastructure and regulations in place, people use mobile phones and have the necessary skills (ITU, 2017a and b), but use of the internet and other ICTs is low and constrained, and the economic and social impacts remain rather low.

What these global actors do with these indicators is to define the reality – they assess and evaluate Botswana's position compared to the rest of the world when it comes to ICT-related issues. This is at the same time objective, normative and a political act. It is objective in the sense that indicators chosen define the criteria for evaluation and on this basis provide objective measures for how a country scores. Of course, it could have been defined in other ways, but given its foundation its information is – in one sense of the word – objective. However, the act of indexing is also normative as it clearly states what the desired goals are. This combination of objectivity and normativity is an act of power and politics. It forces other actors to either comply with or actively dismiss the logic of their constructed reality.

Returning to Botswana, we can clearly see the effects of these globally defined ICT indexes. There are at least four relevant types of roles or functions that are involved in Botswana: assessors, planners, facilitators and users. These can be combined in the same actors. For instance, while ordinary citizens are only ICT users, various institutions within the state apparatus cover all four roles. Let us look at the first three functions, performed by various big actors, before we turn more specifically to the users.

The compilers of data in Botswana are first of all Statistics Botswana (formerly the Central Statistics Office) and various ministry-based institutions. ICT-related statistics have appeared in limited form (primarily focusing on media institutions, telephony, etc.) until recently, although increasingly in focus in official documents after Botswana's first long-term vision (Maitlamo, 2004; Presidential Task Group, 1997). The country's ICT policy, which built on and complemented this framework, formulated three long-term goals: 'to create an enabling environment for ICT industry where numerous small-medium enterprises could prosper', where 'universal ICT services were provided for the population' and to 'become an ICT hub so as to empower Batswana and to make the country's service sector globally competitive' (Ministry of Communications Science and Technology, 2007, p. 5). The subsequent National Development Plan, NDP 10 (covering the period from 2009 to 2016), highlighted the importance of this strategy by signalling massive ICT-related investment (Ministry of Finance and Development Planning, 2009). This NDP 10 was also the first NDP to set up a formal framework for monitoring and evaluating how the defined goals had progressed.

Statistics Botswana completed a series of surveys during NDP 10 to produce data on socio-economic indicators in different sectors, including Botswana's first ICT Household Survey. The ICT Household Survey was conducted in 2014 and has delivered, together with compiled data from service providers (on telecommunications, postal services, print media, radio and television), to an official database from which Botswana's government could assess the current ICT situation. According to Statistics Botswana's own webpages (http://www.statsbots.org.bw/ict-statistics),[4] the specific aim of the 2014 ICT Household Survey (Statistics Botswana, 2017) was to collect data on access and usage that could be used 'to measure the impact of ICT on society and its contributions to the Gross Domestic Product and ICT development index (IDI)'. This explicit reference to the IDI index suggests that Statistics Botswana, as a national actor, understood and constructed the ICT survey partly also to feed into global scaling devices to place Botswana in the world and according to the scaling practices of global actors.

As previous household surveys conducted by Statistics Botswana also contained questions about media ownership of and access to ICT, some figures on the changing ICT scene are now available. These show a strikingly rapid increase in households' access to mobile phones, from 41 per cent in 2003 to a high of 94 per cent in 2014 (Statistics Botswana, 2017), whereas households' access to TV and radio had settled at around 60 per cent. The 2014 survey found that 41 per cent of households had access to the internet (94 per cent of which meant mobile internet), 21 per cent to laptops, 11 per cent to desktop computers, 10 per cent to fixed internet (and WiFi) and 9 per cent to fixed line telephones. Computer ownership and access to the internet was highest within households where the head had tertiary and secondary school education, was below forty-four years of age, and/or lived in the capital Gaborone.

In terms of individual uses of ICT, the 2014 survey found that 85 per cent of the population above the age of ten said they used a mobile phone, 41 per cent used computers and 37 per cent used the internet. It is worth noting that cost was the most commonly stated reason for not using a mobile phone, whereas it was lack of knowledge for computers or the internet. Among the 41 per cent who had access to the internet on their phones, 78 per cent engaged in social media platforms. Among the internet users, 55 per cent claimed to use it daily or almost daily, 77 per cent accessed the internet from their mobile phones and 43 per cent from portable laptops. The highest proportion of internet users had tertiary education (49 per cent) and were in the age group 15–24. The survey also found that print media was used by 76.4 per cent of the population, whereas e-Government services were only used by 7.5 per cent and e-commerce/business by as few as 4.6 per cent (Statistics Botswana, 2017.). More recent statistics suggest that use of mobile broadband has increased to 51 per cent and that 28 per cent are Facebook subscribers. However, most internet traffic still relies on pre-paid subscriptions and many people remain constrained in their use of ICTs (ITU, 2017a).

Other recently compiled data show that there is a steady increase in access to and use of various ICTs among employees, in the media, in schools as well as in households over the last decade (e.g. Statistics Botswana, 2016). But they also point to challenges connected to underutilisation of the infrastructure, high costs and the significant digital divides among the population (e.g. Statistics Botswana, 2017).[5]

ICT in Current National Development Plans

Around 2016, the fiftieth anniversary of its independence, Botswana evaluated its Vision 2016 (formulated in 1996), set up a new vision for the next twenty years and drafted a new NDP 11 for the years 2017–2023. A public opinion study (Lekalake, 2016) ordered by the government indicated that although many Batswana felt the country had done fairly well in relation to a number of the pillars of the old vision – improving access to education, information technology and maintaining social cohesion – they continued to face many of the same economic challenges they had ten years before. Concerns were with skills and with the fairness of national wealth distribution. Taking this into account, goals for the new vision 'Prosperity for All' were set up to achieve sustainable economic development, human social development, sustainable development and governance, peace and security. This new vision also emphasised ICT as a central driver for these changes: 'we will leverage leading information communication technology (ICT) as a key contributor to economic growth and employment whilst also enabling an efficient private and public sector' (Presidential Task Team, 2016, p. 16).

The government of Botswana writes, in the recent NDP 11 set up for the years 2017–2023 (Ministry of Finance and Development Planning, 2016), that it 'has, over the years, invested heavily in the development of ICT' (ibid., p. 23). The emphasis is on how access to ICTs has improved and that, in addition to the 'investments in infrastructure necessary for media and internet access in communities, libraries and schools across the country' there has been an implementation of e-Government systems and services. The government's evaluation of the current situation is, however, that despite their large investments in these areas (not least education), 'Botswana has not been able to sufficiently produce high levels of skilled and productive manpower .... There remains a critical need to develop the human capital and make it more effective and relevant to the needs of the economy' (ibid., p. 54). As for the macro-economic development, they point to how 'limitation and inability to cope with the fast changing global ICT environment have made it difficult for the country to use these virtues to attract FDI [foreign direct investment] to boost overall investment' (ibid.). They also conclude that 'insufficient progress was achieved in the microeconomic environment' and that there were problems with the 'comparable high cost of ICT services; slow implementation of eGovernment programmes; and limited participation and empowerment of citizens in the sector' (ibid., p. 65). Other identified problems are 'inadequate inclusiveness of the education system; sub-optimal utilisation of ICT; low transition rates from secondary to tertiary education; and mismatch between skills produced by the education system and the needs of the economy' (ibid., p. 68).

National statistics on ICT use, together with statistics on demography, economy and other relevant factors, are a common reference for these assessments. It is also with reference to national demographic surveys that the government identifies women and the young as being most vulnerable to unemployment and poverty. Simultaneously, the government sees the youth as presenting 'an opportunity to accelerate socio-economic development' and highlights that 'addressing youth issues such as youth development and economic empowerment are … key to the country's development strategy' (Ministry of Finance and Development Planning, 2016, pp. 11, 17). Emphasis is also put on increased support to small, medium and micro-sized enterprises (SMMEs), with a reference to how this is proven worldwide to promote growth and create employment, not least for women and youth (ibid., p. 117).

The wonders that ICT can do for Botswana nationally and sector-wise are also listed:

> Measures will be put in place to ensure that ICT will continue to play a pivotal role in the development and diversification of the economy. ICT provides a much needed environment for the Botswana economy to prosper. For example, unfettered access and ease of flow of information through modern technology will attract big companies into the country, resulting in job creation, income generation and asset base expansion. The training of ICT personnel will continue to be accorded priority in order to enhance the sector's contribution to economic and export diversification, as well as the creation of high quality jobs. … Connectivity to modern internet infrastructure will be the conduit to enable access to the world, and for Botswana to export her ideas, products and services to the global marketplace thereby opening opportunities for an export-led growth. The effective use of ICT will also boost productivity and growth rates in technology driven sectors, such as Communications, Finance and Business Services, Trade, Hotels and Restaurants, Mining and Manufacturing. (Ministry of Finance and Development Planning, 2016, pp. 65, 68)

These optimistic visions are quite in line with how the challenges and solutions have been portrayed by various international actors (e.g. Esselaar and Sebusang, 2013; ITU, 2017a; World Bank, 2015b, 2016; WEF, 2016). This is not a coincidence, as there is ample evidence of the close coordination between national and international bodies in producing numbers. Global actors (like ITU, World Bank, etc.) need the 'right' kind of statistical groundwork from governments, and the

Botswana authorities need to be favourably assessed by the former. Thus, in the NDP 11 we find statements such as: 'Government will intensify the implementation of the reform roadmap and action plan … with a view to improving Botswana's rankings in both the World Bank Doing Business Report and the World Economic Forum's Global Competitiveness Reports' (Ministry of Finance and Development Planning, 2016, p. 112).

This connection between global and national actors is of course not surprising. Their scaling devices and practices are in many respects alike and connected. The global indexes are in part fed by the latest national statistics, while national statistics are on the other hand partly produced with an eye to feeding into the global indexes, partly as an achievement of connecting to the world itself. In this sense they all engage in an economy of numbers: 'statistics is a medium of communication *and* a species of commodified knowledge, one whose value and veracity accumulates as it circulates' (Comaroff and Comaroff, 2006, pp. 209–10).

However, globally sanctioned figures do not guarantee success. The plans and foresight that the Botswana government have come up with, both long ago and more recently, have not materialised, despite their planning, investments and efforts. A common explanation for why ICT has not yet produced the envisioned impact is lack of skills among the population and problems in the economic environment (e.g. ITU, 2017a). Therefore, Botswana puts its trust in the young – those who can most easily acquire these skills (Ministry of Finance and Development Planning, 2016). However, being young is not sufficient in itself. The young must have access to and use ICTs and must have an attitude that enables them to turn these competences into economic development. Thus, the key actor in official planners' minds is the young entrepreneur.

For this reason, we will use the next section of this chapter to present and discuss three such individuals.

The Vanguards of the Digital Revolution? Young Entrepreneurs

> The development discourse is strong, but it is just a discourse. When you're in school you get big dreams, but when you leave school you meet reality. The economy tells you otherwise. You can't find a job, can't start a business.
>
> —Gosego, age twenty-four, 2017, male graduate aiming to start a supply business

There is a long leap from what the government plans to what actually happens in people's everyday lives. It is safe to say that on a general level what the government and various agencies stated was implemented and working ICT infrastructure was often a mismatch with what the people we met during our fieldwork in Botswana had experienced. Moreover, the ways in which people felt that things were connected, and how they categorised and acted on relationships, did not align well with the classifications and processes depicted by the global and national actors. However, that things were going well and that Botswana was a country in which people's dreams could come true came through as a widely shared opinion among the youth.

A good indication of this government-fed optimism was expressed in essays collected in 2016 from seventh grade (most were thirteen years old) and Form 3 pupils (most were sixteen years old) in two of the schools in the village in which we conducted fieldwork. They were invited to write an essay about 'Myself thirty years from now – what I do and what I did to get there' (Storm-Mathisen, 2017). In the ninety-six essays collected, phrases that clearly echoed Botswana's Vision 2016, hence linked to the official development discourse, were common. Moreover, ICTs were conspicuously present in their imagined futures. The dreams they depicted seemed very distant from the reality in which these pupils lived. They went to schools that did not have working computers, most of them did not have mobile phones and had never been on social media, and only half of them came from homes that owned a TV or radio. Thus, although the majority of these young pupils connected to the discourse about Botswana's digital revolution, they did not take part in its material culture.

The quote that introduces this section was uttered by Gosego, a young educated man who belonged to the active online population of Botswana. The main form of entry into the digital world in Botswana is through tertiary education (Storm-Mathisen, 2019). Due to the country's massive investment in education, students at this level have cheap and comprehensive access to new media. Thus, in comparison to the pupils who wrote the essays, Gosego's view on life and new media is more experienced and in this sense realistic. His view is that school sets big dreams in the minds of young children – thus teaching them to position themselves as just as able as others in the world to prosper and use ICT – while reality and the economy will eventually teach them otherwise.

Gosego (age twenty-four) is one of the three young entrepreneurs we will introduce in more detail to illustrate how the assumed vanguard of the ICT revolution can fare in real life and how their productive activities can link to ICT. The other two are Kabo (age twenty-five) and Atamelang (age thirty). They have all completed a tertiary education degree, and currently reside in the capital. However, whereas Gosego is presently trying to establish a business, but struggling to get it going, Kabo has already established one that gives him economic income, and Atamelang, a woman who is a few years older, has run a business for several years which has expanded, and she receives national and international attention as a successful entrepreneur.

Gosego: ICT, Economy and Gender Trouble

Gosego grew up in a village as the only son of his mother (his father died when he was ten). He was bright and had been among the 20 per cent of his age cohort that had been admitted into university in 2013. We met him for the first time in 2015 when he was in the final year of his bachelor's degree in social science. He was a very articulate and politically engaged person, frustrated with the current government and what he saw as their inability to foster economic development for the people in the country: 'here in Botswana everything is a crisis, lands, jobs … no politics for the middle class, they tax too much, … high inequality, a few people own everything and most very little'. Since 2013 he had received a monthly government allowance of 1400 Pula (126 USD) to pursue his studies, was thankful for this (the sum was more than his mother earnt), but he said it was hard to get by on it, especially for a man, since having a girlfriend required that the man provide for her.

Gosego's dream was to set up a business selling various supplies (computer parts, catering, etc.), and eventually earn enough to be able to buy property and start investing in real estate – which seemed to be every young Motswana's dream. He started to work on this strategy as a student, mostly through learning the processes one needs to go through to get started. He frequently displayed his ambitions on Facebook. Gosego had not had much experience with ICTs when he was growing up, and it was not until he started university that he received an email account, a bank account (including an e-bank account, as the government requires all receivers of the allowance to register for e-banking) and access to computer rooms and free WiFi (at the university). He had learnt to use various online platforms for registration, information and subject submissions and had good ICT skills. He was thus more experienced in using new media devices and internet platforms than most young people.

However, as Gosego had experienced it, setting up a business and getting it going had been difficult. He had applied for plots, a right held by every citizen in Botswana. His idea was to build on it and rent out, but the process of land allocation in Botswana is extremely lengthy (his own mother had at the time of the interview been waiting for fifteen years without receiving a plot). He therefore had higher hopes for registering a company as a means for landing government tenders.[6] According to him, the timing was especially good because 'elections are approaching. They give out lots of tenders, they flush money around so you can vote for them. After that it dries up'. Because of this plan he had become more cautious in the political statements he posted on Facebook (he supported the opposition). The main challenge now, however, was to get a company registered. According to Gosego, just the registering process, the right bank connection and the buying of stock required a minimum of 50,000 Pula. He was not even close to having that kind of money. However, as he had done well in his bachelor's degree at the University of Botswana, he had managed to get a job as a research assistant at a national NGO. He earnt less than he did as a student but he was saving and continued to look for new opportunities.

In Gosego's opinion, new media were very important for his own and his fellow students' futures in business: 'New media is part of starting up a business, the home of every successful business and social media is the new kid on the block. You cannot manage without. For information, advertising, accessing what you want, you need it'. However, his experience – echoed by many others – was that within the realm of business and public management the ICT revolution had a long way to go. The state institutions in particular were to blame as they had not followed up on the promises for a digital future: 'They advertise tenders on social media, but the government gazette is also important. The government still believes in old practices though. You can apply for tenders online, but when you go further the webpage is down …'.

He was clearly frustrated, struggling to keep up his beliefs in a bright future, but for the three years we had known him his ambitions had so far got him nowhere. He felt that he had done all the things that the government had advised him to do, to no avail. His frustrations were fuelled by the fact that his plans were not only about making money – in fact his lack of success was linked to his very existence as a man. His dream was to marry and have children, but:

> you come to the city, want the girls, can't find a job, you run to criminality, drink alcohol, rob people, high number of petty theft, men are doing this … Dreams crashed, it all comes back to politics, the economy, the

> government can't provide, society does not give men the opportunity to provide for women. It is a masculinity crisis, if you are a man and can't provide for your girl or wife they will call you *tinto*, a man who cannot provide … you can't be both poor and respected, it does not work like that.

Thus, his experience, echoed by many others, was that within the realm of business and public management the ICT revolution had so far had little impact. Simultaneously, new media clearly impacted on sociality:

> In the first phase of adulthood social media and Facebook content diverts wants, creates pressures, a new world, speeds up wants, everybody wants to have a Mac, you want to acquire what your friend has acquired, and to brag about it on Facebook and it makes it easier to coordinate infidelity.

New media, as Gosego sees it, brings information more easily, but it also affects dreams and wants. An important factor for him was that he felt that new media have led women to demand more, which he feels puts pressure on his masculinity, while not making it any easier for him to establish a business to make the money he feels he needs in order to be a man.

Kabo: ICT and the Dynamics of Capital Accumulation

Kabo's story has many similarities to that of Gosego, but he ran small businesses that in fact were quite successful and his way of relating to ICT in this respect is different. Kabo grew up in a small village and was the oldest son in a family of four. His parents had no formal education, but ran small businesses and had started using ICTs fairly early. Kabo had done well at school and had two years left of his bachelor's degree in media when we first met him in 2015. At this time, he had already had some success in informal, small-scale business. Since secondary school he had sold goods to peers and was now also arranging events and selling tickets for concerts and festivals, selling self-imported luxury consumer goods from South Africa to lecturers at the university and he lent fellow students money (at very high interest rates). In most of these businesses, new media were important in his strategies: he used them to inform himself, to organise his trips to South Africa and to maintain communication with his customers, by calls and SMS or social media.

With the money he had earnt, he had bought himself a smartphone, a Mac laptop and a car. He said, 'yeah, I try to save up some money to finance my projects' (see also Storm-Mathisen, 2019). Kabo was very interested in business; he posted frequently on Facebook about successful businessmen in Botswana and elsewhere and attended business gatherings when possible. The most successful businessmen in Botswana were Indians, according to Kabo, but among those running medium and smaller businesses there were many Kalanga, like himself, which Kabo believed was because they have the mentality and the networks needed to start new businesses.

He explains:

> For me I also think the contributing factor is my family. My father did not have any formal education so he started doing carpentry and my mother she had a small shop, she sold food, and that got us through university. That's where it all starts from. I don't come from a rich family, no middle class, but they started businesses. During that time they also had houses where people paid rent. Now that's really difficult. We have a plot, we applied for it in 1992, twenty-four years, still waiting. I have also applied for plots. I am on three lists as there was an opening for applications last year. You can get one for free, and buy another one.

One of Kabo's projects had been to register an advertising company together with a friend in his second year of university. However, this ended up being unsuccessful. As he explained to us later:

> We were short on finance. We didn't have equipment and the editing software that we needed to make the adverts up to the standards the clients would require. So we then took a break. And along the way he and I had different visions on the company and we ended up parting. So I decided to open up my own where I was 100 per cent owner. I haven't really started in operation, just saving up money to buy equipment.

Kabo was very knowledgeable about the requirements for starting a business, and what he wanted from it. In his view it was not an expensive process, but a long and complicated one:

> We had to reserve a name and wait for twelve working days. After that you have to get your certificate for cooperation where you pay 360 [Pula]. After that you register with BURS for tax, and then with PPADB enables your company to contend for tenders from the government. Then also you have to get trading licence, then they need to make sure that your premises are up to standards. It's really a long process, up to six months. They come and they look at the premises. Then you can get your trading

> licence. I have to sublet a place and after that I get a trading licence. But I can operate from my bedroom. I just need a computer.

In 2015 he had just started this long process and had not yet earnt any money from his registered company. However, when we met him again in 2017, his business was up and running, and in fact bringing in quite a good income. He ran the promotions for several food products in local store chains, he had bought TV screentime on buses between Gaborone and some other cities, had set up entertainment programmes for travellers and sold advertising breaks to companies and made TV commercials. His view now was that successful businesses did not require much start-up capital: 'I don't need the equipment, I just need to know the people'. And Kabo knew many people. During his university years, he had built up a large network of friends and acquaintances – people in business environments, government employees and some in academia. He was a very pleasant and polite young man, a competent talker who made people feel acknowledged, and he used new media to uphold these relations.

Atamelang: ICT and Gender Connected to National and Global Goals

Atamelang also came from a village, but was a few years older. She had graduated as one of the few female bachelor's students in computer science at the University of Botswana. It was during her time as a student that she developed her business idea to teach use of computers and the internet to the local community. She won an innovation prize for this idea, and secured, after she graduated, some government and NGO funding to rent premises, buy the necessary equipment and set up the business. She constructed a webpage and a Facebook page to advertise for pupils and to inform the public of her services. She started running computer classes in her local community for free, but gradually, as they became popular, she introduced fees and started to earn an income. Over time, Atamelang expanded her business to other cities, advertising her courses on Facebook and on the business webpage. In a Facebook post some years after she established her business, she expressed her gratitude as follows:

> To our mentees I give nothing back but a story, a journey of how God's grace can take a little girl from a small town and shower her with mercy. A story of a little girl from a small town with no eloquent speech nor swift in any of her steps. I tell them always that ALL things are POSSIBLE, that an ordained destiny is fuelled from mysterious reserves. This girl; Her name

> is I. And her name tomorrow can be any of the ones I meet on my journey. In this I do not boast nor do I take any glory. I am eternally grateful and humbled each day. (Atamelang's post, 2017)

> Thank you [Atamelang], Have no words to thank you enough for the impact you had in my career since we meet. You have been such an inspiration to me as a woman making it in the tech industry ma'am. Thank you a million times Mma. (Facebook reply, 2017, from a male, aged twenty-one)

Atamelang connects in this post to the strong development discourse in Botswana. She addresses her mentees – those whom she or others are teaching – to support the idea, build networks and to believe in the dream: that a little girl from a small village can become a business owner. The reply from a male former mentee points to Atamelang's success within such a discourse, and she receives respect in practice. She has, as a woman and an entrepreneur, become a person who inspires not only girls but men too – those like Gosego or Kabo – who have entrepreneurial dreams. Other posts also gave witness to how she had become someone whom the government and some NGOs would point to as an example of new innovations and activities of the sort they were hoping to see more of in Botswana. Atamelang was invited to give speeches and to travel nationally and internationally, something that was also communicated online.

Scaling, Dynamics and Power

A commonality between Gosego, Kabo and Atamelang is that they have all acquired the kinds of entrepreneurial ambitions and basic ICT skills the government hopes to see among the young. They are relating actively and competently to new media and use technology, including the internet other than for social media, to enhance their businesses. However, their strategies, as well as the outcomes of their efforts, are quite varied. In this concluding section of the chapter we will highlight some of the parallels and contrasts in order to assess the question that is contained in the title – namely what the alleged digital revolution in Botswana really implies.

We find it useful to start by distinguishing between three different ways in which new media can affect economic outputs: as a business sector in itself; as tools for increased efficiency in productive processes; and in making connections between actors faster and better.

The ICT Sector

Businesses that deal in ICTs are relatively few in Botswana. The sector consists mainly of high-skilled, high-paid labour, or it involves unskilled, low-paid work, like those who sell SIM cards and other cheap stationery in bus stations, outside shopping malls and so on. Those in the latter category engage many but yield very meagre profits, while those in the former are well paid but very few in number. Atamelang is one example of a young actor who has succeeded in turning ICT into a business by specialising in teaching ICT skills to ordinary people. She came to think of this business idea through her own experience and competence as someone educated in ICT, a factor that also makes her service trustworthy. Hence, as soon as she got her business going, it was relatively easy for her to receive the necessary funding from governmental and non-governmental actors to develop the business and provide a service that could later attract paying customers. Kabo, for his part, is an example of an actor who has succeeded in a certain respect in providing media content, mainly through making and selling TV commercials or editing them into movies that people watch on the long bus rides between the larger cities.

ICT as More Efficient Production

In addition to her entrepreneurship in teaching ICT, Atamelang not only has a business in ICT, but also uses ICTs to make her business more efficient. She has replaced certain manual and physical elements of procedures in her daily running of the business (in management, purchases, billing, customer relations and advertising) with digital solutions. As this helps her perform these tasks more quickly and easily, ICT saves her time so that she can spend more of it on teaching, arranging new courses and on other tasks from which she can earn money. As Gosego notes, new media is also part of starting up a business, something he felt he could not manage without, especially as he was going for government tenders, which were promoted and advertised through digital media. However, the digital platforms for these purposes often malfunctioned, many of the schema were complicated, and the internet is expensive. Thus, more often than not, the young ended up choosing offline, analogue solutions – sometimes after having spent considerable amounts of time trying to do it online. While planners and various global actors often emphasise the lack of digital competence among the population, those who do have this competence complain about the lack of digital infrastructure and content.

Kabo had, like Gosego, experienced the difficulties in starting a business, especially if one wanted to get tenders from the government. His response to these obstacles, however, was different. While Gosego stuck to his plan of basing his business on government tenders – with little success so far – but gave priority to analogue solutions, Kabo decided to move away from doing business with the government and focus only on doing business with private actors. Moreover, his experience had also taught him that he did not need much equipment, or an office. He needed only a computer and could operate his business from his bedroom, thereby keeping expenses down.

ICT and Networking

Our data suggest that the most important effect – at least at this stage of the revolution – is the effect new media have on connecting people (and people and things). First, and most visible, it helps migrants and their families. Swifter, cheaper and more accurate communication is crucial for those on the move, and for those who need to move goods (cf. the chapters by Willems and Helle-Valle in this book). For our entrepreneurs, too, the potential of new media as efficient connectors is important. Maintaining relations and building new relations of relevance has evidently become much easier with mobile calls, SMS, email and not least social media. However, to use the right platforms in the right ways requires competence. Although all three of our entrepreneurs routinely use new media, the ways in which they do so differ. For instance, Gosego has had to tone down his postings on Facebook, out of fear that his oppositional political postings could make him lose tenders for the current government. Atamelang and Kabo seem more cautious in voicing political or private ideas. Their posts relate to their business interests and are used by them to attract people who could become potential customers. Kabo, for instance, used Facebook as a space to advertise his goods and to systematically convey an image as a reliable person and businessman. He had built up a considerable network of friends and acquaintances offline and online over the years. This was a resource for his advertising business. His well-maintained network included individuals with all kinds of skills, and he gave us several examples of how he was able to capitalise on his networks – it became social capital, convertible to economic capital. For instance, when he landed a contract for TV commercials, he could quickly recruit people whom he knew and trusted to produce the media content. This is also why, in his case, establishing a successful business had not required much start-up capital: 'I don't need the equipment, I just need to know the people'. Some of these small jobs were also communicated to people among the network of friends he had gathered on Facebook. For instance: 'Looking for someone with at least two years of experience in events management. Inbox me for further details'.

Kabo is successful in business, and seems to be doing better every year. He is successful not because he was born rich, but because he has the skills to strategically build social networks that are used as social capital, convertible to economic capital, in what seems to be a self-enhancing process.

There is an additional factor that plays into Kabo's success in networking. He belongs to the ethnic group Kalanga, who in Botswana are generally associated with being good businesspeople. Thus, as he himself expressed (see above), his Kalanga ancestry has helped him to acquire the attitudes and outlook on life that are necessary to succeed in business. However, there is little doubt that his ethnicity also provides him with some very important connections; being a Kalanga means you have friends of friends of people who matter. Ethnicity plays a part in another way too. Both Kabo and Gosego – as well as countless others in Botswana – claim that big business in Botswana is controlled by Indians. For Gosego this had no consequences for his business strategy other than dampening his optimism, but Kabo cites Indians' dominance as one important reason for steering clear of government tenders, as well as certain business sectors.

Atamelang is interesting in this respect because of her gender as well as her scaling strategies. Becoming a female computer scientist was obviously a great achievement. According to her, there were only a handful of her kind at the time of her graduation. Moreover, international NGOs were strongly influenced (as they still are) by the ICT4D rhetoric (cf. the introductory chapter in this book), and by the focus on women and their key role in development efforts. Thus, not only did she prove herself to be a highly competent professional, she also became an ideal candidate for NGOs who wanted to dive into this new field, and she was highly attractive as a symbol of what was in vogue in the development business. Thus, she was assisted in applying for funding from NGOs and invited to conferences and meetings. This boosting of her social capital no doubt contributed to her being able to establish a successful business.

In contrast to Kabo and Atamelang, Gosego has none of these resources. His background – both in terms of class and ethnicity – represents no assets, and he seemed to have a hard time breaking into the right circles. Although he is still very young, and may well succeed, he will have to work very hard to build up the networks that are necessary to succeed in the Botswana business world.

Connecting Scales

Our discussions point in the direction of a country that is undergoing a difficult and earnest struggle to work new media into the national economy. Advances have taken place but the planning and foresight have been too optimistic and have had to be adjusted repeatedly. Still, the conviction among policy-makers that ICT is key to a prosperous future seems to be as rock solid as ever. No doubt this perspective is strongly affected by global actors, not least through ICT and development indexes.

In fact, there is a dual relation between the global indexes and national self-assessment scales. As international bodies such as the World Bank set requirements for Botswana to improve its national statistics, Botswana's own scales become oriented to the global scale. As such, there are active interconnections between assessments of the ICT situation in Botswana by the international society and by Botswana itself. Moreover, our cases show how this connection has consequences for the infrastructural development plans, as well as actual investments in Botswana. On the other hand, when aligning the scaling practices of these global and national 'big' actors to the scaling practices of those mundane actors the government sees as the vanguards of the ICT revolution – the young entrepreneurs – many connections disappear. However, as our cases demonstrate, not all connections are severed; some are able to navigate the cumbersome business-related digital landscape. Our three examples point to some of the common mechanisms that obstruct young people's ambitions. These individuals struggle to make productive use of new media. A few are successful, but it is clearly not up to them alone. The big actors' governmental instruments define the world in which these aspiring individuals must act, and the world that is formed by these defining forces is not always to their advantage.

So what is in Botswana's digital revolution? The common conception is that when digital solutions replace the old procedures, they are revolutionary in their effects because new products and services can be developed, production can become more efficient and social capital can grow in civil society. Since there has been a very rapid increase in the use of digital tools in Botswana, it is assumed that there has been a revolution. Our discussion suggests that the explosion in use has not (yet) translated into revolutionary socio-economic change. What has taken place so far is that Botswana has become an information society but not (again: yet) a knowledge economy (Carmody, 2013). There is, however, undoubtedly a potential for radical change. The cases we have presented suggest that there are connections between ICT and things that are happening on the ground in Botswana. As of yet, this is especially strong on the discursive level, whereas the practical impact on entrepreneurship is meagre and primarily for the educated. If our analysis is sound, the situation is that almost 80 per cent of the young generation (i.e. those who have not been admitted to tertiary education) are left behind. Thus, the fact that so much digital competence is developed through tertiary education suggests that the digital divide will widen. Moreover, our discussion also shows that the connection is perceived and acted upon differently and brings about different outcomes among educated young entrepreneurs. There seems to be a lack of connections between the reality for people on the ground, ICT as technology and narrative, and the grand plans and visions. This is clearly visible in the case of Gosego. Whereas Kabo and Atamelang use ICT to scale up their businesses, Gosego speaks of it as something that is necessary for scaling up, but out of his reach. He might never succeed in this, because for him there is no active connection to the 'big' actors – he seems unable to assemble the material and human actors he requires in productive ways (Latour, 2005). Kabo, for his part, could not have succeeded in his early petty trading or in his current advertising business without new technology. It is a connection made possible by new media. However, his practice – selling and continuously making new connections to promote his business – has not significantly changed because of new media. Rather, it seems to be his high level of social competence that enables him to apply ICTs as useful tools. In fact, it is our opinion that apart from Atamelang, who obviously depends on the existence of new media, the other two would likely be in the same situation if digital ICTs had not existed. This suggests that one needs to engage with ICTs because they exist, but that they do not in themselves necessarily make a big difference in who succeeds and who fails.

In all, the three cases point to some challenges for the digital revolution to gain force in Botswana. First of all, there are huge inequalities among groups of Batswana, thus large proportions of the population are inhibited from taking part in the digital revolution. Second, the ICT-related National policies and systems are not attentive enough to the needs of the young up-and-coming entrepreneurs; even the ambitious and qualified struggle. What mattered to these young people was not connecting to the global market through ICT, but connecting to and making a living in their local worlds.

Acknowledgements

We are indebted to Gosego, Kabo, Atamelang and the many other people in Botswana who were willing to share their experiences and help us learn about these processes. The research was funded by the New Media Practices in a Changing Africa project, financed by the Research Council of Norway (grant no. FriPro 240714).

Ardis Storm-Mathisen is Research Professor at Consumption Research Norway and Faculty of Education, Oslo Metropolitan University. Her research has focused on issues of gender, identity and vulnerability among children, youth and families in relation to their everyday, digital media-related practices, currently as Principle Investigator for Relink (Building resilient households through interdisciplinary and multilevel exploration and intervention), a project funded by the Research Council of Norway. She conducted fieldwork in Botswana between 2015 and 2018, giving special attention to gender relations and the lives of the young. During this research she was affiliated to the Centre for Gender Research, University of Oslo as a senior researcher and a visiting researcher at the University of Botswana.

Jo Helle-Valle is a social anthropologist and Professor in the Development Studies Department at Oslo Metropolitan University. He has carried out fieldwork in Botswana, Uganda, Ethiopia and Norway. His main research areas are media practices, gender, local politics and economy, and theoretical issues related to the social sciences. Helle-Valle has served as a Visiting Scholar at Harvard, Oxford, Simon Fraser University, the University of Botswana and Makerere University. He has published in journals such as *Journal of African Media Studies, Africa, Ethnos, History and Anthropology* and *New Media & Society*.

Notes

1. Fieldwork included participant observation, collection of secondary material and reports, interviews, video-assisted self-reporting, digital ethnography (Storm-Mathisen, 2017), essay competitions in primary and secondary schools as well as two door-to-door surveys (with households and individuals) and a web survey.
2. Names and certain characteristics are changed to protect these people's identity.
3. Indicators for access are fixed telephone subscriptions; mobile-cellular telephone subscriptions; international internet bandwidth per internet user; households with a computer; and households with internet access. The indicators for use are individuals using the internet; fixed broadband subscriptions; and mobile broadband subscriptions. For skills, the indicators are adult literacy; gross secondary enrolment; and gross tertiary enrolment.
4. Accessed 21 November 2017.
5. A finding confirmed by various studies by international NGOs in Botswana. InfoDev found, for instance, that ICT had not been implemented much in the educational system and Research ICT Africa concluded that the market for airtime and bundle packages offered by the three mobile operators (Orange, Mascom and beMobile) was difficult to navigate, with higher consumer costs of using telephones and internet than in other African countries (Esselaar and Sebusang, 2013).
6. A government tender is a formal, structured invitation to suppliers to submit a bid to supply products or services.

References

Abram, S., and G. Weszkalnys. 2011. 'Introduction: Anthropologies of Planning – Temporality, Imagination, and Ethnography', *Focaal – Journal of Global and Historical Anthropology* 61: 3–18.

Carmody, P. 2013. 'A Knowledge Economy or an Information Society in Africa? Thintegration and the Mobile Phone Revolution', *Information Technology for Development* 19(1): 24–39. doi:10.1080/02681102.2012.719859.

Christian Michelsens Institutt (CMI). 1988. *Botswana: Country Study and Norwegian Aid Review*. Bergen: DERAP Publication no. 235.

Comaroff, J., and J.L. Comaroff. 2006. 'Figuring Crime: Quantifacts and the Production of the Un/Real', *Public Culture* 19(1): 209–46.

Esselaar, S., and S. Sebusang. 2013. *Understanding What Is Happening in ICT in Botswana: A Supply- and Demand Side Analysis of the ICT Sector. Evidence for ICT Policy Action*. Policy Paper. Research ICT Africa.

Flyvbjerg, B. 2006. 'Five Misunderstandings about Case-Study Research', *Qualitative Inquiry* 12(2): 219–45.

Hacking, I. 1990. *The Taming of Chance*. Cambridge: Cambridge University Press.

Hope, K.R. 2001. 'Population Mobility and Multi-Partner Sex in Botswana: Implications for the Spread of HIV/AIDS', *African Journal of Reproductive Health* 5(3): 73–83.

International Telecommunications Union (ITU). 2017a. *Measuring the Information Society Report 2017 Vol. 1.* Geneva: International Telecommunications Union.

———. 2017b. *Measuring the Information Society Report 2017 Vol. 2.* Geneva: International Telecommunications Union.

Jerven, M. 2018. 'The Art of Medicine. Beyond Precision: Embracing the Politics of Global Health Numbers', *The Lancet* 392 (10146): 468–469

Latour, B. 2005. *Reassembling the Social: An Introduction to Actor-Network-Theory.* Oxford: Oxford University Press.

Lefko-Everett, K. 2004. *Botswana's Changing Migration Patterns.* http://www.migrationpolicy.org/article/botswanas-changing-migration-patterns (accessed 15 April 2017).

Lekalake, R. 2016. 'Evaluating Botswana's Performance on National Vision 2016: Public Opinion on Development Pillars'. *Afrobarometer* Policy Paper no. 33.

Maitlamo. 2004. *Botswana's National ICT Policy: Legislative Framework & Change Report. Final Report, December 2004.* https://www.researchictafrica.net/countries/botswana/MAITLAMO_Botswana_National_ICT_Policy.pdf (accessed 19 November 2017).

Ministry of Communications Science and Technology. 2007. *Draft National Information and Communications Policy.* First draft July 2006, edited July 2007. Republic of Botswana. http://unpan1.un.org/intradoc/groups/public/documents/cpsi/unpan027708.pdf (accessed 15 October 2019).

Ministry of Finance and Development Planning. 2009. *National Development Plan 10 (2009–2016). Volume 1.* Republic of Botswana: Ministry of Finance and Development Planning.

———. 2016. *Draft: National Development Plan 11. April 2017–March 2023. Volume 1* [September 2016]. Republic of Botswana: Ministry of Finance and Development Planning. http://extwprlegs1.fao.org/docs/pdf/bot175398.pdf (accessed 10 November 2017).

Moores, S. 2012. *Media, Place & Mobility.* Basingstoke: Palgrave Macmillan.

———. 2018. *Digital Orientations: Non-Media-Centric Media Studies and Non-Representational Theories of Practice.* New York: Peter Lang.

Morley, D. 2009. 'For a Materialist, Non-Media-Centric Media Studies', *Television & New Media* 10: 114–16.

Mutula, S., B. Grand, S. Zulu and P. Sebina. 2010. *Towards an Information Society in Botswana: ICT4D Country Report.* Thetha: The Sangonet Regional ICT Discussion Forum Project. Gaborone: Department of Library and Information Studies, University of Botswana.

Presidential Task Group. 1997. *Vision 2016: Long Term Vision for Botswana.* Gaborone: Government Printer. http://unpan1.un.org/intradoc/groups/public/documents/cpsi/unpan033260.pdf (accessed 15 April 2017).

Presidential Task Team. 2016. *Vision 2036: Achieving Prosperity for All.* Gaborone: Government Printer. http://www.statsbots.org.bw/sites/default/files/documents/Vision%202036.pdf (accessed 3 August 2018).

Rakner, L. 1996. *Botswana – 30 Years of Economic Growth, Democracy and Aid: Is There a Connection?* Report 1996:8. Bergen: Christian Michelsens Institute. https://www.cmi.no/publications/1222-botswana-30-years-of-economic-growth (accessed 15 September 2017).

Slater, D. 2013. *New Media, Development and Globalization.* Cambridge: Polity Press.

Statistics Botswana. 2016. *Selected Statistical Indicators 1966–2016: Enabling Stakeholders Formulate Policies, Plan and Make Decisions.* http://www.statsbots.org.bw/sites/default/files/publications/Selected%20Statistical%20Indicators%201966-2016-%20Sept%202016.pdf (accessed 15 April 2017).

———. 2017. *Botswana Household Access & Individual Use of Information & Communication Technologies Report-2014.* http://www.statsbots.org.bw/sites/default/files/publications/Botswana%20Household%20Access%20%20%26%20Individual%20Use%20of%20Information%20%26%20Communication%20Technologies%20Report%202014.pdf (accessed 20 April 2017).

Storm-Mathisen, A. 2017. 'Gender Representations and Identity Constructions among Youth in Botswana: Exploring the Influence of Media', in D. Lemish and M. Götz (eds), *Beyond the Stereotypes? Images of Boys and Girls, and Their Consequences.* Göteborg: Nordicom, pp. 173–81.

———. 2019. 'New Media in Everyday Life of Batswana: On Concerns, Consequences and the Educational Factor', *Journal of African Media Studies* 11(2).

UNDP. 2015. *Human Development Report 2015: Work for Human Development.* http://hdr.undp.org/sites/default/files/hdr_2015_statistical_annex.pdf (accessed 20 April 2017).

UNESCO/IFAP. 2016. *ICT Literacy Policy: Botswana.* Study and Report by Botswana IFAP Committee. Geneva: UNESCO. http://www.unesco.org/new/fileadmin/MULTIMEDIA/HQ/CI/CI/pdf/ifap/meetings/council/ifap_botswana_ict_literacy_report_9thifapcouncil.pdf (accessed 10 April 2017).

World Economic Forum (WEF). 2016. *The Global Information Technology Report 2016: Innovating in the Digital Economy.* Geneva: WEF. http://online.wsj.com/public/resources/documents/GITR2016.pdf (accessed 27 April 2017).

World Bank. 2015a. *Botswana Poverty Assessment.* Report no. 88473-BW. http://documents.worldbank.org/curated/en/351721468184754228/Botswana-poverty-assessment (accessed 27 August 2017).

———. 2015b. *Botswana: Systematic Country Diagnostic.* http://documents.worldbank.org/curated/en/489431468012950282/pdf/95304-REPLACEMENT-SCD-P150575-PUBLIC-Botswana-Systematic-Country-Diagnostic-Report.pdf (accessed 27 May 2017).

———. 2015c. *Botswana Country Partnership Framework FY 16-202015.* http://documents.worldbank.org/curated/en/772221468196759090/pdf/104953-WP-P132886-PUBLIC-NON-BOARD-VERSION-World-Bank-indd.pdf (accessed 25 September 2017).
———. 2015d. *Botswana: Country Opinion Survey 2016.* World Bank Group, March. http://microdata.worldbank.org/index.php/catalog/2712 (accessed 27 May 2017).
———. 2016. *World Development Report 2016: Digital Dividends.* http://www.worldbank.org/en/publication/wdr2016 (accessed 7 April 2017).

PART II

Gender and Social Relations

CHAPTER 3

Bolingo ya face

Digital Marriages, Playfulness and the Search for Change in Kinshasa

Katrien Pype

In this chapter, I intend to offer some ethnographic insights into new forms of relating based on data collected in Kinshasa, capital city of DR Congo. In particular, I will explore the idioms of *bolingo ya face*, 'love over Facebook' in Lingala (the city's lingua franca), and *libala ya face*, 'marriage over Facebook'. *Face* is shorthand for 'Facebook', but this internet application has become so important in Kinshasa's public sphere that any form of digital flirtation and romance is called *bolingo ya face* despite the platform on which the flirtatious exchange happens. In the following, I am using the concept of 'romance' in a broader sense than the conventional designation of 'love affair, romantic relationship', which is, according to the Oxford English Dictionary (2010, online version), only the sixth meaning of 'romance'. The other definitions[1] emphasise fictional narrative and the imagination. Both are particularly appropriate to capture the sentiments and metaphoric character of *bolingo ya face* and *libala ya face*. Given the fact that my interlocutors would use *bolingo* and *libala ya face* interchangeably, I will do the same in this chapter. The fact that *bolingo* (love) and *libala* (marriage) have become synonyms here is informative regarding the metaphoric character of the empirical phenomenon.

The ethnographic material will allow me to contribute to the expanding literature on the sociality of new media by linking urban sexual economies and strategies of social mobility to the digital. Platforms such as WhatsApp, Facebook and other social media function for many men and women living in Kinshasa as dating apps. Indeed, introduction to future and potential marriage partners has significantly changed since cellular telephony became more available in Kinshasa. This is not unique to central Africa; anthropologists working on Asian societies have made similar observations. Constable (2003, p. 4) argues in her research on transnational marriages in Asia that 'although meeting marriage partners from abroad is not new, the Internet has fuelled a global imagination and created a time-space compression that has greatly increased the scope and efficiency of introductions and communication between men and women from different parts of the world'. It strikes me that a study of online flirtation has something to teach us theoretically about how sexuality and matrimony are (re-) organised in the era of digital modernity, this moment of the modern era in which digital technologies increasingly shape subjectivities, social networks and aspirations for the future. Its possibilities for expanding social networks into physically unfamiliar worlds have further implications for our understandings of kinship and relatedness. The rubric through which I explore the emergence of digital flirtation is the play-work binary. As will become clear throughout the chapter, 'play' and 'work' provide fundamental insights into digital interaction as well as organising sexuality in Kinshasa. I contend that the material has relevance beyond the ethnographic space of Kinois sociality and argue that in order to better understand the social possibilities of digital interaction anywhere we need to pay attention to the ways in which the apparent opposites of 'play' and 'work', rather than 'online' versus 'offline', or 'virtual' and 'real', feed into the digital sphere.

Scene 1: Flavie's Husband Is Waiting for Her

In July 2016, when I arrived for another field research trip in Kinshasa, Flavie (pseudonym), a young woman in her mid-twenties, was frantic. Three of the various Congolese men living in the diaspora with whom she had been entertaining digital intimate conversations and which sometimes led to actual sex, had *descendu sur le terrain* (literally: entered on the territory[2]), and she had no idea about how best to manage her availability to these men during these weeks. She was nevertheless also desperate to find romantic love, and like many Kinoises[3] (girls from Kinshasa), Flavie believed that her [future] husband was abroad. Thus, she tried to be as available as possible when these *djikas* (the middle part of the word *belgicain*, 'coming from Belgium'[4]), as Congolese men living in the diaspora are called, wanted to meet up. One afternoon, Flavie and I were having one of our almost daily conversations about Facebook. We were sitting in a *nganda* (open air bar) where Flavie is well known, as it is close to her father's house, where she and her three children and two of her siblings reside. As usual, we were having a hard time keeping our conversation going as we were constantly interrupted by men who greeted Flavie, and who offered us drinks. Some would sit down at another table, either on their own or with others, and would from time to time shout towards our table, flirting, teasing, inviting us over and sending us drinks. With many of these men, Flavie had been or still was in an active sexual relationship. A fight nearly started when one of these men called her *mwasi na ngai* (my wife), and another got angry about this public display of 'ownership' over Flavie, to which she only replied with laughter. That day, our conversation ended before I had expected as suddenly Flavie took a phone call. I heard her replying in an almost disinterested way (though that is part of the acoustics of flirtatious conversations): '*Saint Raphaël? heure moko?*' (she sighed and lowered her tone, while slowly turning her head in another direction). '*Ca va*' (at St Raphael's, in one hour. Okay). As soon as Flavie ended this phone conversation, she got up, informing me that one of her *djikas* was picking her up at a particular taxi stop. She needed to go home, bathe, and make sure she was ready in one hour. The next day, she texted me that the *djika* had taken her to a hotel, where they had had sex, and she had come home with only 30 USD, adding a sad smiley.

Scene 2: An STD Bothers Flavie

In early September 2016, I travelled back to Europe for a few weeks. Flavie urged me to bring vaginal cream from the pharmacy in Belgium. Her summer was not going well. By the third week of July, she had begun to suffer from a vaginal infection. As the antibiotics she was supposed to buy were too expensive, she had only bought half of the prescribed amount. The infection did not go away. She certainly could not speak about her condition to the *djikas*, and had been mobilising various strategies to avoid meeting them. After all, she knew that seeing them would lead to sex. So, for days on end, she would make sure she was unavailable on the phone numbers the *djikas* knew; and she was not active on these WhatsApp and Facebook accounts. The three men had all brought her perfume from Paris and London, but they had told her to wait for cash. Now, with her condition, there was no opportunity to meet them and to request money from them. She also assumed that the *djikas* were disappointed in her being unavailable, and thus she began to think about connecting with other *djikas* as soon as I had travelled back with the cream. However, when one of the three *djikas* unexpectedly extended his holiday until the end of September, she set all her hopes on him to pay the school fees for her three children. Flavie clearly had not vested any hopes in matrimony with any of these three *djikas*, even though she was negotiating affect, sexuality and money very much like matrimonial partners do. She knew that the *djikas* were expecting sex, and she did not want to refuse them.

These two vignettes introduce the protagonist of this chapter, Flavie, and the topic of my analysis – urban sexuality in times of digital connectivity. For many social media users in Kinshasa, digital flirtation on social media applications such as Facebook, WhatsApp, Badoo, We Connect and so on ideally leads to 'digital marriages', *libala ya face*. A 'digital marriage' in this context refers to the affective bond that exists between two partners whose courting and communication and perhaps even love-making mainly happen through digital interaction. So, despite the fact that this *libala ya face* is not a 'real' marriage, there is a lot of emotional, discursive and material exchange going on between the two conversation partners that draws on obligations of the matrimonial realm.[5] As such, the *libala ya face* oscillates between a metaphor, because it is not a real marriage and love relationship, but rather a rhetorical device to show a relationship that plays with the idioms of love and matrimony, and a metonym because the concept does evoke the possibility for material exchanges, for practices that materialise within the realm of matrimony.[6] As will become clear, these 'digital marriages' differ from other forms of marriage (Li. *libala*), such as those confirmed by customary, civic and religious rituals, in which lineages, the state and religious communities are involved. Such rituals confirm the two partners as publicly acknowledged partners in matrimony. Other forms of marriage lack this ceremonial confirmation, and are rather marriage by practice, such as the *yaka tofanda* ('come and let's live together').[7] The latter refers to a pseudo-marriage in which the partners share a living space. Often, the *yaka tofanda* follows a pregnancy, and it can speed up the preparations for the marriage ceremonies, although this may take years, even decades. Here, even though they lack the formal approval and confirmation of lineages, the state and religious groups, these matrimonial unions are nevertheless publicly known and confirmed by practice. The 'digital marriages', by contrast, have not (yet) obtained ceremonial and public approval and confirmation. They are not pseudo-marriages either because the relationship between conversation partners engaged in *libala ya face* remains very much restricted to the private lifeworld of the individual interlocutors. Sometimes some information about the conversations and material exchanges within the *libala ya face* is given to friends or neighbours, but these relationships tend to remain rather secretive, mainly to protect the reputation of the (married) *djika*, and also to protect one's privileged contact with that particular man. They are in line with the camouflaged polygamy of urban centres (see Hunt, 1991), or with other forms of playful marriage such as those described by Cousins (2016) in KwaZulu-Natal's timber plantations, where women engage in playful marriages which are spaces of affect, support and attention, but which only rarely translate into physical relationships.

This chapter thus addresses the question of 'new media practices in a changing Africa' on two different levels. First, it identifies the emergence of a new idiom of romance, *bolingo ya face*, and a new realm of exchange of affect, depending on electronic interaction. Second, and intimately tied to the first, the material speaks to the desire for change in the lifeworlds of social media users. Undergirding these dating practices on social media are aspirations for social mobility, both economically and socially, as regards to a betterment of one's personal economic situation, or the transformation of one's identity from a single into a married individual. Digital connectivity has turned the *djika*, the figure of the transnational migrant,[8] into a more prominent future marriage partner for Kinois girls. The concept of 'playfulness' will help me to bring both themes together: flirtation is play, while 'playfulness', as elaborated by Handelman (2001) and as I will explain below, opens up the possibility for (individual) change.

My story will mainly be told through the lens of Flavie, the young woman introduced at the beginning of this chapter. Born and raised in Kinshasa, in her mid-twenties, but already a divorced mother of four children (of which one had died), Flavie needed to take care of her three children who were living with her. Separated from their fathers, and with the secondary school degree (*diplôme d'état*) as her highest qualification, Flavie used sex and flattery to provide for school fees, food for the household, and her own lifestyle. Her mobile phones were indispensable tools in this daily quest. Flavie had more than one smartphone. In July 2016, when I returned for a new stint of fieldwork, she had three, but all three of them had a (different) technical failure, so she usually only used one, changing sim cards constantly. Since 2007, Flavie had been using dating websites such as We Connect, Meetic and Badou to be introduced to men. She entertained minimal, almost phatic conversations with these men (see Pype, 2019a). From time to time, she would invite a photographer to come to her house to take pictures in a variety of poses and clothes. Flavie would then visit cybercafés to upload pictures to these dating websites, and to entertain electronic conversations. When she received her first smartphone, she downloaded dating apps and social media platsforms such as Facebook, Viber and Whatsapp, and it became much easier to manipulate her digital persona and to handle her digital romances. In July 2016, as Flavie showed me her Facebook, WhatsApp, Instagram, We Connect and Badou accounts, I noticed that she was in minimal conversations with at least thirty different men, whom she called her 'husbands from Facebook' (*mibali ya face*). Some of them were living in Kinshasa, and she already had met up in person with some of them, encounters which often led to sex. She decided not to meet up with some of the others who were living in Kinshasa, because she thought these men were either friends of one of her other lovers or of relatives. By avoiding overlap between these social spaces, Flavie tried to prevent deeper entanglements between her, her lovers' and her relatives' affective worlds. She seemed to look for conversations with men living abroad, in Europe and the US, but also South Africa, Togo and Nigeria. While most of her contacts were Congolese, or at least performed as Congolese (conversing in Lingala, referencing key elements of Kinois sociality, etc.), Flavie also engaged in digital flirting with French and Lebanese expats and UN soldiers who were either stationed in the DRC or had been at some point in their career. As she told me, Flavie did not really hold out any hopes that flirting with expats would lead to marriage, though she did when interacting digitally with Congolese men, chatting and exchanging pictures with them.

Flavie's efforts, online and offline, to find men who could offer her a more prosperous future, either temporarily or on a more permanent basis, are fully in line with the importance of transactional relationships in the lifeworlds of sub-Saharan African men and women, as documented by a wide range of social scientists (Bernault, 2015; Cole and Thomas, 2009; Cole and Groes, 2016; Helle-Valle, 1999). These scholars have shown how various forms of exchange (material, spiritual and affective) are constitutive of love and sexual relationships on the African continent. In Kinshasa, but also in many other societies, the realms of courting and matrimony are fully embedded in the circulation of affect, aspirations, commodities, information and money (Pype, 2012, chapters 8 and 9).

Flavie's practices of introduction and courting need to be interpreted against the background of both the urban social environment and the increased availability of electronic communication in Kinshasa. The so-called 'democratisation of cellular telephony' happened in two phases. First, around 2003, cellular telephony became cheaper, and people began to use mobile phones such as the Nokia 3210 and others, calling and beeping (i.e. hanging up after one or two rings and thus avoiding a charge). At this point, sim cards, phone numbers, phone credit and the handset became important features of one's personhood, and contributed to the organisation and expansion of individuals' social networks. The second phase, which started around 2008 when Vodacom began selling smartphones, led to people becoming more active on social media platforms.

From 2003, cybercafés were the spaces where Kinois chatted, but not many people spent hours online. Nowadays, with mobile data being sold on every street corner, and smartphones being important devices to have and/or to give (Pype, 2017a), many manage various online accounts and make gregarious use of the internet to connect with friends and relatives who are nearby or far away, and, probably most importantly, with strangers.

This chapter is structured as follows. First, I will explore the play-work binary, as it has operated within anthropology as a rubric through which to understand social life and social change. Then, I analyse various forms of work that Flavie and other girls engage in when conversing, or preparing to converse, with online contacts. The third part speaks to the transformation of digital contacts into fictive matrimonial partners, the 'kinning' of social media contacts. In the final parts of this chapter, I pick up the binary 'play' versus 'work' again, yet do so from an emic perspective since this opposition also operates in Kinshasa in order to make sense of intimate lifeworlds and social reproduction. Here, I also explore the desirability of the *djika* and his role in aspirations to hypergamy. In the concluding section, I bring the analysis back to the question of change, in particular the desire to marry up.

The material was collected during intensive fieldwork in the summers of 2015 and 2016, April 2017 and August 2017. Interviews with men and women, both online and offline, but also observations of men and women when visiting or being visited by friends, being around them before and after dates, and in certain instances even being around during these dates, introduced me to the world of play, flirtatious sociality and digital identities. These data are complemented with an analysis of diaries written by Flavie upon my request over a period of eight months, and with a study of internet communications of several female research participants. The material is biased towards women's experiences of digital romance. All names are pseudonyms in order to protect my interlocutors' privacy.

Play and Work

Flavie would often tell me that she was only 'playing' (*kosakana, kosala bajeu*) when discussing her social media practices. Like many others, she reacted initially with surprise when I told her that I was investigating Facebook, WhatsApp and various forms of social media interactivity. I would quickly be shown Facebook pages of users such as 'perle noire' (black pearl), 'Alice la Mignonne' (Alice, the cute girl), 'Marlon Elegantizimo' (Marlon the very elegant one) and 'Vraie Vraie Epice' (extremely hot spice). These pages served as examples of how their friends would play with their digital alter egos. Sexually explicit pictures sent privately would be shown as well. I would constantly be reminded that this was 'only play'. However, play can be serious. We are all familiar with trolls, fake accounts and fictive names as illustrations of playful digital activity, and take for granted how social media platforms are a space of playful interaction among peers.[9] The assumed licence provided by social media also loosens up other forms of social interaction. In industrial China (Wang, 2016; also, in Miller, 2016, p. 106), for example, social media may offer a space for more easy-going and funny interactions between junior and senior generations, while face-to-face encounters are supposed to be more serious and respectful.

Furthermore, debates in Kinshasa about social media rapidly evolve into assessments of moral behaviour, as referenced in my paper on Blackberry Girls (Pype, 2016a), a label assigned to girls who are assumed to have obtained their smartphones from sugar daddies. Very quickly, my interlocutors would start telling stories about being duped over social media, and how they had learnt the hard way not to share intimate details (information, pictures) too eagerly with digital others. I would be oriented towards YouTube clips in which Kinois women were complaining about how *mibali ya poto* (husbands from Europe) did not respect Kinshasa's women, or about sex tapes circulating on WhatsApp and Facebook and turning high-profile Congolese into the laughing stock of the moment. Less sensational but still dramatic warnings about social media practices causing distress, disappointment and frustration were also voiced in religious circles (Pype, 2016a, 2017a, b). For many Kinois, it is clear that while the virtual space seems to be a zone of unlimited possibilities, digital interaction can have serious repercussions in individuals' lives. This confusion about the social relevance of social media has also been observed elsewhere. In *The Break Up 2.0*, for example, Gershon (2010) shows how US-based college students sometimes tend to think of relationship statuses on Facebook as jokes, and most of Gershon's interlocutors doubted the seriousness of information communicated over Facebook. Yet the heartbreak and emotional investment these same interlocutors displayed when someone had 'broken up over Facebook', or when they were trying to make sense of likes, emojis and comments on status changes, new profile pictures or memes on one's wall, are evidence of the social dilemmas that emerge with new media, and these testify to the social costs that digital play can accrue.

Given these initial observations about social media and play, and in particular about the 'offline' experiences of online interactivity, it is important to situate the analysis in a wider analytical conversation about sociality and play. The dialectical relationship between play and social life has inspired many anthropologists. While the language of play led to concepts through which to study social behaviour (Geertz's 'deep play', 1973; Bourdieu's 'game', 1984; Ortner's serious games, 1996), anthropologists have also explored the role of play and games in society. From Huizinga's essay on 'homo ludens' (1949) to Turner's (1987) attention to the subjunctive mood of games, imagination and fiction in society, and more recently Hamayon's (2016) *Why We Play*, the discipline has always taken play, fun and creativity seriously. For some scholars, following Bateson's essay on play and fantasy (1987), there are strong boundaries between the play frame and daily reality, analogous with the online-offline divide. This is perpetuated in game studies, where scholars explore the rules, plotlines and protagonists of virtual realities without relating these to the flesh, sweat and currency of social life.

Yet Handelman's and Appadurai's understanding of the formative role of play and the fictive in everyday life speaks productively to the strong investment of everyday social media users in digital communication, and informs us about the possibility of social change – the major question of this edited volume. For Handelman, the playful and social change are intimately connected, like a braid or a moebius, because the playful weaves reality with the imaginative, the possible. Critiquing the all too rigid boundary between 'play' and 'daily reality', and drawing on though also remedying Bateson's study of framing, Handelman prefers the notion of 'the playful'. Playfulness, Handelman (2001, pp. 145–46) argues, is a 'condition of being in the world on its way to becoming someone or something else'. Furthermore, 'playfulness folds realities into one another, into the smallest, most expansive spaces of possibility – ludic spaces – that exist through their inflections of lineal reality' (ibid.).

Similar attention to the productive role for (social) change of new media was formulated by Appadurai in *Modernity at Large* (1996). Writing in the early 1990s, Appadurai focused on radio, television, cinema and other electronic platforms such as VHS tapes, audiotapes and so on, and touched upon a central element of electronic modernity that has only intensified with the emergence of the internet and social media. For Appadurai, electronic media

> are resources for experiments with self-making in all sorts of societies, for all sorts of persons. ... Because of the sheer multiplicity of the forms in which they appear (cinema, television, computers, and telephones) and because of the rapid way in which they move through daily life routines, electronic media provide resources for self-imagining as an everyday social project. (1996, pp. 3–4)

Self-making, agency for the individual and the possibility of new futures are central in Appadurai's understanding of the social role of the imagination in electronic modernity.

Recently, scholars have started to pay attention to the economic opportunities that online interactivity can bring. For example, concepts such as 'playbour' ('play' + 'labour') and 'weisure' ('work' + 'leisure') have been coined in order to draw attention to the fact that so-called play and leisure also produce value (see, among others, Kücklich, 2005; Conley, 2009). Observing the popularity of the sharing economy and the entertainment industry, it is impossible to ignore how the subjunctive has become a space of politics (Bernal, 2014; Bräuchler, 2013; Postill, 2018), money making (Steel, 2017) and career making (Abidin, 2018).

Anthropologists also attend to various forms of engagement with digital personae and electronic visual culture (Boellstorff, 2008; Deger, 2016; Lukacs, 2010). In her fascinating analysis of Aboriginal Yolgnu's work on digital photographs in which (deceased) relatives are depicted, Deger (2016, p. 113) observed that her research participants would sometimes work for days on one photograph, assembling photos, using screen-based photo applications and turning family photographs into 'something wider, something deeper ... than the original, unadorned images'. This is 'spectral labour', as performed in the 'cutting and pasting by finger, searching through web archives for frames and background that suit (the) subject matter' (ibid.). This work then produces 'thick photography', that is, visual data that mobilise 'affect, image, and meaning to significant effect' (ibid.).

It seems to me that a perspective combining Handelman's 'playfulness' in the digital sphere, Deger's 'spectral labour', and the various forms of effort, investment and expectations of return (material and immaterial) that undergird Kinshasa's sexual economy provides the perfect analytical angle to explore *libala ya face*. With a nod to Hardt (1999) and Hardt and Negri's (2000) 'affective labour',[10] I reference Flavie's and others' spectral labour, time and efforts spent online and offline in order to attract digital lovers and entertain these relationships as 'affective work'. The sexual economy in which *bolingo ya face* thrives is not embedded in the capitalist society that Hardt and Negri (2000) have described,[11] though there is an immediate manipulation of affect and sentiment going on in order to obtain money and material benefits.

The Work of (Digital) Flirting

Communicating over Facebook and other social media platforms requires situated knowledge which is culturally, socially and gender-dependent. Much of my fieldwork conversations turned into instructive moments in which I was taught about the arsenal of tactics and strategies Flavie and others deploy in the management of digital sexual relationships. These draw to a high degree on spectacles of the intimate. I am using 'spectacle' here in the way Bernault (2015, p. 754) defines it: 'an exhibition specially prepared or arranged for the visual senses'. The preparations for the arrangement of digital exchanges of sounds, images and affect require effort, skill and attention.[12] In Flavie's world, (electronic) conversations and magical powders combine into an assemblage of persuasive powers that draw on the powers of the word, spirits and photographs.

The first level of work is defined by the opening of digital communications, which can involve the exchange of phone numbers, initial greetings and so on. Indeed, there are various stages in digital flirting, especially on Facebook. One starts by looking at the pictures of one's Facebook friends, and sending short text messages in the Messenger app saying 'hi', or 'you look pretty' and so on. Sometimes the recipient responds quickly, and after some banter and initial flirting phone numbers are exchanged. From that moment on, the flirtatious conversation is continued on another platform, usually WhatsApp. Insofar as one's phone number is considered part of one's social persona (Pype, 2017b), the move onto WhatsApp signals the possibility of a deeper connection (see Miller et al., 2016 on 'scalable sociality').[13]

Unsurprisingly, the economy of social media shapes the rhythm of the flirting. Many cellular phone companies operating in the DRC offer extremely cheap bundles of mobile data only to be used between 11p.m. and 5 a.m. As mobile data are rather expensive, people tend to wait until the night to chat, have phone conversations and upload or download photographs and videos (Pype 2019b). In various Kinois households, where people usually share beds and bedrooms with (classificatory) siblings or friends, whispering over the phone can often be heard after midnight.[14] Linguistic and visual codes are developed between chat partners in order to maintain some intimacy, and to keep others (often siblings or children) unaware of the content.[15]

Closer, affective ties are not only maintained, nourished and expressed via private written and spoken conversations, but pictures play a significant role as well. Here, a second phase in the digital flirting sets in. Nude or semi-nude pictures are the main types of pictures that are requested over Facebook Messenger or via WhatsApp among electronic husbands and wives. To that extent, Flavie has a whole range of *photos sexy*, in varying degrees of nudeness, stored on her mobile phones, which she can quickly send. These pictures are usually taken by other lovers, though they are also the product of attention, preparation and organisation. As Flavie recounted, she is careful to take a white sheet to her hotel encounters, so that the pictures always display similar bedding. In this way, her digital husbands never see that the pictures are actually taken in different rooms. Flavie thus literally works on the décor of the nude pictures.

Other digital work in which girls engage is the composition of digital love couple photo collages that mimic matrimony and marital union. These are often composed of two photographs of the two love interests. Flavie would pull a picture of the *mobali* (digital husband) from his Facebook account and insert it into a drawing of a golden ring, red heart, or animation and words such as 'l'amour', 'love you', 'you will forever be mine always', 'only you' and so on. These assemblages are made with apps such as love couple photo collage or canva. Flavie regularly sends similar collages to her digital husbands, only changing the picture of the man. This spectacle of matrimony is an important strategy in entertaining intense relationships with digital contacts. Having the significant other's photo as one's profile picture is another strategy of signalling to the other his or her importance.

Flavie, however, was not really into public displays of having men's pictures as her profile picture. She was involved with too many men, and wanted to maintain an image of being serious and available to each of them. Yet posting and sharing words and photographs constitutes only one (and very visible) practice of affective work. Flavie had other, more mystical means to bind the men she encountered through Facebook and other online dating apps to her: the *nkisi ya mibali*, 'the medicine of men', meaning magical substances that would help her to bind men to her. The usage of this particular medicine is not much different from other strategies people deploy to influence people or manipulate reality: many Kinois use – at certain times in their lives – magical powders (*poussière*). These are for sale on the streets and in spiritual shops, and circulate among relatives and people who one trusts.

In the summer of 2016, Flavie was raving about a *poussière* she had been able to reclaim from her (classificatory) sister who had just got married. As the sister deemed herself a 'true Christian',[16] she declined the gift of the *nkisi ya mibali* (medicine for men) which her aunt had sent to her from Moba via a domestic transfer agency. The new bride distributed the powder among her sisters (as it was only for women) who had gathered for the customary wedding.

The substance, called *poudre ya dominance* (a powder to dominate, *korègner*, *kodondwa*), is used in the following way: in its simplest form, one puts a drop of it on one's tongue just before making a phone call to ask for money. When in dire need of money, however, as Flavie told me, a three-day morning ritual has to be performed. In one of our conversations, Flavie described vividly how powerful this powder was. Around June 2016, she had followed her aunt's instructions: for three days in a row, she had washed herself with water to which some of the powder had been added. She had then discreetly deposited her briefs, which she had been wearing while washing herself, in a small gateway between houses (*tunnel*) in her street. While applying the *poudre ya dominance*, Flavie requested that 'all men that had been giving her money in the old days [pre-crisis], that they would return to her and fight over her. Even if they are at home, with their wife, "I want them to think of me. I want their money "'. So, during those three mornings of applying the powder, Flavie tried to dominate men, and make sure that they would spend money on her. Very quickly she began to see the effect of the *poudre ya dominance*: dormant ties were reawakened, men would come and drop off food for her and the children, would pay for hospital bills, and would beg her for sex. Cars were lined up in the street, and she had to bribe boys from her street in order to manage these visits – to whisk some of them off to a bar, to lie that she was not at home while in fact another man was visiting and so on. In fact, so strong was her attraction for men that the neighbouring women, who all knew of Flavie's reputation of having many lovers and to whom these lines of cars were only additional confirmation, would come to her house and ask what her secret was. It was just a few days later that she encountered four men, all members of parliament, who were all seated at separate tables in the restaurant where she was supposed to meet up with another man. Three out of the four were casual lovers of Flavie. The sight of four love interests in the same space frightened her, and she had no idea how to move around in that space anonymously and to avoid conflict between these men who – as she assumed – would send her discreet signs of familiarity. Flavie quickly left the restaurant. As she told me later, with much amusement, she became afraid of the *nkisi,* and there and then decided to stop using the *poudre* for a while. She kept it in her bedroom, hidden in a small wooden chalice usually used to store *pili pili* (red pepper spices).[17]

It is probably in the combination of working with digital images and applying magical substances that we see the most intimate forms of affective work in which Flavie and others are engaged. This work is discursive (textual), visual (working with the images), spiritual (use of magic) and physical (sexual intercourse). In the *bolingo ya face,* the first three dimensions of flirting are fundamental. These are part of the 'affective work' that Kinois girls act out in order to turn digital contacts into 'digital husbands'. Through this work, (digital) connectivity gains deeper meanings, becomes persuasive and beneficial.

Kinning Contacts

This possibility of change in the most intimate spheres of their lives – to find new (metaphorical) husbands digitally, thus altering one's life prospects – attracted many of my interlocutors to online flirting, even to the extent that they invested a lot of money and time in being digitally available (see also Nyamnjoh, 2004; Tazanu, 2012), setting up and managing online accounts. If Flavie's digital conversations with new online contacts (*contact*; *branchement*) survived the first days of small talk ('you look pretty'; 'where do you live?'; 'can I have your phone number?'), a certain degree of intimacy would be achieved rather quickly. This happened with José, who one night, as they were chatting until her phone credit ran out, asked Flavie for a *photo sexy* (nude picture). Although the request did not surprise her, and she had many such pictures stored in her phone, Flavie first responded as a 'decent girl' (*mwasi ya malamu*) should: she acted surprised, told him that they don't know each other well enough, and that she 'is not like that'. However, after a few insistent texts, she sent a photo, making sure that her face was not fully visible so that she could always deny later that the depicted body was hers. Once such a picture is sent, the electronic conversation partners enter into a sexual relationship, in which not only explicit sexual content is shared, but the two call one another *mobali* (husband) and *mwasi* (wife).

The emergence of digital 'husbands' and 'wives' in Kinshasa's social media sphere provides a striking difference with another trend that has been observed in the digital world: Miller (2017) describes a shift from fictive kinship to fictive friendship in the social media era. Platforms such as Friendster, Facebook and others have given prominence to the friendship realm as a dominant rubric through which to express relationality digitally. In the digital flirting that I describe here, something else is happening. Digital *contacts* (or 'friends'; see Pype, 2012, p. 65) become identified as matrimonial partners. This 'kinning of strangers', and in particular the linguistic game of turning them into affines, is embedded within a society that places a lot of weight on the obligations between spouses.[18] Husbands are supposed to cater for the material well-being of their wives, while wives need to perform domestic duties for their husbands, in terms of cooking, cleaning and being sexually available.

The kinning of strangers and casual sexual partners is not limited to the digital world; it is part of everyday interactions in the city, and some scholars argue that African kinship systems have always been 'muddied by the fragilities and ambiguities of relatedness' (Manderson and Block, 2016, p. 206). In particular, the Manchester School, with scholars such as Gluckman (1950) and Van Velzen (1964), and later Epstein (1981), have studied how urbanisation and migration for education and employment allowed people to extend 'old forms of fictive and intentional kinship and so have created new ways of being kin, with care often being the basis of closeness' (ibid., p. 208). Kinois do not perceive the city as a space inhabited by anonymous strangers with whom one does not have any significant ties beyond the sheer fact that they are sharing the same urban space. Very often, when people meet, they will try to identify kin relationships between one another. If these do not exist, then via metaphorical language people will draw each other into their kin world. This happens in the most banal of everyday interactions. For example, when asking an adult for directions, one will say *maman* or *papa, mbuta* ('elder', even 'genitor', in kiKongo), *noko* (uncle) or conversely *yaya* (older brother/sister). Friendship relations also very often evolve into the metaphorical language of affinal relationships. Someone quickly becomes someone else's fictive husband or wife, or a *bokilo* (an in-law). The city thus is a space full of kin, either real or fictive consanguines or affines. The following anecdote illustrates this poignantly. One day in August 2016, when driving to meet a friend of mine, Flavie and I were stuck in a traffic jam. At one major road, Flavie pointed at a large billboard on which a well-known local politician was regretting the death of Papa Wemba, one of Congo's most famous musicians who had died a few months earlier. Flavie jokingly said, '*bokilo na ngai*', my father-in-law. I knew she was in a casual sexual relationship with one of the politician's sons. His father had probably never heard of Flavie, but the fact that she transformed this man into an affine is significant as it points to the usage of thick relationship labels in contexts where one of the relationship poles is unaware of the tie.

The kinship space (fictive kinship included) constitutes a social realm of obligations and debt relations. This relatedness is important in an urban locale characterised by precarity, violence and lack of trust in others. It thus becomes important to establish a large pool of relationships that can be instrumental. For Simmel ([1908] 2009), a major theorist of urban sociality, the stranger does not have any obligations to anyone else. However, in Kinshasa, many men and women have an expanded network of former lovers who can be contacted and reminded about their connection, and thus can be mobilised when looking for a solution to a particular problem (solutions do not always materialise, but these are indeed routes to explore).[19] The fictive agnatic and affinal relationships are fundamental spaces for resources. Calling someone fictively 'my husband' is not necessarily a way of promising sexual intimacy, but first and foremost a way of announcing that claims will be made on that person.

Making claims on the digital husband/wife plays out in further interactions once two digital conversation partners have defined each other as their (digital) spouse. Despite the lack of public acknowledgement, these 'digital marriages' do not always remain metaphorical, and are very often shot through with obligations and commitment. In the end, both parties hope to transform the metaphor into a metonym, that is, they want the relationship to move from a mere discursive reality to a more practical and material experience. In other words, they want to experience a particular kind of commitment that goes beyond flirtatious talk.[20] Flavie is indeed a regular visitor to one of the Western Union offices in the neighbourhood, where she can collect 100 or even 200 USD sent from men abroad. When her son was dying in 2012, however, she was disappointed when one of her *mibali ya face* did not respond to her request for money, only making promises and keeping her waiting while her son was dying in hospital. She deleted him from her Facebook account and thus ended the *libala ya face* with that man. Others do manage to translate the electronic marriage into a material relationship. At play here is exactly the affective work in which others are identified as either fictive agnatic or affinal kin. 'Digital marriage' with reliable concrete financial obligations is the ideal result of the affective work described above.

Play and the City

'I am playing', Flavie repeatedly told me, *nazosala bajeu,* when I asked her to what extent she was hoping to find matrimony with one of her many digital husbands. The playing, *kosakana,* here obscures various layers of meaning that speak in variegated ways to the urban sexual economy. First of all, 'play' refers to Flavie's efforts to try out various possible venues for novel futures, with or without matrimony. Yet ethnographic research about social life in Kinshasa brings in 'play' (*lisano*) from two different spheres: (a) sexuality performed outside of matrimony; and (b) the sociality of Kinshasa's *ambiance* culture. These form the background of Flavie's affective work and will be discussed in the following paragraphs.

First of all, in Congolese marriage culture, flirting and sexual practices before or outside marriage are practices coined as 'playing', *kosakana.* By contrast, sexuality within the space of a couple that has been wed customarily (and possibly legally and/or religiously) is referred to as *mosala,* 'work'. The latter rubric emphasises the duty (towards the family, towards ancestors, towards God) of a married couple to reproduce the lineage and/or the Christian community in the case of a couple that is married in church as well (Pype, 2012). In this play (*lisano/liseki*)/work (*mosala*) opposition, 'work' refers to the labour of reproduction of the community. Even though pleasure and fun are not absent from this intimate realm of domestic sex (i.e. within a married couple), it should lead to the reproduction of the lineage.

Rules of decency and respect dictate that the *kosakana,* flirting, should not happen in front of one's elders, that is, (classificatory) parents, uncles and aunts. So, even though *kosakana* is allowed with various partners until one is engaged (*kokanga lopango,* 'closing the compound') and married, usually the family does not intervene, nor are they formally informed about the nature of the relationship. *Kosakana* is carried out in a space of social and intimate activity that is kept outside of the family/lineage; relatives only come in when a *masta* (friend) turns into a *fiancé* (a designated marriage interest). Even if (classificatory) parents might have an idea that their son/daughter is sexually involved with someone, they will usually not comment, or if they do, it will be in an indirect way, through proverbs or through intermediaries (other relatives, religious leaders, etc.).[21] Therefore, it is unsurprising that Flavie had never encountered the politician whose photograph was on the billboard (see above). *Kosakana* is thus a space of individual autonomy.[22]

While many Kinois argue that respectfulness towards one's (social) elders requires that the flirtation and playing occur without them being confronted with it, gossip and personal histories are rife with moments in which these taboos have not been observed. Here, we arrive at the second dimension of play – urban sociality. Many hold that city life itself, captured in Kinshasa's culture of *ambiance*, renders it difficult to adhere to this scaling of play and work in the sexual sphere. In particular, urban life and interactions in Kinshasa are often assessed as *bajeu* (games).[23] The city is readily identified as a promotor of sexual play, that is, of flirting and courting without the necessity of any commitment towards matrimony. Urban architecture and codes of secrecy among friends, colleagues and peers accommodate the possibility of extra-marital sex.[24] As I observed in previous research, urban (masculine) adulthood is often perceived as characterised by 'play', despite normative demands of seriousness, fidelity, monogamy and discipline.[25] Papa Wemba, one of Kinshasa's most iconic musicians, and deemed by many to be a representative of Kinshasa's *ambiance* culture, would often call himself a 'player' (using the English word), perhaps first and foremost because of his notorious number of offspring born out of wedlock. Indeed, male adulthood is not devoid of play, or of 'sexual play' (i.e. extra-marital sexuality); nor is 'play' limited to men's sexuality. Playful female sexuality undergirds informal urban polyandry, coined in the concept of *Chique, Choque, Chèque*. This phenomenon, in which sex and exchange of commodities and money undergird the relationship, is also publicly denounced as immoral. This culture of urban sexual play has led to various categorisations in Kinshasa's society, such as teenage mothers (Li. Sg. *maman ya mwana*) and 'false lovers' (men or women who have carried out the first steps of formal engagement, but break it off before any of the formal wedding rituals can take place).

The choice of the French *jeu*, instead of the Lingala *lisano*, to assess the non-serious attitude of Kinois social life communicates a cultural distance, as it references a modern, urban, not typically Congolese practice. Kinois life is often described as guided by *anti-valeurs*, asocial actions like corruption, immodesty and looseness (see also Petit and Mulambwa Mutambwa, 2005; Pype, 2017b, pp. 123–24). *Bajeu*, then, refers to this 'playful' behaviour, which is considered to be immoral though typical and perhaps necessary for survival in Kinshasa. Here we arrive at a dimension of economic survival, in which urban sexuality plays an important role. Jackson (2010, p. 53) has observed a general trend in Congolese society which he calls 'trickster entrepreneurialism', referencing the 'negotiating and managing [of] multiple identities, allegiances, affinities and profiles'. This has become 'a source of pride in Congo, a lifestyle, a cultural value, and a political act' (ibid.), and is certainly also valid in Kinshasa's urban economy. Many young people are economically autonomous, sometimes even providing for the livelihoods of the household (De Boeck and Plissart, 2005). In a city where formal marriage is becoming more and more difficult, due to the rise of bride prices among other factors, and where transactional sex is an important strategy of self-making, girls and women are highly autonomous in their sexual lives, and perform various types of work – also sexual work – to get by.

Social media have enlarged this terrain of urban sexual play. The virtual world, as a space of play and trying one's luck, as Flavie does, appears as a variant on the urban spaces of sexual play and pleasure, like hotel rooms, nightclub corners and dark alleys. Closed Facebook groups in particular,[26] accessible through individual accounts (which are not shared), are spaces in which explicit sexual content circulates. These virtual closed circles,[27] often highly pornographic, are only intensifying what the urban lifeworld already accommodates.

Playing with (Married) *Djikas*

'Play' has not only gained new meanings and forms in the contemporary urban context, which social media have only have epitomised; rather, the playing field has been enlarged. One consequence of this is that the *djika* as a preferred (metaphorical) husband has become an increasingly real *possibility* for Kinshasa's girls. With the democratisation of the internet and the ubiquity of smartphones, Kinshasa's women can more easily enter into electronic marriages. They accept that it is most likely they will not get married to any of these far-away digital lovers, but the possibility is always there, and they need to remain available for all opportunities that come their way.

Global hypergamy builds on longer traditions of the higher social value of 'people who have travelled'.[28] The hunter, as one of the prototypical figures who travel, has for a long time been a cultural hero in ethnographies of rural communities. As a traveller by excellence, the hunter brings food to the village, after having conquered the danger and risks of the forests. The *djika*, or the migrant, has often been called a contemporary hunter, hunting in the Global North, yet always claiming to come back with game to the homestead, either by sending remittances or later, upon retirement, returning and settling back 'home' (see Sumata, 2002).

While more research needs to be done on the emergence of the *djika* as a desired marriage partner, it is clearly a phenomenon that people talk about as having increased with and been facilitated by social media. In pre-social media days, television celebrity was seen as the most important route to embark on in order to attract a *djika*. During field research among evangelising TV actors in the early 2000s, actresses mentioned how they hoped that VHS tapes and DVDs of their work that circulate among the diaspora would attract 'serious lovers' from the diaspora and would lead to marriage. Stories circulated about *djikas* returning for marriage to television celebrities, installing these women in flats in a fancy part of town until all the paperwork had been arranged, and then travelling to Europe with them. These actresses I worked with anticipated hypergamy through media celebrity. Certainly, since the availability of social media, being introduced to a *djika* is far easier than before. Now, everybody can have his/her *djika*. The *djikas* themselves also like to entertain fictitious love relationships with girls at home (in Kinshasa) so that these relationships can be consumed when on a short trip back home for a funeral, business affairs or holidays.

The scale of transcontinental communication made possible via social media adds a particular temporality to the sexual life of unmarried Kinois. Each year, around mid-June, excitement and anticipation are in the air in Kinshasa. As the holidays are coming closer, many girls in Kinshasa eagerly await phone calls or text messages from their *mibali ya face*. The months of July and August, summer months in the Global North, are the months of the year (dry season in Kinshasa) when Congolese of the diaspora visit their home country. Many of these *djikas* spend some time in Kinshasa. If the men are coming on their own, either because they are bachelors or because they did not have the funds to travel with their spouses and/or children, they will usually stay in *des flats-hôtels*. These new buildings, often two, sometimes three storeys high, and always walled, have increasingly sprung up in the city since 2010. Most often built with remittances, these places double as a source of income for the *djika* and/or his relatives in Kinshasa, and as a place of residence during their visits to *le bled* (slang for home). Other *djikas*, those who do not own a *flat-hôtel*, usually rent a room (sometimes with a kitchen) in one of these buildings owned by one of their contacts in the diaspora.

Most girls are usually aware of the married status of the *djika* with whom they are chatting and meeting when they are in town, and to whom they are sending (teasing and nude) pictures, though most of them do not really care about their marital status and do not want to cause a divorce. Rather, the relationship is attractive as long as it is beneficial, that is, as long as the girl can send requests for money or goods.[29] It was clear that Flavie invested much more time and effort in digital communication with men living abroad. Most of these she had never encountered in person, and she assumed that she never actually would. Yet some of them had already travelled to Kinshasa, and she had met them a few times, mostly also leading to sexual play. Although Flavie assumed that in most cases their stories about being single and serious were lies, she did cherish the hope that one day she would meet a man who would take her and her children away from DR Congo.

Ultimately, the increased efforts of Kinois girls to set up deep connections with digital contacts signal a transformation of the role of the extended family/lineage in the establishment of matrimony. Kinois men and women enjoy a high degree of autonomy when choosing a marriage partner (see Pype, 2012), though approval by relatives remains necessary for the various ceremonial confirmations.[30] Some wo/men are preferred marriage partners or prohibited marriage partners along ethnic lines, although urbanisation, which diminishes the knowledge of ethnic taboos and prescriptions, has tended to change this; churches have also established their own set of preferred marriage partners for their believers (Pype, 2012, pp. 232–56). While individual choice and preference for marriage partners is not new, it seems that social media emphasises the individual, and, at least as long as the romance remains in the 'play phase', the *libala ya face* remains isolated from the girl's family network.

Flavie's digital accounts on dating websites had been initiated by two female friends – twins – living in her street. When Flavie's relationship with the father of her children had ended, these girls had introduced her to Kinshasa's expat communities, where *bamindele* ('white men', usually Belgian, French or others working in diplomatic and humanitarian circles) pay good money for sexual intercourse.[31] In the early days, Flavie and the twins would split the money they received from these trysts. When Facebook became more accessible, it made introductions easier, and she no longer needed the twins. She also observed that the girls did not always inform her of their meetings with men. Flavie therefore began to manage this segment of her love life, that was mainly lived digitally, on her own. Her children were not supposed to touch her smartphones, and according to the *kipe ya yo* sociality ('mind your own business'; Pype, 2016b), Flavie's elder brothers and sisters apparently did not ask any questions either. These observations on Flavie's autonomous handling of her sexual life connect to Appadurai's earlier-mentioned emphasis on the social consequences for the individual: electronic modernity allows for novel opportunities for self-making. Flavie indeed entertains multiple 'husbands from Facebook' and she has sexual relationships with various men (not only those she meets online), but this is all hidden from her relatives' sight.

This, however, does not mean that girls' relatives are always ignorant of the affective work the girl performs digitally. Sometimes they wilfully ignore it (see Archambault, 2017), yet at certain occasions they also facilitate, and even encourage it. I am frequently reminded of the fact that many families are keen for their daughter to find a *djika*.[32] Indeed, the investment in the affective work for one woman to get married is not always limited to the individual. Flavie, however, invested a lot of time and phone credit in keeping her online lovers secret, mainly in an effort to protect her reputation. As a divorced mother with children, she also did not perceive much pressure from her relatives to get married again.

Of Change and Digital Playfulness

Concentrating on how Flavie and others initiate digital romance, how these electronic liaisons are (successfully and sometimes unsuccessfully) managed, and interrogating the pragmatic qualities of the rubrics of *bolingo ya face* and *libala ya face*, I have attempted to shed light on how the realm of kinship, here the sphere of matrimony, is mobilised in a digital world. This attention to kinship and matrimony is significant as the ideology of friendship (Miller, 2017) dominates on social media.

At the beginning of this chapter, I argued that *bolingo ya face* has something to teach us theoretically about how sexuality and matrimony are (re-)organised in the era of digital modernity. It has become clear that *libala* (matrimony; marriage) in Kinshasa is, like in many other megacities, a complex affair in which urban livelihoods and the desirability of the *djika* are negotiated. I have situated the emergence of the *bolingo ya face* within the urban sexual economy, and highlighted the continuities of the affective work defining Kinois sociality. Therefore, this chapter has discussed some of the laborious practices which Flavie mobilises to gain the affect, attention and money of her *husbands from Facebook*. These are strategies and tactics in which she combines flattery, suggestion, magic and seduction. The affective work thus aims at enhancing social connectivity, by establishing deep, meaningful, marriage-like relationships that can become beneficial.

In the 'kinning' of strangers, especially turning them into affines, *libala* (marriage) is used as a metaphor to emphasise the exchange of affect and intimacy. In the words of Manderson and Block (2016, p. 210), discussing the mobilisation of kinship idioms in spaces of care: 'To invoke a kinship idiom … sets in place a relationship of kinship and care, typically of mutual responsibility, in the present and the future'. The idiom of *libala ya face* draws attention to the imagination of 'matrimony' in Kinois society. It is exactly the notion of *libala* as a space of solidarity and support that is mobilised in these digital flirtations. I believe this is the major contribution of this chapter: we observe how a particular social form, marriage, appears in unexpected spaces (the digital media platform) and does so without the classically assumed social context, being the ceremonies, the public expression of expectations and the required involvements of social groups (the extended families).

This attention to continuity and transformation with regard to social forms in 'offline' environments vis-à-vis digital communications counters the idea of a radical shift in social life since the introduction of new media (although in the perceptions of Kinois this might actually be experienced as such). As I see it, the stranger sociality of online networking is fully in line with urban sociality, and builds further on that. *Bolingo ya face* and *libala ya face* increase the responsibility of the individual in an urban setting to survive, while there are nevertheless pull factors from the family. In addition, these new idioms relate to the ideal of global hypergamy as currently thriving in Kinshasa, with its emphasis on the *djika* as a preferential marriage partner for women, and the ideal of marrying 'a girl from home' for the Congolese men in the diaspora. Therefore, I have argued that the 'play' versus 'work' binary is more relevant to understand digital flirting, rather than the 'offline' versus 'online' and 'virtual' versus 'real' binaries. I have tried to show that analytical attention to the various forms of play that appear in Kinshasa's social universe, in particular in the urban environment, and in the imagination of sexuality and the organisation of matrimony, inform Flavie's digital performances.

One major question that remains to be answered is if, and how, these 'digital marriages' turn into marriages confirmed by customary, religious and civil rituals. Insofar as the practices of exchanging money, attention, commodities and time occur in and through the digitally mediated communication, the union between the two partners of the *libala ya face* is real. Even if these digital marriages have not been ritually confirmed through customary, civil and/or religious ceremonies, these are interactions in which the responsibilities, obligations and benefits of partners are expressed and used as claims in order to achieve certain goals. The fact that digital marriages are polygamous and polygynous – in that there is a strong distribution of attention, commodities, words and promises and sometimes actual sex among multiple partners – does not set them apart from so-called 'real marriages'.[33] Yet it is rather rare that *bolingo ya face* turns into matrimony confirmed by the various rituals organised by kin, religious communities and the state.

At the time of finishing this chapter, in the autumn of 2019, Flavie was still single, and continued to converse online with men living in Kinshasa and abroad. She was still in search of a potential marriage partner who can provide a better future for herself and her children, preferably abroad. In the sixteen years that I have been visiting Kinshasa, less than a handful of couples that I know have turned the *libala ya face* into ritually confirmed matrimony. I have collected numerous stories about men and women being duped by people they had met online, and with whom they had been talking about marriage. Time and again, it transpired that offline realities – such as the distance, rumours about the other's alleged marital status, or impositions made by the family – interfered and prevented the transformation of the digital connection into matrimony. I would often hear, with a sigh, 'It are all *bajeu*'. On the one hand, *bajeu* refers to the fact that people cannot trust others, but will be played with. On the other hand, the game itself has an aspect of chance. By playing games, one tests the waters for one's chance, one's luck.[34] And maybe here we come to the heart of the idea of change, opportunity and mobility, as experienced by many Kinois: if it is not in your destiny, then it will not happen. However, you can always test the waters to see where your luck is situated. And this is what (digital) play allows: it has expanded the spaces in which people can test their luck.

Finally, I want to introduce again Handelman's distinction between 'play' and 'playful'. Insofar as sexuality remains within a space of pleasure, then we can consider it as 'play'. However, when sexuality and the metaphorical language of 'husbands' and 'wives' are mobilised in order to bring about new realities and new futures, then this behaviour can be framed as 'playful', situated on the borders between 'play' and 'seriousness'. It is in this border zone, oscillating between pleasure seeking and attempting to produce new futures, that Flavie navigates. She is well aware of the possibility that her *mibali ya face* are playing, while she is playful. Playfulness, as a space of becoming, brings in a time dimension that extends beyond the moment of play. It allows for change to set in gradually.

Acknowledgements

I am indebted to Flavie and many other Kinois friends and research interlocutors who have helped me to make sense of digital conversations. Likewise, the members of the 'New Media Practices in a Changing Africa' team have offered insightful comments during the Marrakech discussions. Jeroen Cuvelier, Ilana Gershon, Ewa Majczak and Steven Van Wolputte offered invaluable feedback on previous versions of this chapter. The material has been presented at the University of Birmingham (May–June 2017) and at the Annual Meeting of the African Studies Association (Atlanta, 2018). I wish to thank Karin Barber, Jennifer Cole, Juliet Gilbert and others for their questions and reflections. Funding for this research was offered by the Norwegian Research Council and the Flemish Fund for Scientific Research (G.A005.14N, ERC-Runner Up Budget).

Katrien Pype is associate professor (*hoofddocent*) in anthropology at the KU Leuven University. Since 2003, she has been studying Kinshasa's media worlds and popular culture. Her work engages in particular with aesthetics and material infrastructures. In 2012, her ethnography of the production of television serials was published by Berghahn Books (*The Making of the Pentecostal Melodrama: Religion, Media, and Gender in Kinshasa*), and articles have appeared in, among others, *Journal of the Royal Anthropological Institute, Ethnos: Journal of Anthropology, Africa: Journal of the International Africa Institute, Media, Culture & Society, Journal of African Cultural Studies, Journal of African Media Studies* and *Visual Anthropology*.

Notes

1. The OED (2010, online edition) gives as explanation for the entry 'romance', as a noun: 1. A medieval narrative ...; 2. Music, balled, epic poem ...; 3. A fictitious narrative, usually in prose, in which the settings or the events depicted are remote from everyday life, or in which sensational or exciting adventures form the central theme ... The genre of literature which consists of romances; 4. An extravagant fabrication; a wild falsehood, a fantasy ...; 5. A. The character or quality that makes something appeal strongly to the imagination and sets it apart from the mundane, an air, feeling, or sense of wonder, mystery, and remoteness from everyday life; ... B. ardour or warmth of feeling in a love affair; 6. A love affair; a romantic relationship; 7. A story of romantic love ... literature of this kind.
2. *Terrain* references a battle ground. The word speaks to the imagination of life as a constant struggle.

3. The desire to marry a man from abroad seems to be pretty general among various social groups in Kinshasa.
4. A *belgicain* is someone who has travelled to Belgium (and by extension the Global North). A synonym is *mikiliste.* There are different socio-economic categories of *djikas,* each speaking in different ways to Kinois girls' aspirations.
5. *Bolingo ya face* is thus different from virtual romance, as described, for example, by Barker (2008) on interkom, an analogue chat system used in urban and peri-urban Bandung (Indonesia), where conversation partners – usually married in real life – engage in flirtation and sexually suggestive interaction, with no consequences for the matrimonial lives of each conversation partner. Rather, as interkom cannot provide one-on-one dialogue, and a wide range of others can listen along, 'interkom is only for entertainment' and 'does not cause any major domestic conflicts' (Barker, 2008, p. 140), at least so long the boundaries between the 'on-air society' and the 'on-land society' are kept clear (ibid.).
6. See Hendriks (2016) for a similar linguistic play with regards to telephony devices and accessories ('sim cards') and urban homo-erotic interactions in Kinshasa.
7. In Katanga, the idiom *kuingia pa fenêtre* (to enter through the window – instead of the door) is used to express this informal marriage.
8. See Tazanu (2012) for an incisive study of the role of new media in transnational sociality for the Cameroonian community.
9. In one of the first anthropological engagements with Facebook, Miller (2011, p. 554) already emphasised that 'a good deal of posting consists of jokes and innuendoes'. Humphrey (2009) also makes playfulness central to her analysis of online sociality in Russian chatrooms.
10. Hardt (1999) and Hardt and Negri (2000) have observed an increasing dominance of immaterial labour, of which affective labour is only one type, in contemporary postmodern society. According to Hardt (1999), immaterial labour, which produces an immaterial good such as a service, knowledge or communication, is central in contemporary regimes of value production and the economy at large. Especially with the advance of computer technologies, 'jobs of routine symbol manipulation such as data entry and word processing' have become crucial. Also, the entertainment and culture industries rely heavily on the creation and manipulation of affects. 'Affective labour', or 'labour that produces or manipulates affects' (Hardt and Negri 2000, p. 99), is thus not confined to the kinship realm and spaces of care work. Rather, 'in global society, the contemporary economy aims at producing feelings of ease, well-being, satisfaction, excitement, passion – even a sense of connectedness or community' (ibid.).
11. In Kinshasa, an informal economy reigns. Capitalism thus thrives in Kinshasa in a different fashion than the societies described by Hardt and Negri (2000).
12. See Macjzak (2019) for a fascinating investigation of Bamileke women's usage of digital photography (Cameroon).
13. On certain occasions, if the new contact is physically present in Kinshasa, a meeting can be arranged the same day or within the same week. In many instances, sexual interaction occurs during these initial encounters.
14. Calling during the day would mean that one has money to spend.

15. Codes are formed through written explanations in text, thus sometimes interrupting the spoken conversations.
16. The concept of a 'true Christian' (*chrétien ya solo*) is here used in contrast to 'false Christian' (*chrétien ya lokuta*) and 'Christian of the flesh' (*chrétien ya misuni*), various categories that Christians use to define the different levels of commitment to Christianity (Pype, 2012, p. 77).
17. Flavie uses other powders from time to time to protect her against the angry legitimate wives of her 'husbands', and especially against the powders women use so that their husbands become impotent when trying to have sex with a *mbanda* (rival). A battle of spiritual powers is thus played out between women over the man's sexual potency.
18. An interesting comparison can be made with the Indonesian interkom (see notes 5 and 20), where 'users described interkom relationships in an idiom of kinship and neighbourly relations' (Barker, 2008, p. 136), thus showing the need to enlarge 'one's circle of relations' (ibid., p. 137); and Cousins' (2016) exploration of play marriages among female labourers working on KwaZulu-Natal's timber plantations.
19. This is also the reason why sexual and love relationships are rarely broken up in Kinshasa. Rather, people prefer to let them fade out. Disconnecting with people – stopping speaking, or blocking them on social media – are radical social acts that signal a major social conflict. The ideal is to maintain harmonious relationships with others, even with former lovers. Thus, the best strategy is not to disrupt but merely to temporarily interrupt relationships.
20. Gershon (2010) describes the frustrations some US-based college students experience when a Facebook or other digital relationship remains trapped within the online sphere, and does not evolve into a physical relationship. Barker (2008), by contrast, provides a fascinating description of 'couples' that only exist within the communicative sphere of interkom (see notes 5 and 18). It is expected that every interkom user has one privileged conversation partner, with whom affect is exchanged, and which can be quite possessive. Nevertheless, these relationships are limited to the interkom sphere, as most of them are married or involved in an exclusive, intimate relationship with someone else in 'real life'.
21. See Archambault (2017) on wilful ignorance.
22. One wonders how the rules of the game have changed through time and with different phases of urbanisation. This seems to beg an alternative history of urban sociality.
23. *Bajeu* combines the Lingala prefix *ba-* indicating the plural and the French *jeu* (game, play).
24. Around town there are many rendezvous hotels where one can rent a room for half an hour at cheap rates; bars and nightclubs have separate rooms for sexual encounters, separated either by walls, curtains or dark windows. These are called *kuzu* (or *kousou*) (Pype, 2016a, fn5). There is also a general mood in the city that people should mind their own business (*kipe ya yo*; Pype, 2016b), so certain questions are not to be asked or are easily left unanswered.
25. These *bajeu* also explain the dominance of the rubric of 'youth', in contrast to 'adulthood' (see Pype, 2012).

26. *Basi ya Facebook* (translated from Lingala: 'Girls from Facebook') is a hit on the internet, and refers to closed social media groups on WhatsApp, Facebook and elsewhere containing sexually explicit content.
27. Access to these groups is via circulation of phone numbers. It is often pointed out that members need to be over eighteen, though this is difficult to verify.
28. Customary marriage rituals in Kinshasa during which the bride price (*dot*) is transmitted from the groom's family to the bride's relatives illustrate the social (and economic) value attached to those who have travelled. Often, a fictitious cosmopolitan identity is used for the bride as a way to increase the money that her relatives can get. After all the goods have been transferred literally from one side of the table to the other, and when the groom's relatives then start to claim 'their wife', in the banter and joking at play, the bride's relatives will usually playfully say that she is still in Beijing, Brussels or Cape Town, and that money for a plane ticket is needed. Usually, the groom's relatives – who have calculated this in their budget as it is very common during customary weddings – add another 100 or 200 USD to the bride price. The bride's family then brings out the bride from the room in which she has been hiding during the whole ritual. While a fictitious cosmopolitan identity is used here to raise the bride price, the ritual itself also allows the physical absence of one of the two marriage partners. It sometimes happens that a *djika* cannot travel back to Kinshasa for his customary wedding, and needs to be physically represented by a brother. Marriage by proxy is allowed in the customary and civil wedding celebrations. In these cases, a representative (often a brother or cousin) of the absent marriage partner (and a lawyer, for the civil marriage) stands in. There is an important gendered dimension here: usually it is men that are absent. Absence needs to be justified, and it can be pricey.
29. Other *djika* prefer to marry 'girls from home', very often from the same region as them. This is a very complex matter which I cannot develop further here. I have heard numerous accounts of Congolese men living in Brussels, Boston or London, requesting their relatives in Kinshasa to find a girl to marry for them, on their behalf. The 'girls from home' seem to have a better reputation than the *basi ya poto* (the girls from Europe); they are perceived to be more moral, uncontaminated by feminism, and more obedient.
30. There are various tactics that people use, however, in order to enforce approval from the lineage. That is a topic for a separate manuscript.
31. See Cole (2010) for an exploration of Malgasy women and their interactions with white men.
32. Anecdotal evidence here is provided by a television serial in which I starred in 2015, called *Mbutu Mbutu* (groupe de théâtre Sai Sai), in which I played the role of a white woman who had travelled to Kinshasa to marry a Kinois man whom she had met over Facebook. The serial shows in comedic ways the lengths to which relatives would go in order to flatter and accommodate the *mundele* (white person). Relatives encourage their son to lie and to deceive his local love interest and the white woman. *Mbutu Mbutu* thus portrays, among other things, how morals are quickly put aside within the extended family when confronted with one of the children's possibilities of wealth, travel and prestige.
33. Many married Kinois women assume that their husbands have extra-marital affairs.

34. McGovern (2010) observed a similar usage of 'play' in Ivory Coast when interpreting war and conflict. His analysis points at the moral distancing that the mobilisation of the play frame brings: for those saying 'he is merely playing', a sense of responsibility is denied, while for those making sense of painful events as 'play', it speaks to the difficult acceptance of conflict and war.

References

Abidin, C. 2018. *Internet Celebrity: Understanding Fame Online*. Bradford: Emerald Publishing.

Appadurai, A. 1996. *Modernity at Large: Cultural Dimensions of Globalization*. Minnesota: University of Minneapolis Press.

Archambault, J.-S. 2017. *Mobile Secrets: Youth, Intimacy, and the Politics of Pretense in Mozambique*. Chicago: Chicago University Press.

Barker, J. 2008. 'Playing with Publics: Technology, Talk and Sociability in Indonesia', *Language and Communication* 28(2): 127–42.

Bateson, G. 1987. 'A Theory of Play and Fantasy', In G. Bateson, *Steps to an Ecology of Mind: Collected Essays in Anthropology, Psychiatry, Evolution, And Epistemology*. Northvale: Jason Aronson, pp. 138–48.

Bernal, V. 2014. *Nation as Network: Diaspora, Cyberspace, and Citizenship*. Chicago: Chicago University Press.

Bernault, F. 2015. 'Aesthetics of Acquisition: Gabonese Spectacles and the Transactional Life of Bodies and Things', *Comparative Studies in Society and History* 57(3): 753–79.

Boellstorff, T. 2008. *Coming of Age in Second Life: An Anthropologist Explores the Virtually Human*. Princeton, NJ: Princeton University Press.

Bourdieu, P. 1984. *Distinction: A Social Critique of the Judgement of Taste*. London: Routledge.

Bräuchler, B. 2013. *Cyberidentities at War: The Moluccan Conflict on The Internet*. Oxford/New York: Berghahn Books.

Cole, J. 2010. *Sex and Salvation: Imagining the Future in Madagascar*. Chicago: Chicago University Press.

Cole, J., and C. Groes. 2016. *Affective Circuits: African Migrations to Europe and the Pursuit of Social Regeneration*. Chicago: University of Chicago Press.

Cole, J., and L.M. Thomas. 2009. *Love in Africa*. Chicago: Chicago University Press.

Conley, D. 2009. *Elsewhere, U.S.A.: How We Got from the Company Man, Family Dinners, and the Affluent Society to the Home Office, Blackberry Moms, and Economic Anxiety*. New York: Pantheon Books.

Constable, N. 2003. *Romance on a Global Stage: Pen Pals, Virtual Ethnography, and 'Mail Order' Marriages*. Oakland: University of California Press.

Cousins, T. 2016. 'Sex, Gender and Marriage in the Timber Plantations of KwaZulu-Natal, South Africa: A Minor Otherwise', *Social Dynamics* 42(2): 218–36.

De Boeck, F., and M.-F. Plissart. 2005. *Kinshasa: Tales of the Invisible City*. Ghent: Ludion.

Deger, J. 2016. 'Thick Photography', *Journal of Material Culture* 21(1): 111–32.

Epstein, A.L. 1981. *Urbanization and Kinship: The Domestic Domain on the Copperbelt of Zambia, 1950–1956*. London: Academic Press.

Geertz, C. 1973. *The Interpretation of Cultures: Selected Essays*. New York: Basic Books.

Gershon, I. 2010. *The Break-Up 2.0*. Ithaca, NY: Cornell University Press.

Gluckman, M. 1950. 'Kinship and Marriage among the Lozi of Northern Rhodesia and the Zulu of Natal', in A.R. Radcliffe-Brown and D. Forde (eds), *African Systems of Kinship and Marriage*. London: Oxford University Press, pp. 166–206.

Hamayon, R. 2016. *Why We Play: An Anthropological Study*. Hau Book Series. Chicago: Chicago University Press.

Handelman, D. 2001. 'Postlude: Framing, Braiding, and Killing Play', *Focaal: European Journal of Anthropology* 37: 145–56.

Hardt, M. 1999. 'Affective Labour', *boundary 2* 26(2): 89–100.

Hardt, M. and A. Negri. 2000. *Empire*. Cambridge, MA: Cambridge University Press.

Helle-Valle, J. 1999. 'Sexual Mores, Promiscuity and Prostitution in Botswana', *Ethnos* 64(3–4): 372–96.

Hendriks, T. 2016. 'Sim Cards of Desire: Sexual Versatility and the Male Homoerotic Economy in Urban Congo', *American Ethnologist* 43(2): 230–42.

Huizinga, J. 1949. *Homo Ludens: A Study of the Play Element in Culture*. London: Routledge & Kegan Paul.

Humphrey, C. 2009. 'The Mask and the Face: Imagination and Social Life in Russian Chat Rooms and Beyond', *Ethnos: Journal of Anthropology* 74(1): 31–50.

Hunt, N.R. 1991. 'Noise Over Camouflaged Polygamy, Colonial Morality Taxation, and a Woman-Naming Crisis in Belgian Africa', *The Journal of African History* 32(3): 471–94.

Jackson, S. 2010. 'It Seems to Be Going: The Genius of Survival in Wartime DR Congo', in A.-M. Makhulu, B. Buggenhagen and S. Jackson (eds), *Hard Work, Hard Times: Ethnographies of Volatility and African Being-in-the-World*. Berkeley: University of California Press, pp. 48–68.

Küchlich J. 2005. 'Precarious Playbour: Modders and the Digital Games Industry', *Fibreculture Journal* 5, http://five.fibreculturejournal.org/fcj-025-precarious-playbour-modders-and-the-digital-games-industry/ (accessed 20 September 2019).

Lukacs, G. 2010. *Scripted Affects, Branded Selves: Television, Subjectivity, and Capitalism in 1990s Japan*. Durham, NC: Duke University Press.

Macjzak, E. 2019. 'Entrepreneurs of Love: Digital Photographic Displays and Reconfiguration of Intimate Relations among Young Bamileke Women Living in Yaounde (Cameroon)', paper presented at the 8th European Conference of African Studies, University of Edinburgh, 14 June.

Manderson, L., and E. Block. 2016. 'Relatedness and Care in Southern Africa and Beyond', *Social Dynamics* 42(2): 205–17.

McGovern, M. 2010. 'This Is Play: Popular Culture and Politics in Côte d'Ivoire', in A.-M. Makhulu, B. Buggenhagen and S. Jackson (eds), *Hard Work, Hard Times: Ethnographies of Volatility and African Being-in-the-World.* Berkeley: University of California Press, pp. 69–90.

Miller, D. 2011. *Tales from Facebook.* Malden, MA: Polity Press.

———. 2017. 'The Ideology of Friendship in the Era of Facebook', *Hau. Journal of Ethnographic Theory* 7(1). https://www.haujournal.org/index.php/hau/article/view/hau7.1.025 (accessed 15 April 2018).

Miller, D., E. Costa, N. Haynes, T. McDonald, R. Nicolescu, J. Sinanan, J. Spyer, S. Venkatraman and X. Wang. 2016. *How the World Changed Social Media.* London: UCL Press.

Nyamnjoh, F. 2004. *Married but Available.* Bamenda, Cameroon: Langaa RPCIG.

Ortner, S. 1996. *Anthropology and Social Theory: Culture, Power, and the Acting Subject.* Durham, NC: Duke University Press.

Petit, P., and G. Mulambwa Mutambwa. 2005. '"La Crise": Lexicon and Ethos of the Second Economy in Lubumbashi', *Africa: Journal of the International African Institute* 75(4): 467–87.

Postill, J. 2018. *The Rise of Nerd Politics: Digital Activism and Political Change.* London: Pluto Press.

Pype, K. 2012. *The Making of the Pentecostal Melodrama: Religion, Media, & Gender in Kinshasa.* New York: Berghahn Books.

———. 2016a. 'Blackberry Girls and Jesus's Brides: Pentecostal-Charismatic Christianity and the (Im-)Moralization of Urban Femininities in Contemporary Kinshasa', *Journal of Religion in Africa* 46(4): 390–416.

———. 2016b. 'On Interference and Hotspots: Ethnographic Explorations of Rural-Urban Connectivity in and around Kinshasa's *Phonie* Cabins', *Mededelingen der Zittingen van Koninklijke Academie voor Overzeese Wetenschappen* 62 (2): 229–260. doi: 10.5281/zenodo.3379983.

———. 2017a. 'Brokers of Belonging: Elders and Intermediaries in Kinshasa's Mobile Phone Culture', in W. Mano and W. Willems (eds), *From Media Audiences to Users: Everyday Media in Africa.* London: Routledge, pp. 198–219.

———. 2017b. 'Branhamist Kindoki: Ethnographic Notes on Connectivity, Technology and Urban Witchcraft in Contemporary Kinshasa', in K. Rio, M. MacCarthy and R. Blanes (eds), *Pentecostalism and Witchcraft: Spiritual Warfare in Africa and Melanesia.* Cham, Switzerland: Palgrave Macmillan, pp. 115–44.

———. 2019a. 'Benda Bilili na Toile: Ethnographic Reflections on Sociality and Cryptic Digital Communication in Kinshasa', paper presented at the 8th European Conference of African Studies, University of Edinburgh, 14 June.

———. 2019b. '(Not) in Sync – Digital Time and Forms of (Dis-)Connecting: Ethnographic Notes from Kinshasa (DR Congo)', *Media, Culture & Society* (Online First): 1–16. doi: 10.1177/0163443719867854.

Simmel, G. [1908] 2009. *Sociology: Inquiries into the Construction of Social Forms*, vols 1 and 2, trans. and ed. A.J. Blasi, A.K. Jacobs and M. Kanjirathinkal. Leiden and Boston: Brill.

Steel, G. 2017. 'Navigating (Im)mobility: Female Entrepreneurship and Social Media in Khartoum', *Africa: Journal of the International African Institute* 87(2): 233–252.

Sumata, C. 2002. 'Migradollars and Poverty Alleviation Strategy Issues in Congo-DRC', *Review of African Political Economy* 23(93/94): 619–28.

Tazanu, P.M. 2012. *Being Available and Reachable: New Media and Cameroonian Transnational Sociality*. Mankon, Cameroon: Langaa Research & Publishing.

Turner, V. 1987. *The Anthropology of Performance*. New York: PAJ Publishers.

Van Velzen, T. 1964. *The Politics of Kinship: A Study in Social Manipulation among the Lakeside Tonga of Nyasaland*. Manchester: Manchester University Press for Rhodes-Livingstone Institute.

Wang, X. 2016. *Social Media in Industrial China*. London: UCL Press.

CHAPTER 4

Texting Like a State

Knowledge and Change in a National mHealth Programme

Nanna Schneidermann

It is Tuesday morning at the antenatal clinic at the Midwife Obstetric Unit somewhere on the Cape Flats, the flatlands of former townships on the outskirts of Cape Town. On rows of benches, maybe eight pregnant women sit waiting to see a nurse, either to 'book', to register their pregnancy and get an initial examination, or to get a scheduled check-up. Some have been here since before seven o'clock and some will wait until midday, if it gets busy. There are those who are smartly dressed in dresses and pumps, as if going to work in an office in town, others wearing tattered and torn leggings and jerseys. A few have brought their male partners. All are black.[1] I sit in the corner, under the television mounted on the wall, waiting to see Africa's first national mobile health programme in action.

After a while, Susan, the community nurse, comes in and says, 'Okay, mommies! Today I want to talk to you about MomConnect'. A stout, short woman with small square spectacles, she stands in front of the rows of women like a teacher, and speaks in a commanding voice, in clean English with a Cape Flats accent. 'It is a very good programme that gives you all of the good information', she proclaims, and smiles to the expecting parents.

This chapter examines how ideas of change are inscribed into the first national mobile health (mHealth) programme in Africa (Innovation Working Group [IWG], n.d.). Over the past ten years, mobile health – organised and intentional uses of mobile phones for health purposes – has mushroomed across the continent (Aranda-Jan et al., 2014). NGOs and other institutions have created programmes and apps using mobile technologies for use by health professionals and patients (Bloomfield et al., 2014; Forrest et al., 2015), but the field also includes institutionalised inventive uses of mobile phones as part of giving and receiving health care (Watkins et al., 2018). Recently, the focus of international policy in the field has been on how to scale up mHealth and make it sustainable (Fölster, 2017; Haas, 2016; Lundin and Dumont, 2017; Seebregts et al., 2018). MomConnect is an example of bringing an mHealth programme with patients as end users to national scale, and this raises questions about changing relations between digital imaginaries (see Willems' chapter in this book), media use and governance in Africa.[2]

Recent studies of the impact of mHealth initiatives in South Africa focus narrowly on the intended users of interventions and rely largely on quantitative data such as downloads or page views, held against diachronic statistical data on, for example, the spread of HIV or child mortality (e.g. Coleman, 2013). Such studies document change in relation to specific mHealth interventions, but say little of the how mHealth initiatives are part of everyday media use, or of how users place value, if any, on using their phones for purposes of health care. Neither do they confront the context in which the mHealth programmes are developed and implemented in practice.

Yet the context of use also shapes the access and use of mHealth, as offline inequalities are reproduced and at times entrenched in mHealth initiatives (Waldman and Stevens, 2015, p. 7). Investigating situations of use of mHealth in its various contexts moves the analysis beyond quantitative measures and into more complex understandings of how these interventions work in very different settings.

In this chapter, I ask how ideas of social change take shape in situated uses of mHealth. I ask this from the vantage point of five sites in which the MomConnect programme was at stake: the everyday lives of the intended users; the working spaces of frontline health care workers like Susan; the content of the messages; the technological infrastructure of the programme in its encounter with maternal health clinics; and lastly, the research produced about mHealth. These 'sites' differ in quality, but they are bound together in that they are sites in which change in maternal and child health and well-being is conceptualised in relation to mobile technologies. When Susan spoke about the 'good information' that MomConnect gives, she gave a clue about a central factor in all of these sites: knowledge. This comes to refer to very different phenomena: 'not-knowing' among intended users, 'information' at the antenatal clinic, 'stats' at the Midwife Obstetric Unit, 'data' for MomConnect scientists. I use these emic concepts of knowledge as a lens through which to examine how the relationship between mHealth and change is articulated and experienced in different contexts of use.

In so doing, I revisit insights from James Scott (1998) about the relationship between statecraft, knowledge and power, suggesting that 'texting like a state' might be an approach to understanding projects of up-scaling mHealth in context. Scott analyses how state projects to transform nature, space and sociality to improve the human condition have failed, and in particular how the gaze of the state onto its territories and populations itself seeks to remake the world in its own image of bureaucratic and scientific knowledge. He contrasts these fictions of order with a kind of practical knowledge that he calls metis – the rules of experience (Scott, 1998, p. 333) or 'the science of muddling through' (ibid., p. 327). While these distinctions are useful, and I will draw on them below, they also place the writer in a position of making disembodied diagnoses of successes and failures of various projects. By examining how ideas of 'knowledge' animate the relationship between digital technologies and social change in different sites of one specific project, I wish to push Scott's project forward, beyond success and failure and into situated practices of stateness (Hansen and Stepputat, 2001, pp. 8–9). This also means that the present ethnography is in no way a comprehensive analysis of the impact of MomConnect, but rather a list of situations that each in their way relate to it. I start by contextualising MomConnect before presenting the five sites in which mobile technology, pregnancy, motherhood and health were put at stake in relation to different forms of knowledge. I conclude by drawing together some reflections from these situations of texting like a state.

mHealth in Context

The MomConnect programme is a flagship project of the National Department of Health (NDoH) in South Africa. It was developed in partnership with USAID, Johnson and Johnson,[3] South African telecommunications providers and non-profits in the tech development sector, and scaled up the pilot programme, MAMA (Skinner et al., 2018). For MomConnect, women using the public health system sign up via a mobile phone to receive stage-based text messages with health information and reminders throughout their pregnancy and the first year of their baby's life. A central aim is to get women to attend four or more clinic appointments for early detection of risks and complications. There is an option in the programme to send feedback about health services, and possibly to engage in dialogue by text messaging

(Barron et al., 2018; NDoH, 2015a). In turn, users are registered in a national digital patient database – and building a low-cost and flexible technological infrastructure for this is considered by some to be the main accomplishment of the project (Seebregts et al., 2018). More than one million women have been registered since the programme's launch in 2014 (ibid.).

The health care system in South Africa is two-tiered: the services in the public health care sector are free to residents, while health care insurance gives access to private health care facilities – usually with an aspect of self/co-payment. Private health insurance is usually referred to as a 'medical plan' and provided by employers in stable wage-earning jobs. The public health care system is permanently understaffed and underfunded, but serves about 80 per cent of the population. Over recent years, around one million births have been reported annually and 93.5 per cent of women give birth in a medical facility, while over 90 per cent of these have attended one or more antenatal appointments (see also Chadwick and Foster, 2013, p. 321).

Colonial and apartheid health regimes enabled and perpetrated systematic mass violence, including various forms of obstetric violence and forced contraception (Lewis and Salo, 1993). The state now seeks to extend health care to all residents regardless of background. Yet according to Zerucelli Rucell, the imagery and morality of past regimes is still shaping practice in the reproductive health care of the public sector, as justification for obstetric violence towards pregnant black women and girls (Zerucelli Rucell, 2017; see also Digby, 2006). This violence can take many forms, from physical and verbal abuse in clinics to more indirect forms such as lack of access to clinics and other health resources (Ferreira, 2016), and underlines the extreme inequality in health care in South Africa. Despite improvements of outcomes in maternal and child health over the past ten years, the NDoH notes that maternal and infant mortality and morbidity rates in South Africa are far from the Sustainable Development Goals (Innovation Working Group [IWG], n.d.) and that there are great inequalities in access and quality in maternal health care services (Silal et al., 2012).

The aim here is not to contest the efficacy of national mHealth programmes, but to begin to notice the processes by which what at a national level is considered a political and culturally sensitive technological solution to problems of maternal health and patient data is given meaning in specific sites of use by histories and ideals about women's health and motherhood. In the next two sections I explore two sites in which MomConnect became meaningful in everyday life and in the antenatal clinic in the Midwife Obstetric Unit on the Cape Flats.

Site One: Everyday Lives and Ambiguous Knowledge

As we were sitting on the battered couches in the iron sheet extension of her mother's Reconstruction and Development Programme (RDP) house, Aisha fiddled with her phone. She was not on MomConnect, but her phone was still crucial for her path towards motherhood. She was quiet and seemed shy when we asked her about her pregnancy and expectations of motherhood. 'Every child is a blessing', she said, perhaps to remind herself of this. She was seventeen, out of school, living with her mother and two younger siblings. At times her older sister would also live with them, always reminding Aisha that her condition was also a sign of her own lack of moral fabric. Aisha had only found out that she was pregnant when it was too late to get an abortion, after twenty weeks. She might have wanted an abortion, and other family members had urged her to try remedies outside of the formal health system to terminate the pregnancy. But now, seven months along, Aisha had accepted that she would become a mother.

Her boyfriend, who was ten years older than her and lived in a different part of town, had broken up with her when he learnt about the pregnancy. He claimed that the child was not his. Aisha, however, insisted that he was the only man she had ever been with. Their romance started on WhatsApp. He got her phone number from a mutual friend and started sending her flirtatious messages. After a while she responded, and they chatted for weeks on WhatsApp before meeting in real life. He had not been in touch for a while, and Aisha's phone, as it shifted between her hands, was no longer a site for romance and adventure.

Aisha's story is complex but somehow paradigmatic for my fieldwork among pregnant women and new mothers on the Cape Flats. The ambiguity of giving life to a new human being seeped through the stories they shared with us. The upsetting of social relations through the arrival of a new person into families with limited resources was obvious and tension ridden. The blessing of a child was something that they needed to be reminded of, while perhaps hoping for a message on the phone that could make it all better.

My field assistant Shari Thanjan and I went looking for MomConnect in everyday life on the Cape Flats. It turned out to be elusive. We met women like Aisha in their everyday lives, through local community workers, NGOs and personal networks, and we conducted over one hundred interviews, mostly with coloured and a few Xhosa mothers who used the public health care system in Cape Town's southern suburbs and on the Cape Flats, in the periods from September 2016 to June 2017 and from January to May 2018. Of these women, fifty-two were recent mothers or, like Aisha, pregnant, and thus the target group for MomConnect.[4] Of the women we talked to, only two had heard of MomConnect. One had attempted to register with MomConnect and failed, and one was enrolled in the MomConnect programme. She enjoyed receiving the messages and felt they were inspiring. However, she then turned to more pressing matters: difficult kin relations, cramped living situations, lack of employment and fear of personal violence.

When we insisted on meeting and learning about health concerns and media use from pregnant women and recent mothers outside of the clinic, in NGOs in their neighbourhoods, or through friends or kin, it was an effort to place everyday forms of knowledge about health and its mediation at the centre of the study. Like Aisha, many of the first-time mothers we interviewed, and a few of the others, told stories of not knowing that they were pregnant until they were four to seven months along. Others had known but out of shame had not felt able to tell their families. Still others had known but not gone to the clinic to avoid the moral stigma of being seen by other community members at the local Midwife Obstetric Unit (MOU). These forms of ambiguous knowledge about pregnancy, and the women's navigation of the social and moral landscapes of what Ferreira calls 'un-knowing', clash with the biomedical understandings of pregnancy as a linear timeline and with the health system's focus on knowledge, education and disclosure as always positive and desirable (Ferreira, 2016; see also Houmøller, 2015).

While Aisha's phone played an important role in her pregnancy, her engagement with the medical system had not led her to MomConnect. Her story here is intended to highlight that knowledge about pregnancy, birth and motherhood is not only a biomedical project of maternal and child health. It is socio-cultural, embodied and embedded in everyday life. It is therefore relevant to examine how MomConnect was spun into webs of everyday knowledge of health and motherhood in the clinics on the Cape Flats.

Site Two: The Clinic and Health Information

At the Midwife Obstetric Unit, Susan continues her presentation. She asks how many of the women are registered and have a blue sticker on their folder that says 'I am connected', together with the MomConnect logo. A few raise their hands and Susan nods. She continues to explain that the service is free, it does not cost airtime or data, but mothers will receive text messages twice a week according to their stage of pregnancy. The women listen to the talk, chat on WhatsApp on their phones or stare blankly into space. All the while, nurse-midwives call the women in for their check-ups, by their last names. 'MomConnect is walking the path with you through the nine months', says Susan. 'And even after baby is born it will send you all the good information that you need to keep baby healthy and happy. Even if there is a bleeding or if baby gets sick, then you get advice there.' She explains how to register and encourages the women to take out their phones and register now, if they have not done so already: 'Dial *134*550*2# then you must fill in the questions, your own informations. Your ID number and that. You must do it yourself. Then you fill in the clinic code'. She points to a handwritten cardboard sign mounted with tape on a MomConnect poster in Xhosa. 'Show some interest in your baby and register', she implores.

When she is done with the presentation, Susan disappears into a tiny office. It is not much bigger than a broom closet and she sits down heavily in a chair next to the cabinet. She says she is tired, her feet ache. She has diabetes, and she knows that this is one of the symptoms. The aches and pains of routine, of giving the same talk every day, counselling women with the same kinds of problems every day – HIV, drug and alcohol use during the pregnancy, depression, violence in the home, unwanted pregnancies – seep through her silence as she organises the blue stickers for the patient files.[5] She complains that there are not enough staff allocated, so although all are present, and there are even a few students working, they are still constantly one nurse short in the antenatal clinic and one in the labour ward.

'It is a good programme', she tells me about MomConnect, 'it gives mommy all the good advice that mommy needs'. There is information and advice for the nine months of the pregnancy and then after the birth there are messages about how to care for the baby. If there is a miscarriage or a stillbirth, 'they counsel you through the trauma', she adds. 'Especially if it's mommy's first baby, it is very good.'

She takes out a battered feature phone and shows me some of the messages. She and her colleagues signed up to MomConnect so that they know what they are talking about and promoting. 'Most of the mommies are very good', Susan nods, now rubbing her leg as if to squeeze out the discomfort. 'But then there are the ignorant ones that don't care. They don't care about good information on their phone, they will rather just play a game on the phone. They will say "Ag man, another thing to fill up the phone".'

At the antenatal clinic, MomConnect was an educational programme, and 'information' from it was a form of knowledge that good pregnant women would accept, and ignorant and careless pregnant women reject for the sake of their own pleasure, playing games on the phone instead.

Receiving information about health transformed pregnant women into 'good mommies'. This idea of the transformative power of information plays into the social and moral landscapes of pregnancy and motherhood on the Cape Flats, invoking an entrenched alliance between women as respectable mothers and the state.

Elaine Salo in her ethnography of personhood and changing gender relations among women in Manenberg focuses on the local term for respectability, *ordenlikheid* (Salo, 2003; see also Jensen, 2008; Ross, 2010, 2015). She describes how the implementation of apartheid labour, housing and welfare policies located adult coloured women in a unique relation to the state, and how these structures unfolded after apartheid. The labour market favoured women, only families – with wives and children – were eligible for housing schemes, and women were recipients of child grants which were often the only stable income for the household, 'emphasizing adult women's importance in their roles as mothers' (Salo, 2003, p. 349). This role was extended beyond the household as practices of 'mothering' the community, which meant mediating local residents' relationship with the state to access services or get help with problems.

Young women, in contrast to mothers, were expected to conform to what Salo terms 'the local ideology of domesticity', where motherhood and domestic responsibilities were considered feminine ideals and girls are expected to 'confine themselves to the domestic arena' and 'restrict their mobility to within the local community' (Salo, 2003, p. 350). Falling pregnant before twenty-one years of age, and outside of marriage or a stable partnership, is the ultimate sign of a young woman's failure to be a good daughter and stay in the home. Young women, like Aisha above, seeking adventure, romance and pleasure beyond the home and the neighbourhood are seen as careless, and less deserving of help and care. Aisha's mother confirmed her own respectable motherhood, as she resignedly scolded her daughter: 'You don't listen to your mother. Then you must take the consequences!'

Though Salo suggests that the moral power of respectable mothers in the townships was waning in the late 1990s as welfare and housing policies changed (Salo, 2003, p. 354), both Aisha's story and Susan's presentation of MomConnect, along with so many of the other stories we heard about pregnancy and birth in Cape Town, invoked ideals of *ordenlikheid* and respectable motherhood. Women were seen as being responsible for ensuring the respectability and health of their families, despite obvious structural constraints. As Jensen notes, ideals of respectable motherhood are not mechanical scripts for social action, but rather a gendered cultural repertoire from which women and their families draw (Jensen, 2008, p. 147). Both Aisha's story and Susan's presentation show how these subject positions are inhabited in everyday life.

Moral rules related to the social category 'mother' shape experiences of maternal health in Cape Town in somewhat more forceful ways than individual encounters at the clinic. For Aisha, and other women we interviewed, motherhood presented a moral paradox: to become a valuable social person as a woman one must be a mother, but it is morally problematic and socially upsetting to be pregnant. When Susan promoted the programme to the expecting mothers, MomConnect became meaningful in the clinic by being placed within this paradox of pregnancies, as a tool to transform women from being problematic – and careless – pregnant women into good and caring mothers by way of 'information'.

Site Three: The Messages and a Theory of Change

Delving further into MomConnect as a health information programme, I will here consider how the content of MomConnect was understood as having the potential to change how subscribers act in relation to maternal and child health. The premise of MomConnect is that almost every citizen is within reach via mobile phone, and that delivery of information changes problematic 'behaviours' of individuals, leading to better health outcomes for mothers and children (Barron et al., 2016). That is, if the messages from MomConnect are read by the subscribers, they will adopt healthier practices. This theory of how to bring about change was also known as Social and Behaviour Change Communication Theory among the health professionals working with the programme at the National Department of Health level. It positioned the sender (the NDoH) and the receivers (pregnant women and new mothers in the public health system) in a relation in which the former possessed the knowledge needed for pregnancy and motherhood and the latter lacked this knowledge. If receivers were given knowledge, their attitudes and then their practices would change, apparently regardless of whatever else might be at stake in their lives. This resonates with James Scott's remarks on how large-scale modernist development projects make plans for an abstract citizen, a kind of standardised subject with no history, no values and no ideas – blank slates onto which the state can inscribe visions of a better future in its own image (Scott, 1998, pp. 345, 349). Asking about what kinds of knowledge are transmitted in the programme also means asking about what kinds of subject positions this knowledge assumes.[6]

The first message available in MomConnect (NDoH, 2015b) is in week five: 'Congrats on your pregnancy! Your baby is just the size of a small seed but you can help your baby grow. Eat vegetables and fruit, don't smoke or drink alcohol'. The message initiates a narrative about a welcome and wanted pregnancy, taking for granted the relations of the mother-child dyad as already existing and positive. It also personifies the embryo in the woman's womb as a baby, and prescribes specific courses of actions for 'mother' and 'baby'. The imagery of an already formed human, here being the size of a grain, a human being in need of the mother's help to grow into a full social person, runs through the messages of the MomConnect programme. The kinds of ambivalence and choices that women like Aisha face in their pregnancy have little space in MomConnect. Rather, these messages seem to reflect political choices made in the NDoH promoting a pronatalist stance and conforming to national ideals of respectable South African motherhood in a biomedical sense.

Altogether, 162 messages are sent by MomConnect during pregnancy, the first year after birth, and in cases of miscarriage, stillbirth or the loss of a baby. Fifty-three (one-third) of the messages encourage the reader to go to the clinic, either for regular appointments or if mother or child are showing signs of illness. Descriptions of the size and abilities of the unborn foetus or born child are the second most prominent theme in the messages, followed by encouragement and information about breastfeeding. Other recurring themes are healthy eating, keeping oneself and the baby clean by washing hands, taking the medicine prescribed by the clinic, avoiding traditional and alternative medicines, and avoiding alcohol, smoking and illegal drugs. Saving money for transport to the hospital and shopping to prepare for the birth of the child are also mentioned in the messages. Throughout the messages, the foetus is articulated as a baby with human features in need of the help, care and safekeeping of the mother: 'Your baby is growing fingers! If you feel unwell, have a fever, bleeding or vomiting, go to the clinic to make sure you and your baby are safe' (week 10 of pregnancy). Many of the messages, like this one, seem to have several concerns in mind: to congratulate the mother on 'growing' her 'baby' in a friendly way, and at the same time managing the perceived risk involved with pregnancy by encouragements to go to the clinic.

After birth, messages focus on breastfeeding and feeding, as well as on activities that help the child to develop: 'Your baby loves the sound of your voice. She may stop moving when you speak. Talk and sing to her every day. Make eye contact and smile. She will smile back!' (week 11 after birth). The conclusion of the messages at week 51 after birth instigates a new period of life: 'You have done a great job! Keep being a great mother to your sweet child. If you miss a period, you may be pregnant again. Go to the clinic for pregnancy care'. The baby has now become a child, and the mother has proved herself a capable mother. But motherhood is not without risks, another pregnancy may occur, and again the clinic is where to get help.

The messages themselves contain few actual medical facts about pregnancy and risk, but the focus remains on the mother-child dyad and the mother as responsible for the well-being of both, with the possibility of getting help at the clinic. The recipient is placed within the narrative as responsible for the foetus's and the child's growth and well-being and as manager of environmental risks from illnesses to negative personal relationships.

O'Rourke (2016) describes a similar notion of individualised responsibility as a central – albeit unarticulated – objective in a moms and babies educational programme at a Christian NGO in Cape Town. She describes how participants internalise notions of 'ideal motherhood' so that 'the influence of political economy and local context become less visible than the individual responsibility' (O'Rourke, 2016, p. 27). She draws a parallel between this internalisation of moral ideals of motherhood and Steven Robins' notion of 'responsibilised citizenship' in relation to HIV/AIDS (2006), and shows that 'responsibilization works to disguise the political- economic context that shapes health by making the maternal body the source of both harm and well-being' (O'Rourke, 2016, p. 42). For MomConnect, the 'responsibilised citizenship' of maternal health is intensely present as well. The texting state in MomConnect speaks directly to 'mothers' in the spaces of their everyday lives where they use their mobile phones, not through officials at the Home Affairs office or the clinic or through court orders and case numbers.

The theory of change that underpins MomConnect puts the National Department of Health in direct 'conversation' with expecting and new mothers all over the country. The 140 characters of the text messages tell subscribers stories about how to bring new life into the world, not merely nudging, but hailing pregnant women to act and feel in particular ways towards their pregnancy and motherhood. Whether it is the NDoH partnership with USAID or other partners in MomConnect, or attempts at being culturally appropriate, the pronatalist messages focusing on women as empowered and responsible citizens make little space for considerations of abortion, doubts and ambivalence in relation to pregnancy, or for structural constraints and the social context of being pregnant and having a child. The 'information' transmitted is as much about placing recipients in a particular relation with the state, within a narrative of respectable and responsible South African motherhood.

Two related issues further troubled the idea of MomConnect as media technology delivering depoliticised 'information' to mothers: connection and voice. The fourth site that I examine here – encounters between MomConnect and the antenatal clinics – has two parts: the first highlights the role of health workers in making the connection between the technological infrastructure of MomConnect and its users; the second shows how those same people intermingled with the technology and shaped how subscribers understood the text messages.

Site Four A: A Connection and Institutional Metis

Some MOUs in the Western Cape had not taken up MomConnect, despite public health facilitators presenting and introducing the service to managing and working nurse-midwives at the clinic. As Susan, the community health nurse, told us at the beginning of the chapter, pregnant women must sign up to MomConnect using the specific clinic code of the place where they receive antenatal care. There is a bit more to it: women can sign themselves up without the code, and they will then receive a limited number of messages encouraging them to go to the clinic to register fully. The information registered in the national patient database for MomConnect must be accurate, and so women must be diagnosed as pregnant in a public health facility, and register their gestational age accordingly, to receive the stage-based push messages. For that reason, the clinic code is needed for full registration, and because the clinic code is, in principle, confidential, the registration needs to be overseen by a health professional. For this to happen, nurses must spend time registering their patients. This may be a challenge in an overburdened health system where nurse-midwives are constantly pressed for time, torn between seeing as many patients as possible and correctly monitoring and diagnosing potentially fatal conditions in their patients.

Registration of users in the MomConnect database could be experienced as a burden for nurses at the understaffed MOUs, and as beyond the scope of their professional duties. One woman working as a counsellor at an MOU commented: 'Ag, every week it is some new project. They come in with a new study or bring new people from charities, and in the end, how does it help?' She went on to say that she understood why managers were reluctant to take on new projects that required already overworked staff to run faster (see also Wolff-Pigott, 2015; Wolf-Piggot and Rivett, 2016, p. 7).[7] Thinking with Scott's terminology, the ideals of the state's scientific knowledge and its projects of sending health information to patients and registering their information in a national database in some ways clashed with the practical knowledge of running an under-resourced maternity clinic in the Western Cape Province. In this way, MomConnect became part of a gendered political struggle for institutional hegemony and medical legitimacy between often male experts and doctors and often female nurses and midwives (Scott, 1998, p. 311; see Deacon, 1998 and Digby, 2006 for a history of maternal and health care in the Western Cape).

At the MOU where Susan worked, they had solved the problem by making the Community Health Workers responsible for enrolling patients in MomConnect while they were waiting to see a nurse in the antenatal ward. Community Health Workers (CHWs) are lay health workers employed by NGOs, subsidised by the government, usually in home-based care programmes for HIV/AIDS and tuberculosis patients and in health support and counselling programmes. Susan and her colleagues' main task at the MOU was to counsel and support pregnant women in relation to HIV/AIDS, as HIV tests are a routine component of antenatal care. They spoke individually with each woman who registered her pregnancy at the clinic, either in the tiny broom-closet-like office next to the waiting room or down the hall in the actual cleaning supply room, where Susan had placed two folding chairs. CHWs are, not surprisingly, placed lowest within clinic hierarchies and have only recently been placed on the National Health Insurance payroll.

That MomConnect fell under the purview of CHWs in their work to inform and counsel might be a pragmatic solution in a situation where the staff struggle to provide essential services at antenatal clinics. MomConnect depends on the staff at the MOUs to collaborate with the technological infrastructure of the programme by 'connecting' patients' phones with the programme, and here it seems that the practical knowledge – metis in James Scott's parlance – to run a maternity clinic was incompatible with the envisioned workflow of MomConnect. Yet that same flexibility meant that at some clinics the programme was accommodated in inventive ways. At the clinic where Susan worked, it was done by writing the 'confidential' clinic code on the wall in the waiting room and by letting CHWs promote the programme during otherwise unused waiting time (Marais, 2017). Texting like a state entails imaginaries of centralised dissemination of scientific knowledge and organisational structures, but also metis and non-conforming practice as a condition for the formal order (Scott, 1998, p. 352).

Site Four B: The Voice of Technology and 'Local Knowledge'

The role of clinic staff in MomConnect was even more difficult to manage when it came to how subscribers read and made sense of the messages. The 'voice' of MomConnect messages was a mysterious thing, said one of the public health doctors who had worked on developing the programme. The voice was essential for effecting behavioural changes in the women, he suggested, and differentiated between the 'tone' of messages – the wording and intentions put into the messages by the producers – and the voice of the messages heard by the receivers.

The developers had developed the tone of the messages by drawing on what they called 'local knowledge'. With the vantage point of the existing, smaller mHealth project MAMA, which was based on a programme developed by Johnson and Johnson, they had tried to develop a set of messages that would be friendly and encouraging across cultures and languages in South Africa. To deliver messages with the right tone, they were developed in collaboration with midwives, doctors, communication specialists and a range of other professionals. MomConnect is available in South Africa's eleven official languages, translated from the original set of English messages. This use of local knowledge was considered by the researchers working within the MomConnect programme to be one of the strengths of MomConnect; it was designed with 'local experts to make it compatible with the local South African context' (Seebregts et al., 2016, p. 131).

The tone of the text itself seemed not to be all that mattered to the receivers, as the researchers working with MomConnect had discovered. When the subscribers read the messages, would they hear a voice that was friendly and caring, or a shrill, patronising one? Apparently, users read the messages in the voice of the person who had helped them sign up for the programme. People like Susan were not only connecting patients to the infrastructure of the programme in material and bureaucratic terms, but their voices became part of the technology itself. The relationship between patients and caregivers, a relationship placed outside the control of the carefully crafted MomConnect system, in the signing up processes became entangled with the system itself.

Frontline clinic staff are needed to connect MomConnect with the mothers it seeks to connect with. But they also became uncontrollable elements as the voice of the MomConnect technology; despite the same standardised messages being sent to all subscribers, individual encounters at the clinic shaped how they were understood. 'We can do everything and design everything, except for the thing that matters!' remarked one of the MomConnect developers. Despite the best preparations, drawing on 'local knowledge' and designing messages for the cultural diversity of South Africa, the texting state shares with James Scott's modern states 'the utopian, immanent, and continually frustrated goal ... to reduce the chaotic, disorderly, constantly changing social reality beneath it to something more closely resembling the administrative grid of its observations' (Scott, 1998, p. 82).

Site Five: Policy, Research and Data

In the course of seeking out knowledge about mHealth in South Africa, I was invited to speak at a workshop for researchers, practitioners and policy-makers from across Africa on technology for maternal, newborn and child health as part of a conference on mobile technologies and health in low resource settings. More than fifty presentations in total articulated how digital technologies, and mHealth in particular, might change health care for the better. Fragments of conversations from the event illuminate how mobile health was made meaningful among policy-makers, members of international think tanks, clinical and IT researchers and developers as potentially changing health systems, and the role of knowledge in this site.

The conference presentations gave two overall points of view. The first stance towards the potential of mHealth was extremely optimistic. The title of one presentation was simply 'Technology: The Promise', while another was: 'M-Health: Only the Imagination Sets the Limit'. Another presentation made these high expectations more explicit: 'Digital technology will reduce health spending by 25%' and 'improve accessibility and equity'. Rather than developing large and costly physical infrastructures of health care, places like Africa would 'go straight to digital'. 'Africa is increasingly a networked society, we have connected places, people and devices', one presentation stated, 'it is going to be the future of health care'.

The other approach to digital technologies was more tempered. 'Everybody is talking about it, nobody knows what it does', one presenter said as the introduction to his presentation, pointing to the mushrooming number of projects and the lack of documentation of their effects. Another presentation criticised the theories of change used in mHealth interventions, like the Behaviour Information Change Model: 'We have a theory that access to information will produce care. We have no evidence to back that up'. A third presentation lamented how techno-optimism shaped policy and funding structures to the detriment of funding projects focusing on delivering basic health care: 'Technology is sexy, but not so sexy that it solves all our problems. It is sexy and fun to write your name on it [as a politician] but it is not the core of services'. In particular, clinicians who had worked on research projects over decades to develop mobile, digital solutions for front-line health workers presented nuanced views on the promise of their projects. For instance: 'Tools are tools, none of these tools will save patients on their own'. While policy literature on mHealth in Africa may be extremely optimistic about the potential for improving health outcomes (Haas, 2016), the conference and the subsequent special issue (Laflamme, 2017) presented more moderated expectations.

MomConnect was also one of the cases presented at the conference, and the success of the programme was noted by the participants. The NDoH and its partners had successfully scaled up mHealth based on global public-private partnerships in a programme that the end users loved. One survey from 2015 examined the users' experiences with MomConnect via an SMS-based survey sent to those registered with the programme. Ninety-seven per cent of respondents liked the programme (Skinner et al., 2018). The same research showed that respondents answered that they had followed advice in the messages to go to the clinic, suggesting success in 'behavioural change'. One NDoH affiliate noted that although the women were enthusiastic about the programme, as the market research showed, it appears that despite the informational qualities of the text messages, there was no measurable change in the 'knowledge' that the users had about pregnancy and childbirth before and after they had completed the programme (see also Lau et al., 2014). As noted above, the messages from MomConnect are arguably not about medical information as such, but about confirming the relationship between women-as-mothers and the state, supporting the subject position of respectable motherhood.

What was also discussed as an important feature of MomConnect at the conference was the amount of data MomConnect produced about its user and about itself. For the Community Health Worker Susan, MomConnect was primarily a health information programme. For developers and public health planners, it was a unique digital patient database on a national level, and an infrastructure that could inexpensively produce large quantities of data about users as well as about the programme itself (Seebregts et al., 2016).

Although this 'data' remained far removed from her everyday work, Susan explained to me that a very important aspect of getting pregnant women connected to MomConnect was to write their names on a list and give them to the sister in charge. 'We need it for the stats', she said – the 'statistics' that the MOU needed to report to the Department of Health each month. These stats would be used to measure the level and quality of care at the clinic, and aggregated into regional and national overviews. Possibly, future funding and support would be contingent on these stats. From the way Susan and her colleagues spoke about them, stats were important but for uncertain reasons. Knowledge in the form of 'data' and 'stats' is becoming increasingly important in how work is organised in places like the MOU, without having an immediate value for health care workers. Rather, it increases the experience of unfair workloads, control and uncertainty about the future. Meanwhile, the stats and data make these spaces more legible and thereby open them up for far more nuanced interventions and control.

The team behind MomConnect did indeed realise the difficult working situations of those working with maternal and child health, and launched NurseConnect, another text-based programme hoping 'to improve medical knowledge and professional skills development, encourage personal growth and self-improvement, and provide inspiration and recognition for work well done'.[8] Although it is beyond the scope of this chapter to discuss it in detail, the extension of the bio-politics of respectable motherhood through personal growth and self-improvement from patients in MomConnect to health care workers in NurseConnect is remarkable. Rather than addressing structural problems in the health care system, nurses are here positioned as in need of the benign care and 'self-improvement' that the state offers through text messages.

Scientific knowledge in the form of data produced to be read and used by the NDoH to improve services places power and authority to define good care as well as methods of improving care at the centre of the health system. More data means more possibilities of 'seeing' and intervening with improvements. Texting like a state concentrates power at the centre of national health care and displaces or devalues other ways of knowing about care and health as well as more decentralised forms of learning and sharing (cf. Scott, 1998, p. 93). At the conference about mobile health technologies, some presentations emphasised data and big data as the future of health governance. 'The most powerful tool is going to be the data, not the technology itself', remarked one policy-maker, while a tech developer claimed that a central aim of interventions should be 'translating doctor-patient relations into big data relations'.

Concluding Remarks

'That is it', Susan sighs and winks at me, 'this is what we do. And tomorrow we do it all again'. It is the end of her shift at the Midwife Obstetric Unit on the outskirts of Cape Town. She has counselled and registered eight women today, carefully placing the blue MomConnect stickers on their patient files. She has written their names on a small piece of paper and handed it to the sister in charge. In her small office she gathers her things in a shopping net and straightens her white uniform before she walks through the waiting room, still full of waiting mothers, across the parking lot and out into the township street.

In the South African context, the idea that detailed centralised knowledge and control of the population is inherently positive is of course nothing new. More than ten years ago, Keith Breckenridge described efforts by the South African state to develop a fully digital national identification system using biometrics (fingerprints) (Breckenridge, 2005, 2014). Similar to the public health planners behind MomConnect, administrators implementing new digital biometrics in late-1990s South Africa believed that with more detailed and centralised digital data collection they would 'radically improve the state's grasp of the identity, and history, of its elusive citizens' (Breckenridge, 2005, p. 271). Despite using similar technologies and ideas about legibility and control to those used previously by colonial and apartheid governments, in 'contemporary South Africa the state's interest in digital biometrics is very largely driven by a desire to repair a broken bureaucracy, to deliver grants and other benefits to the poorest and most vulnerable of its citizens' (Breckenridge, 2005, p. 270). Breckenridge notes that there is a certain irony to this, as previously coercive technologies were being applied to improve the distribution of benefits 'to those they were originally designed to subjugate' (ibid.). The biometric state, in its digital form of smart cards, digital fingerprint readers, computers and databases that can seamlessly merge data streams, produces state fantasies of 'information panopticons' that eliminate possibilities to subvert the disciplinary intent of the system (ibid., p. 271). Breckenridge's analysis is a reminder of how on one hand technology has no inherent meaning but is given meaning by the context of use, and on the other how aspirations of states are continuous despite radical political changes.

In this chapter I have described how the use of mobile technology for maternal and child health was associated in different ways with notions of change: changing life courses, changing morally problematic women, changing behaviours, changing routines of care at the clinic, changing technologies, changing governance. These relations between digital technologies and change each constituted particular forms of knowledge. The different ways of conceiving of knowledge and what kinds of knowledge are legitimate and relevant in pregnancies, birth and child rearing point to how actors engage mHealth with widely different concerns, and therefore different hopes of change. Texting like a state means attempting to entrench singular, standardised state-sanctioned knowledge-generating techniques into all of these settings. It is perhaps not surprising, then, that when MomConnect sends text messages to women across the country, what seems to be at stake is not medical information that exists in a political vacuum, but rather what Hansen and Stepputat would call languages of stateness (2001, p. 7), pressing questions of moral subject positions and citizenship in a changing South Africa.

Acknowledgements

I would like to thank the mothers, nurses, midwives and doulas who shared their stories and taught me about motherhood and birth in Cape Town, in particular the women of the Zoe Project who became family to me. Thanks to MediAfrica colleagues, Fiona Ross, Michelle Pentecost, Nicole Daniels and Tessa Moll for their ideas and comments on previous drafts of this chapter and to Shari Thanjan for coming along on unlikely adventures. Thanks to the Norwegian Research Council for financial support for fieldwork in South Africa and for supporting the overall project New Media Practices in a Changing Africa (grant no. FriPro 240714).

Nanna Schneidermann was previously a postdoctoral researcher in the MediAfrica project in the Section for Development Studies at Oslo Metropolitan University and at the University of Cape Town Department of Anthropology. She is currently Assistant Professor in Anthropology at Aarhus University.

Notes

1. Racial categories are difficult and tension fraught in the context of South Africa. I try here to use the categories used by my interlocutors themselves when self-identifying and identifying others. Black here refers to 'non-white' people, under apartheid classified as African and Coloured.
2. An earlier version of this chapter was published as a blog post on somatosphere.net as part of the First 1000 Days series. Parts of Aisha's story also appear

in a forthcoming article entitled 'Romance and Respectability: The Intimate Infopolitics of Township Sociality in Cape Town'.

3. Johnson and Johnson is an American multinational medical conglomerate operating more than 250 companies in the fields of consumer health, medical devices and pharmaceuticals.
4. We also advertised for participants who were MomConnect users on Facebook groups for Capetonian mothers and with flyers on the noticeboards in supermarkets on the Cape Flats, but these strategies yielded no results.
5. See Meintjes et al. (2015) for a case study of the kinds of problems facing women attending perinatal mental health counselling at an MOU on the Cape Flats.
6. MomConnect functions primarily as a broadcast from a national, centralised database in the Department of Health directly to subscribers' phones. But it also has a feedback option through which subscribers, via text messages, can report problems or abuse and ask questions about their own health and that of their offspring. In project reports based on the self-generated data of MomConnect, this feature has been used to translate messages, call for materials for local clinics and a range of other uses (Barron et al., 2016, 2018). Here I focus on the text messages sent to subscribers.
7. The NGO workers whom I interviewed, working to support mothers, were extremely positive about MomConnect but frustrated by not having the possibility to help pregnant women to sign up for the full programme.
8. See https://www.praekelt.org/nurseconnect/ (accessed 23 June 2019).

References

Aranda-Jan, C.B., N. Mohutsiwa-Dibe and S. Loukanova. 2014. 'Systematic Review on What Works, What Does Not Work and Why of Implementation of Mobile Health (mHealth) Projects in Africa', *BMC Public Health* 14(188): 1–15.

Barron, P., J. Peter, A.E. LeFevre et al. 2018. 'Mobile Health Messaging Service and Helpdesk for South African Mothers (MomConnect): History, Successes and Challenges', *BMJ Global Health* 3(suppl. 2): e000559.

Barron, P., Y. Pillay, A. Fernandes, J. Sebidi and R. Allen. 2016. 'The MomConnect mHealth Initiative in South Africa: Early Impact on the Supply Side of MCH Services', *Journal of Public Health Policy* 37(2): 201–12.

Bateman, C. 2014. 'Using Basic Technology and Corporate Social Responsibility to Save Lives', *South African Medical Journal* 104(12): 839–40.

Benjamin, P. 2014. 'MomConnect: The First National Public mHealth Service in South Africa'. GSMA. https://www.gsma.com/mobilefordevelopment/programme/mhealth/momconnect-the-first-national-public-mhealth-service-in-south-africa/ (accessed 20 June 2018).

Bloomfield, G.S., R. Vedanthan, L. Vasudevan, A. Kithei, M. Were and E.J. Velazquez. 2014. 'Mobile Health for Non-communicable Diseases in

Sub-Saharan Africa: A Systematic Review of the Literature and Strategic Framework for Research', *Globalization and Health* 10(49): 1–9.

Breckenridge, K. 2005. 'The Biometric State: The Promise and Peril of Digital Government in the New South Africa', *Journal of Southern African Studies* 31(2): 267–82.

———. 2014. *Biometric State: The Global Politics of Identification and Surveillance in South Africa, 1850 to the Present.* Cambridge: Cambridge University Press.

Brown, B. 1987. 'Facing the "Black Peril": The Politics of Population Control in South Africa', *Journal of Southern African Studies* 13(3): 256–73.

Chadwick, R.J., and D. Foster. 2013. 'Technologies of Gender and Childbirth Choices: Home Birth, Elective Caesarean and White Femininities in South Africa', *Feminism & Psychology* 23(3): 317–38.

Coleman, J. 2013. 'Monitoring MAMA: Gauging the Impact of MAMA South Africa', *Journal of Mobile Technology in Medicine* 2(4S): 9.

Deacon, H. 1998. 'Midwives and Medical Men in the Cape Colony before 1860', *The Journal of African History* 39(2): 271–92.

Digby, A. 2006. *Diversity and Division in Medicine: Health Care in South Africa from the 1800s*, vol. 5. Oxford: Peter Lang.

Ferreira, N. 2016. 'Enduring "Lateness": Biomedicalisation and the Unfolding of Reproductive Life, Sociality, and Antenatal Care', Dissertation for Master of Social Science, Anthropology, School of African and Gender studies, Anthropology and Linguistics, University of Cape Town.

Fölster, S. 2017. 'Viral mHealth', *Global Health Action* 10(suppl. 3): 1336006, 18–21.

Forrest, J.I., M. Wiens, S. Kanters, S. Nsanzimana, R.T. Lester and E.J. Mills. 2015. 'Mobile Health Applications for HIV Prevention and Care in Africa', *Current Opinion in HIV and AIDS* 10(6): 464–71.

Haas, S. 2016. *mHealth Compendium, Special Edition 2016: Reaching Scale.* Arlington, VA: African Strategies for Health, Management Sciences for Health.

Hansen, T.B., and F. Stepputat. 2001. 'Introduction: States of Imagination', in T.B. Hansen and F. Stepputat (eds), *States of Imagination: Ethnographic Explorations of the Postcolonial State.* Durham, NC: Duke University Press, pp. 1–40.

Houmøller, K. 2015. 'Ambiguous Intimacy: Aids Medicine and the Everyday in Khayelitsha, South Africa', Unpublished PhD dissertation, Institute for Culture and Society, Aarhus University.

Innovation Working Group [IWG]. N.d. *MOMCONNECT: Launching a National Digital Health Program in South Africa.* United Nations Foundation and the Human Reproduction Programme.

Jensen, S. 2008. *Gangs, Politics and Dignity in Cape Town.* Oxford: James Currey.

Laflamme, L. 2017. 'Image-Based mHealth for Remote Diagnostic Assistance a Means to Promote Equity in Quality Care', *Global Health Action* 10(suppl. 3) (mHealth for Improved Access and Equity in Health Care): 1344004, 3–5.

Lau, Y.K., T. Cassidy, D. Hacking, K. Brittain, H.J. Haricharan and M. Heap. 2014. 'Antenatal Health Promotion via Short Message Service at a Midwife

Obstetrics Unit in South Africa: A Mixed Methods Study', *BMC Pregnancy and Childbirth* 14(1): 1–8.

Lewis, D., and E. Salo. 1993. 'Birth Control Contraception and Women's Rights in SA: A Cape Town Case Study', *Agenda* 9(17): 59–68.

Lundin, J., and G. Dumont. 2017. 'Medical Mobile Technologies: What Is Needed for a Sustainable and Scalable Implementation on a Global Scale?' *Global Health Action* 10(suppl. 3): 1344046, 14–17.

Marais, K. 2017. 'Mothers Matter: A Critical Exploration of Motherhood and Development through a Video Card Intervention in a Local Clinic', Dissertation for Master of Social Science, Anthropology, School of African and Gender studies, Anthropology and Linguistics, University of Cape Town.

Meintjes, I., S. Field, T. Van Heyningen and S. Honikman. 2015. 'Creating Capabilities through Maternal Mental Health Interventions: A Case Study at Hanover Park, Cape Town', *Journal of International Development* 27(2): 234–50.

National Department of Health (NDoH). 2015a. *MomConnect One Year of Operation: A Case Study*. Report by Health Enabled, Text and Photos by Miriam Mannak.

———. 2015b. *MomConnect Messages for Trainees* (unpublished).

O'Rourke, S.L. 2016. '"We Must Be Responsible for Our Children": The Makings of Motherhood in Ocean View', Dissertation for Master of Social Science, Anthropology, School of African and Gender studies, Anthropology and Linguistics, University of Cape Town.

Robins, S. 2006. 'From "Rights" to "Ritual": AIDS Activism in South Africa', *American Anthropologist* 108(2): 312–23.

Ross, F.C. 2010. *Raw Life, New Hope: Decency, Housing and Everyday Life in a Post-Apartheid Community*. Cape Town: UCT Press.

———. 2015. 'Raw Life and Respectability: Poverty and Everyday Life in a Post-Apartheid Community', *Current Anthropology* 56: 97–107.

Salo, E. 2003. 'Negotiating Gender and Personhood in the New South Africa: Adolescent Women and Gangsters in Manenberg Township on the Cape Flats', *European Journal of Cultural Studies* 6(3): 345–65.

Scott, J.C. 1998. *Seeing Like a State: How Certain Schemes to Improve the Human Condition Have Failed*. Yale University Press.

Seebregts, C., P. Barron, G. Tanna, P. Benjamin and T. Fogwill. 2016. 'MomConnect: An Exemplar Implementation of the Health Normative Standards Framework in South Africa', *South African Health Review* 2016(1): 125–36.

Seebregts, C., P. Dane, A.N. Parsons et al. 2018. 'Designing for Scale: Optimising the Health Information System Architecture for Mobile Maternal Health Messaging in South Africa (MomConnect)', *BMJ Global Health* 3(suppl. 2): e000563, 1–7.

Silal, S.P., L. Penn-Kekana, B. Harris, S. Birch and D. McIntyre. 2012. 'Exploring Inequalities in Access to and Use of Maternal Health Services in South Africa', *BMC Health Services Research* 12(120): 1–12.

Skinner, D., P. Delobelle, M. Pappin, D. Pieterse, T.M. Esterhuizen, P. Barron and L. Dudley. 2018. 'User Assessments and the Use of Information from MomConnect, a Mobile Phone Text-Based Information Service, by Pregnant Women and New Mothers in South Africa', *BMJ Global Health* 3(suppl. 2): e000561, 1–6.

Waldman, L., and M. Stevens. 2015. *Sexual and Reproductive Health Rights and Information and Communications Technologies: A Policy Review and Case Study from South Africa.* Institute of Development Studies Evidence Report 113. Cape Town: IDS.

Watkins, J.O.T.A., J. Goudge, F.X. Gómez-Olivé and F. Griffiths. 2018. 'Mobile Phone Use among Patients and Health Workers to Enhance Primary Healthcare: A Qualitative Study in Rural South Africa', *Social Science & Medicine* 198: 139–47.

Wolff-Piggott, B. 2015. 'Towards an Affordance Perspective on mHealth Usage: A Clinic-Level View', *Proceedings of SIG GlobDev Eighth Annual Workshop, Münster, Germany*, vol. 26.

Wolff-Piggott, B., and U. Rivett. 2016. 'An Activity Theory Approach to Affordance Actualisation in mHealth: The Case of MomConnect', Paper presented at the 24th European Conference on Information Systems, ECIS 2016, Istanbul, Turkey, 12–15 June.

Zerucelli Rucell, J. 2017. 'Obstetric Violence and Colonial Conditioning in South Africa's Reproductive Health System', Unpublished PhD thesis, University of Leeds.

CHAPTER 5

New Ways of Making Ends Meet?

On Batswana Women, Their Uses of the Mobile Phone and Connections through Education

Ardis Storm-Mathisen

> 'Yes!' Malebogo looks up at me, waves her little, worn black mobile phone in the air and says, 'It's very, very important. I use it for everything! Every day!'

It is November 2017 and I am with Malebogo, a single mother in her forties with four children, in a household to which she often came to do piece jobs – and to charge her phone. Malebogo had just ended an incoming call and tucked her simple mobile phone back into her pocket, when I asked her, 'Do you feel the mobile phone has helped you make ends meet in new ways?' Malebogo's answer was – as quoted above – highly affective and confirmative, not very specific, and conveyed surprise and frustration with me. We had known each other for two years; I should know. Nevertheless, she patiently entered into an explanation: how she used her mobile phone to keep in touch with and receive money transfers from her two eldest sons who were away at school, to coordinate various piece jobs, the babysitting for her youngest daughter and various community activities.

A few weeks later, I met with Patsimo, a woman in her thirties, in the open kitchen/living room of her condo-apartment in one of the new fashionable areas of Botswana's capital Gaborone. Patsimo had, when we first got acquainted in 2015, talked very enthusiastically about her manufacturing business, a new branch she was setting up in Gaborone, and of a software app that let her administer from her smartphone the stock, budget, employees' work hours and payments. This time, the main topic of our conversation was her 'new diamond', a year-old son. Patsimo was preparing a Chinese dinner while we talked. She was constantly consulting her smartphone and seemed very busy, so I asked, 'Is your business demanding these days?' She replied, 'No, I put that on hold when I found out I was pregnant. I am full time mother now. This is Pinterest,[1] I use it for the recipe. You know it, right?' She pointed to the screen, I shook my head and she looked at me surprised: 'It's an app, you should check it out – I use it for everything'.

The idea that the mobile phone is providing new opportunities for people in their everyday lives and that it is taking part in societal changes is a strong contemporary idiom worldwide (e.g. World Bank, 2016). Botswana is no exception. The vision that people's use of new media, and particularly the mobile phone as the most commonly used device, brings about change in the economic situation flourishes in current public discourse, policies, implementation initiatives, research agendas and – as the examples above suggest – in people's everyday ways of talking, thinking and acting (Storm-Mathisen, 2016, 2018). Yet, although the mobile phone beyond doubt can make many tasks easier and faster, and people use it and say it is important, what their use of the mobile phone entails, and the kinds of difference it in fact makes in their lives, is varied and not always obvious (e.g. Carmody, 2012; Miller et al., 2016; Slater, 2013). In this chapter I investigate how people's use of their mobile phone connects to their economic activities, concerns and outcomes. The aim is to bring insights into how mobile phone use plays into the dynamics that create different economic situations for variously positioned people in Botswana.

The discussion will focus on women. In its National Development Plans, the government in Botswana highlights women as important for development and a group for which they envision the mobile phone playing a particularly significant change-making role, enabling them to become more active in businesses and self-sustained economic activities (Ministry of Finance and Development Planning, 2009, 2016). The question is, however, through which processes mobile phone use may or may not play a role, for which women, and under what circumstances. A majority of households in Botswana today are female headed, and more women than men have the double burden of being affected by the high levels of unemployment, poverty and HIV while also taking responsibility for the care and sustenance of children and kin (Statistics Botswana, 2016; World Bank, 2015). Women are therefore often conceived as a vulnerable group. Without dismissing the challenges that women face, it is important to point out that there is high socio-economic inequality in Botswana. The variations of livelihoods among women can be as significant as they are between women and men (Peters, 1983; Statistics Botswana, 2017; Storm-Mathisen, 2018; World Bank, 2015).[2] It is in an attempt to grasp the breadth of such variations, and move beyond taken-for-granted gender stereotypes, that I focus on women.

Reaching an understanding of what mobile phone use entails and how it is involved in women's economic activities is a complex issue that requires a holistic approach. The challenge is how to make sense of an empirical reality where 'everything' is entangled, under constant change and where – as the quote from my dialogue with Malebogo suggests – words alone often fall short in grasping what mobile phone use entails and the concerns to which these uses are oriented (Storm-Mathisen, 2016). The approach here gives supremacy to practice (Helle-Valle, 2010), the processes that bring things together and constellations that make things happen in people's worlds (Latour, 2005). The term 'making ends meet' is to point to such processes.[3]

My discussion draws on experience from recent fieldwork conducted in the capital Gaborone (population approx. 200,000) and in a fast-growing semi-urban village (population approx. 8000) in Kweneng District.[4] The fieldwork was case-based (Flyvbjerg, 2006; Helle-Valle and Borchgrevink, 2018) and used participant observation – learning from 'being with' people and taking part in activities – as the core method. To learn from people in different ways, a wide variety of complementary methods were engaged: surveys,[5] formal interviews (with household members, students, business owners and employees in business and government), written and video-accounted diaries from participants (Storm-Mathisen, 2018), essays from primary and secondary school pupils on their futures (Storm-Mathisen, 2017), digital ethnography and reviews of various documents and reports.

The first section below provides a background to how the mobile phone has entered into Botswana society and the broader user patterns today in terms of gender and socio-economic situation. I then present the cases of three women – Malebogo and Patsimo who have already been introduced, and Masego – and use these to show the different mechanisms that link mobile phone usage to different life situations, focusing on how mobile phone usage connects to economic activities. Through these cases, I point to how various factors – most notably education – play into the dynamics and outcomes of their mobile phone use. Lastly, I compile the three cases to discuss the complex dynamics involved in how these women's use of the mobile phone has had an impact on how they make ends meet.

Mobile Phone Use in Botswana: The Broad Socio-economic Patterns

Botswana is a large country (the size of France) and sparsely populated (2.2 million inhabitants) with a rich state and a relatively poor, highly mobile population (Hope, 2001; Statistics Botswana, 2017). When mobile communication services started to be offered in 1998, infrastructure was still underdeveloped, with fewer than 5 per cent of households having fixed line telephone and internet (Esselaar and Sebusang, 2013). The spread of mobile phones was rapid in the years to come.[6] Penetration of sim cards rose to 57 per cent in 2006 and reached a high of 157 per cent in 2016. This high subscription rate – predominantly pre-paid – is due to people's constant shifting between sim cards from different providers in order to maximise benefits from offers made by the three competing service operators (ibid.; International Telecommunications Union [ITU], 2017). Whereas the typical mobile phone user group during the first years were urban men, the uptake among women has been more rapid than among men and higher in urban than in rural areas. By 2007, equal shares of women and men had become mobile phone owners and by 2010 more women (83 per cent) than men (76 per cent) owned a mobile phone (Deen-Swarray et al., 2012; Esselaar and Sebusang, 2013). Today almost every adult Motswana has access to a mobile phone, there are few gender or urban/rural differences in ownership, and the mobile phone is the main device through which people access the internet (Statistics Botswana, 2017).

User patterns are, however, quite diverse and digital divides remain significant (cf. Storm-Mathisen and Helle-Valle's chapter in this book). There is no official overview of how many people own smartphones, but as costs for phones and use are high, many restrict their use mainly to SMS and call services (Esselaar and Sebusang, 2013). Use of mobile money and Facebook services – both possible to use from simple phones – is around 30 per cent and on the rise (with the former highest in the rural population and the latter highest in the younger age groups) (Botswana Communications Regulatory Authority [Bocra], 2017; ITU, 2017). Such services offer new opportunities for a population among which many still do not have access to other new media tools (such as TV, PC), where only 30 per cent have bank accounts and 39 per cent are internet users (Statistics Botswana, 2016). Nevertheless, usage of the mobile phone for internet-related activities – such as sending/receiving emails, paying bills/buying utilities, mobile banking, sending/receiving money and surfing the internet – remains most common among individuals who have tertiary education, belong to the younger adult age groups and live in urban areas (Statistics Botswana, 2017).

These statistics indicate that the significant factors for mobile phone use in Botswana are linked to higher education and income, young age and urban belonging. Gender, on the other hand, is not statistically significant in this respect. However, the variations in socio-economic situations have for a long time been larger between women than between women and men in Botswana (Peters, 1983) and this can play into the dynamics of mobile phone usage and its economic outcomes. On the one hand, more women than men are unemployed and live in poverty in Botswana, and 58 per cent of poor households are headed by women (United Nations Development Program [UNDP], 2016; World Bank, 2015). On the other hand, the core characteristic of economically vulnerable households in Botswana today is not that they are headed by women but that the household head has low or no education (ibid.). Since Batswana girls for decades have performed better than boys in primary and secondary school, there are now more women than men among the 20 per cent of youth who are enrolled in tertiary education. Thus, the proportion of women who obtain a higher education degree, and hence higher income, is steadily rising (Southern African Development Community [SADC], 2015; Statistics Botswana, 2016; World Bank, 2015). Furthermore, many Batswana have a flexible way of relating to the household unit, so who belongs and contributes and what constitutes expense and income sources can vary over time (Helle-Valle, 1997; Peters, 1983). The various more or less short-term educational and employment schemes funded by the government and international NGOs to bring people out of poverty – many of which are attuned to women – contribute to this pattern. Thus, some women move steadily through increasingly improved living conditions, while others have changing and unpredictable trajectories in and out of different socio-economic situations. The large group who have not obtained tertiary education are more likely to experience the latter, hence there are also generational differences.

Three Women: Different Life Situations, Mobile Phones and Everyday Uses

The three women I present below share an enthusiasm for and long experience with their phones. All have familial connections to the same village and are mothers.[7] Otherwise they are very differently positioned socio-economically, and their mobile phone user patterns also vary considerably. The maximum variation is between Malebogo, an unemployed middle-aged household head who for years has lived on the threshold of poverty, and Patsimo, an educated businesswoman in her thirties, living in one of Gaborone's most expensive areas. Masego, a woman in her twenties and currently a college student (the first in her family) in a government scheme, illustrates a third position, between the two others.

Malebogo: An Unemployed Household Head with a Simple Phone

Malebogo, a woman in her forties, has been the head and only breadwinner of her household since she gave birth to her first child at age twenty-two. At the time of the fieldwork she had four children: three boys and a girl.[8] She lived in a one-room house. She did not have water, a pit latrine or electricity, but it was her house, built in 2004 from income she herself had earnt working in the capital.

Malebogo had, when we first met in 2015, been unemployed for a long time. She lived off piece jobs, government feeding schemes for children, government temporary employment schemes (*Namolo Leuba*) and with help from her closest kin. Most importantly, her aunt (her deceased mother's sister whom she called 'grandmother') looked after the youngest children when Malebogo worked. Also important were her cousin (her grandmother's brother's grandson) – a retired migrant miner to South Africa – and his family. This cousin lived nearby and let her use the water outlet and pit latrine in his yard, charge her mobile phone on his electricity grid and watch news and entertainment programmes with the family. Malebogo, as a third-generation uneducated and unemployed female head, is among the poor in her country and has for long periods lived on an income below the poverty line. This life situation has, however, gradually changed for the better, as her oldest children have started to contribute to the sustenance of the family, something I will come back to later.

Malebogo never went anywhere without her simple mobile phone, her third of the kind and a year old. She got her first one in 2003 from her employer in the capital so that he could reach her easily if he had a piece job for her. She had bought the next two mobile phones herself, the second after giving her eldest son her first phone when he left for secondary boarding school, and the third after her second son received hers when he left for the same boarding school a few years later.

When Malebogo said she used her mobile phone for everything, the services she referred to were calls and SMS-based. She only used one sim card and had never used services over the internet. Moreover, although she used her phone on a daily basis – and had done so for fifteen years – her use was restricted to calls, text messages or money transfers from others and keeping track of time and date. As she usually did not have much money, she kept her total monthly airtime spending to around 40 to 60 Pula (4–6 USD), and was rarely the one who called or sent things to others.

Malebogo said she used to receive calls from her children's fathers, but the most frequent calls were from her two eldest sons who were away at school. In fact, she expected them to call her every day. Each of these two sons – the firstborn who was studying at the university to become a nurse and the second-born who had started on a diploma in accounting – also sent her monthly mobile money transfers of 200 Pula (20 USD), one-seventh of their monthly government-sponsored student allowance. Malebogo's aunt also had a phone but they only called each other rarely, mostly to coordinate the care of Malebogo's youngest child. Malebogo had for a long time been engaged on the parental board at her children's schools, so teachers or parents sometimes called her. She had also recently become active in village politics, and was often called by villagers regarding different issues. She had in fact now become so active that she proclaimed she had an ambition to run for a political position by the next election (in 2019). One of the party candidates, against whom she would be running, had set up a Facebook account and posted pictures of himself posing in a nice suit behind a huge office desk as part of his campaign. Malebogo, for her part, who in any case had little opportunity to follow up on this, said that it was the people in the village who elected their representatives and most of these people were not on Facebook, so why bother. Better, then, to call and use SMS. She knew an impressive number of villagers and had their phone numbers stored in her phone.

Malebogo's main use of her mobile phone was thus to coordinate and maintain relations with her children in the city, her kin (when she herself was away) and with the local school and community. Although she had never used Facebook, WhatsApp or the internet herself, she said proudly that her two eldest sons knew how to, and they would teach her one day.

Patsimo: An Educated Businesswoman with the Latest iPhone

Patsimo, a woman in her late thirties, had lived with her grandparents in the village for long periods during her pre-primary school years, but had later grown up in one of Botswana's larger cities (where her parents, who both had tertiary education degrees, worked and owned a house). Patsimo got her first phone as a present from her parents when she went away to study at a private English Medium boarding school as a teenager. This phone was replaced with a smartphone, bought from her own student allowance, when she a few year later enrolled in tertiary education at a college abroad. Patsimo had started a small manufacturing business at nineteen, a business she had been running ever since. She had also worked in Asia for a year, but had eventually come back and started a new branch of her manufacturing business in the capital. She had steady customers and reliable investors and said that it was going well. She lived alone when we met for the first time in 2015, but moved in with a real estate businessman when she got pregnant the following year. She closed down her business after her son was born and was planning to be a full-time mother until the son started school and 'only do a little real-estate business on the side'.

Patsimo could not remember how many phones she had had since her first smartphone. She preferred the iPhone and bought new models as soon as they appeared on the market. She estimated in 2015 that she spent roughly 500 Pula (50 USD) per month on mobile internet and had a wide range of apps installed that she used for various tasks. At the time, she was particularly enthusiastic about 'this great software program that comes with an app' that had made it 'so much easier to administer the stock, budget, employees' work hours, payments and the like as I can do it all on my phone'. This app had, according to Patsimo, made the daily running of her manufacturing business more efficient. Patsimo was evidently an experienced user of the internet and it took her no time to google for answers to things that came up in our conversations. As for social media apps she said that 'I refuse to use Facebook, it's so irritating' and rather preferred Instagram for posting pictures and following the activities of friends and people she knew. Patsimo was quite secretive about her private relations. She preferred WhatsApp for private conversations and Skype to stay in touch with her closest friends and family when she was abroad. It was apparent that Patsimo, after becoming a mother, had changed her phone use slightly, and that this was connected to her new concern as a homemaker. For instance, her favourite app in 2017 was Pinterest: 'I like the food to be good and healthy and you can find ideas for everything there'. She was still a user of online banking (only occasionally mobile money when there was no other option), had continued using Instagram and WhatsApp for social updates, and thought of her mobile phone as a memory and entertainment box (with calendar, pictures, videos and the like) always at hand. She used SMS frequently with her mother and made the occasional call to her grandparents in the village.

The mobile phone was far from Patsimo's only media access point. Her home was filled with computers, laptops, a smart TV, WiFi and so on. The people with whom she connected through her media devices were primarily in Gaborone or outside the country, rather than in the village. Thus, Patsimo engaged with a much more complex, differentiated, expanded – and not least, ten times more costly – type of media use than Malebogo was able to.

Masego: A Student Mother with a Tablet

Masego, was in her late twenties and enrolled as a student on a government-sponsored two-year diploma in tourism at a vocational college in the capital. Our paths crossed when she was back in the village for a holiday in 2015. Her first term had ended and she was very happy to reunite with her two-year-old son, whom her older sister took care of while Masego was in the capital. The sister was the oldest of four siblings, and head of their late parents' household in the village. Their parents had been farmers and the household, with eight adults and several small children, struggled to sustain themselves on the income they earnt from cultivation and other sources. Masego herself had been unemployed for several years, living off income from piece jobs and her kin. She hoped the recent educational opportunity would help her to eventually get a job in Botswana's growing tourist industry and earn a better future for herself and her son. The student allowance of 1400 Pula (140 USD) that she presently received was more than she could hope to earn from any job and amounted to more than the total income of her sisters' household.

Masego had a rather fancy tablet phone, bought with money from her first student allowance in 2015. She had used it a lot; the screen had already become scratched and the internal storage was full. This was not her first phone, however. Her boyfriend (the father of her son) had given her a simple phone five years earlier so that they could keep in touch after he left the village to work as a soldier. He still occasionally sent her money to buy airtime, so they could talk or send messages. Masego's most regular use of her tablet was for calls and SMSs. She also used it as storage for photos and music to entertain herself in the long periods when she was away from home. Moreover, she used mobile money to send her sister 200 Pula (20 USD) every month for caring for her son. It was with the enrolment at the college that Masego had started using the internet. Becoming a student provided her with an email account and an e-bank account with a mobile money service attached for transfer of her student allowance. In addition, there was free access to WiFi and computers at the college. This had made it easier for her to use Facebook and WhatsApp, although her economic situation severely limited her use of these apps. If she could afford it, she bought a one-day, week or month bundle (the latter approx. 60 Pula) for free use of these social media, but she complained that living in the capital was expensive and that she often did not have the money. So, even though she sometimes posted on Facebook – pictures of herself, her friends, her son and the family – there were long periods (months or more) when she did not post at all. I learnt that the best way to reach her was to call, rather than email or message. In 2017 her tablet phone was stolen and as she had no money to replace it, she went back to using a simple phone.

Making Ends Meet: Dynamics whereby the Mobile Phone Connects

These three cases provide examples of the large variations in actual mobile phone use among differently positioned women. Malebogo engages in the basic use of calls and SMS-based services from a simple mobile phone and is wary of costs. Masego does the same but also engages sporadically with internet activities from a smartphone when at college. Patsimo is not concerned with costs and engages continuously with a whole range of mobile phone and internet-related services from her smartphone as well as from other personal new media devices. I now turn to a discussion of the connections and the dynamics of what is brought together through these women's mobile phone practices. With emphasis on the core question of this chapter – how women's use of the mobile phone connects to their economic activities and outcomes – I first discuss direct connections between their mobile phone use and economic activities, then indirect connections, through education and women's wider concerns.

Direct Connections to Economic Ends

Economic activities can take many forms but typically involve money or the exchange (production, distribution, consumption) of products and services. When Malebogo, Patsimo and Masego make their choices in spending money on mobile phones and mobile phone services, these are consumption activities that derive their meaning from what is possible in their specific economic situations. My primary interest here, however, is more in how their mobile phone use connects to their specific productive economic activities (and outcomes). Three aspects of this are considered below: the use of the mobile phone as business, as an enabler for money transfers and as a tool for income generation.

None of the three women presented were engaged in uses of the mobile phone or other new media *as a business* that provided a source of income in itself. We did encounter other women during the fieldwork who did earn money from their use of the mobile phone: selling sim cards, airtime, mobile phone parts from tuck-shops, doing online sales and advertisement, providing repair or sales services or ICT skills training. The major impression, however, was that they either earnt very little money from it (the tuck-shops) or that it required a degree of investment, knowledge and networks that most people did not have. In fact, we met only one woman who – after a long education – had made a decent living from such a business (see Storm-Mathisen and Helle-Valle's chapter in this book). The direct connections between uses of the mobile phone/new media and productive income from business seemed in this sense to be weak for most women.

Using the mobile phone as an enabler for quick, easy and cost-reducing *money transfers* was, on the other hand, common to a wide range of women's economic activities, yet in slightly different ways (see also Kusimba et al., 2016). Whereas Patsimo and Masego had electronic bank accounts and means to use them, the SMS-based mobile money services were particularly central to Malebogo, Masego and many others in the village because there was no bank, and as there was severe underemployment in the village many depended on remittances from household members working elsewhere. That Malebogo's sons and Masego use mobile money to send a portion of their monthly allowance to their kin in the village was typical of the important redistributive function of mobile phones. It is exactly these contributions that had moved Malebogo's income level above the poverty threshold. The money would likely also have found its way to the families in the village without the mobile money service, but the cost would have been much higher and the speed much slower. The new mobile money transfer system is therefore not really changing the ways things are done, but is only making the process more efficient and reducing transactional costs. With the mobile money service people can rely on the transfer to go through without taking the risk of paying somebody to transport it, and they do not have to wait for it.

Another important function of the mobile phone is as *a tool* for income-generating activities, to make the production of activities more efficient. For instance, Patsimo engaged with her phone in a range of ways related to her business: to manage the budget, manage production, advertise to customers, place orders and make payments and so on. Malebogo increased her chances of earning an income from informal piece jobs by being available through a mobile phone number, which is why she was so concerned with keeping it within reach at all times. This orientation to the mobile phone was shared by all the women we encountered who had a business or business relations. Simple calling and SMS (i.e. to check on employees, probe customers, order deliveries) and mobile money services (i.e. to make or check on payments) were core to most women's business activities (see also Willems' chapter in this book). Webpages or social media were also used by some (i.e. setting up a Facebook page with pictures of things they had for sale), but engagements with professional business solutions of the kind that Patsimo used were rare. The centrality of using a mobile phone in business, even if it is a simple phone and the business is of the smallest kind, can nevertheless be significant. The example of a woman in the village who had started to raise goats a few years previously, with funding from a government-sponsored income programme, can highlight this. The woman had been able to earn some money from these goats, but faced challenges when new sanitary regulations prohibited her from keeping her goats within the village. In order to keep her business going, she was thus forced to move the goats some distance away from the village. Since she could not move herself (she was a single mother with five children), her options were either to hire a herd boy or close down her business. She chose the former, but a widely shared view among villagers is that herd boys are often not to be trusted. Hence, she called the herd boy every day to check how things were going. Although this daily calling cost what was to her a substantial sum of money (2.50 USD every week), she saw it as absolutely necessary to keep her goats healthy and gain some income from them. The mobile phone can thus be said to be directly connected to the woman's economic activities.

Yet surveys conducted during fieldwork suggest that it was more typical for people – regardless of gender, social position and local belonging – to connect their mobile phone use to social rather than economic concerns (Storm-Mathisen, 2019). For instance, in the household survey, to the question 'Are personal media used [by the household] in relation to *income-generating activities*?' only 34 per cent of households in the capital and 39 per cent of households in the village answered 'yes'. Conversely, to the question 'Are personal media used [by the household] to *stay in touch with family and friends*?' an overwhelming 95 per cent of households in the capital and 85 per cent in the village answered 'yes'.[9] Similarly, what kept Malebogo, Masego and Patsimo busy with their phones seemed to be linked more to their social concerns – keeping up relations and coordinating activities with children and family, with people at school, in the community and with friends and lovers and other acquaintances – than to their economic concerns per se. This is not to say, however, that the mobile phone is less important for people's economic than social activities. Rather, as I have argued in a previous analysis (Storm-Mathisen, 2019), usage of the mobile phone seems to have changed the dynamics of people's practices and routines around concerns. By using mobile phones, people can deal with their various concerns in new ways, which for some can have significant longer-term economic outputs. Three interlinked factors – mobility, social capital (Bourdieu, 1986) and, not least, education as a gateway for access to and engagement with new media in more complex ways – seem to be crucial in the processes that produce these different outcomes. In the next two sections, I follow up on this, tracing how connections between the mobile phone use and economic activities of these three women indirectly interlink with changes in education in their families over generations and their present wider concerns.

Indirect Connections through Education

Malebogo's mother and Patsimo's and Masego's grandmothers were in their twenties when Botswana became independent in 1966. The country was then poor and predominantly a patriarchal tribal Tswana society. Most people lived off farming (by women) and cattle herding (by men) and only two out of ten children were enrolled in primary school (Christian Michelsens Institutt [CMI], 1988, p. 9). Patsimo's grandmother was among the few who went to school during this time, whereas Malebogo's mother and Masego's grandmother did not. Although women by tradition were subordinate to male kin (Comaroff and Comaroff, 2001), many women in practice were in charge of the households since a large number of men were absent, due to labour migration or due to a steep increase in children born out of wedlock (Helle-Valle, 1997; Griffith, 1997). The latter was also the case for Malebogo's mother, as it had been for her grandmother: they all had children without being married and had to make a living for themselves and their children. The situation was very different for Patsimo's grandmother as she, having been one among the few who went through primary school at that time, could take on work as a teacher, gained a formal income of her own and was also later married to a man who himself had formal income.

Economic realities and processes were under rapid change when Malebogo and the mothers of Patsimo and Masego grew up in the 1970s and 1980s. Botswana had become rich from the mining of mineral deposits and used this, through stable governance, to invest in infrastructure and public education to increase the domestic skills and opportunities of both genders and all classes (Lefko-Everett, 2004). That both Malebogo and Patsimo's mother went to school – although their parents' socio-economic resources were very different – was thus not remarkable. However, Malebogo, who was a very bright student, got pregnant and was expelled from school. Patsimo's mother, on the other hand, completed secondary school, moved to the city to continue tertiary education and established a relationship with the educated middle-class man who later became Patsimo's father and to networks that eventually gave her a well-paid job.

When Masego, Patsimo and Malebogo's first son were born in the late 1980s and early 1990s, Botswana had become a middle-income country. All three enrolled in primary school along with nine out of ten of their peers (and on a gender equal basis) and continued to secondary level. However, whereas the other two attended public school, Patsimo was among the 10 per cent who attended a private English Medium school, a school attended by children of the country's elites. Both Malebogo's son and Patsimo were among the 20 per cent in their age group who obtained sufficient grades to start tertiary education (SADC, 2015), although Patsimo undertook hers abroad. What they share is having grown up in the decade when urbanisation accelerated, more work and education were offered, the AIDS epidemic struck many families severely, the media landscape expanded rapidly and – not least significant to the discussion here – the mobile phone was introduced in Botswana.

This context provides insights into *education* as a factor that indirectly links to the differences in how Malebogo, Patsimo and Masego use their phones to connect to economic activities today. The most striking differentiating element in their mobile phone user pattern is whether or not they use internet services. Whereas an obvious factor in how much they use their phone actively is how much money they can afford to spend on it, it is more than money that restricts Malebogo from expanding her mobile phone use or keeps her from engaging with the internet. There are cheap smartphones she could have afforded and free WiFi available at the library in the village. What restricts her is rather the idea that there is nothing much for her to gain from such use. What motivates her to use the mobile phone's SMS and call-based services is that these are the services used by the people who are important to her, and they have functions that she feels she needs. In her mind, the people with whom she wants to connect do not use the internet. For Patsimo, money is not the prime factor that shapes her varied and expanded use of her mobile phone. Although her use certainly requires a level of cost (and competence) that neither Malebogo nor Masego can dream of, it is the fact that Patsimo's significant others are also on the internet and using the services she is using that primarily shapes her use.

Education is thus a crucial factor in explaining the variations in Malebogo's, Patsimo's and Masego's socio-economic situations today. Their cases illustrate how education has affected the socio-economic conditions for the different generations in different ways. The difference between Masego's situation today and Malebogo's situation in the 1990s is telling. They are both from poor backgrounds and became single mothers around the age of twenty. However, whereas Masego is given an opportunity to undertake tertiary education through a government scheme and thus has the prospect of earning more money for herself and her family in the future, Malebogo was not given this chance a generation earlier, even though she was a very bright student with high ambitions. Masego thus seems to be climbing up the class ladder: in an economical sense both directly through her student allowance and indirectly through getting an education which she hopes will secure her a well-paid job; and socially by connecting to people who might be important for her future. Patsimo has – through her parents' monetary ability and ambition for her to attend schools with pupils in an upper-class position, the education itself and her own school achievements – accumulated assets that put her in an upper-class position.

Furthermore, it is education that has provided Masego with access to a new media environment, a tablet phone, free WiFi, an email account and beneficial social networks. Patsimo has in addition efficiently put to productive use the social relations with which her educational background has provided her to maintain and expand her connections to people with money. For instance, the customers of her manufacturing business, as well as the father of her child, all come from a social network to which the other two have no access.

Indirect Connections through Mobility and Wider Concerns

Education is in itself a central factor in explaining social and economic differentiation. However, it also indirectly affects other differentiating factors. One such factor of relevance to the discussion here is geographical *mobility*, moving away from home to acquire education or work. It was moving away from their significant others that caused Malebogo, Patsimo and Masego to acquire their first phones and start using them. Malebogo got her phone as a present from her employer when she went home to the village to have her third child; Patsimo was given hers as a present from her parents when she went away to secondary school; and Masego received hers as a present from her boyfriend when he left the village. The mobile phone, even of the simplest kind, has made such situations less difficult and acts as an *intermediary* (Latour, 2005), reconnecting important relations to children, lovers, family and friends through immediate and relatively cheap communication.

To be able to use such an intermediary is not the least significant for the many women with children (92 per cent of women aged between fifteen and forty-nine; Statistics Botswana, 2016). When Patsimo became a mother, she decided to end her business and stay home with her child until she started school. She could choose to do this because she, contrary to most women, was in a financial situation that allowed it (she lived with a wealthy man). Her current use of her mobile phone was adapted to her combined strategy of 'nest building' and maintaining her social networks. Malebogo and Masego, on the other hand, do not have this option. Their economic standing forces them to combine education and/or work with their status as mothers. In this respect, the mobile phone is crucial. Both have experienced long periods away from their children, having left them in the village under the care of a sister or mother when they moved to the city. Masego makes her studies possible and life alone in the capital less difficult by use of the mobile phone: she could coordinate and uphold a close relationship with her son with relative ease, despite the distance; feel safe that she would be alerted quickly by her sister if she was needed; send money to her sister cheaply and efficiently; and concentrate on completing an education that might one day give her a decently paid job.

How such conflicting concerns are handled has economic consequences. For instance, since she became a mother, Malebogo's major concerns have been related to building a home and supporting her children's education, a project she had to embark on by herself as the father of her first three children had married another woman. While Masego is still hoping to get married and build a home with her soldier boyfriend, Malebogo's dream for the future is to get water in the yard, a pit latrine, electricity and a bigger house. However, for these dreams to come true, they have to uphold relationships – Malebogo to her children, Masego to her boyfriend and their son. It is through steady communication and interaction that long-distance relationships are maintained. This was much more difficult before the era of the mobile phone: it could be weeks or months between contact between the woman and a working or schooling spouse or child, and the weaker the links, the bigger the chance of household fissions (Helle-Valle, 1997, pp. 145ff). Such fissions of course still routinely occur, but with the mobile phone as a tool, the women can intensify the communication flow and hence do their best to prevent themselves from breaking away from their family. For instance, it is the mobile phone, together with personal social networks, that has made it possible for Malebogo to uphold a rather intense communication with her sons, and although one example cannot serve as proof of the crucial role of the mobile phone, it is nevertheless striking to see how loyal Malebogo's sons are in relation to their mother. More precisely, it is the combination of earning money to make it possible for her sons to get an education (in which the mobile phone was crucial as she was working outside the village) while simultaneously using her mobile phone to keep up good and regular relations with them over the years that produced a situation where they have now literally started to 'pay her back', an output that is significant as it has changed her socio-economic situation to a level above the poverty threshold.

Services such as mobile money and transfers of airtime have made these transfers of money from her sons easier and quicker (and her requests for help harder to reject or postpone with referral to not being able to or being out of reach). The most important aspect, however, is that Malebogo has used her mobile phone to strengthen the intergenerational relations in her family, a form of social capital (Bourdieu, 1986) or 'wealth in people' (Guyer, 1995) that has now been converted into cash, and likely will increasingly do so as her boys grow older. Hence, whereas the link between Malebogo's use of her mobile phone and her economic situation and activities remains mainly indirect, the links between her economic concerns and her use of the mobile phone are – although indirect – intimate and important.[10] Mobile money would have been of little use to Malebogo had it not been that she had sons who could send her some. The significant change lies in Malebogo's new sources of income – most notably her sons – not in the technology, but it was the technology that made the maintenance and administration of these relations, and the economic transfers, easier and faster from a distance.[11]

This exemplifies how not only education and generation, but also wider concerns with mobility and maintaining relations to children and social networks are important interlinked factors in the dynamics whereby mobile phone use indirectly connects to women's economic activities and in a way that can have significant socio-economic consequences.

New Ways of Making Ends Meet?

The ambition of this chapter has been to reflect on how mobile phone use is involved in the dynamics that create different economic situations for women in this setting today. I have used three individual women as illustrations of the very different socio-economic situations in which women in Botswana find themselves, to give examples of how their uses of their mobile phones connected to their economic activities and concerns, and to point to central factors involved in the dynamics that produce different outcomes.

What these cases show is firstly that the large difference in their socio-economic situations has a bearing on how these women use the mobile phone: the type of phone they have, what services they can use, the frequency of use and the networks they connect to and uphold through it. Across these differences, however, women's uses of the mobile phone do not seem to be primarily oriented to economic activities. Their engagement with their mobile phone was oriented more to upholding various significant social relations – as social capital – which can then be transformed into economic gain. In this respect the mobile phone is central, and my analysis suggests that education and mobility are crucial factors in these dynamics. Although the mobile phone has not directly influenced the economic standing of most women, we can safely contend that it has indirectly introduced new ways for women to make ends meet. Mobile phone use has changed how different concerns in the everyday can be handled and brought together, something which sometimes reduces costs, sometimes accumulates capital and sometimes has a long-term economic outcome. The meaning of using the mobile phone is thus situated – as Malebogo phrased it – in the everything of everyday.

Acknowledgements

I am indebted to Malebogo, Masego and Patsimo, as well as other friends and people in Botswana who shared, discussed and reflected on their experiences with me. Elements of this analysis have been presented to research groups in the past few years and in a series of discussions on New Media Practices in a Changing Africa in 2018, and I thank participating colleagues for their comments. Special appreciation goes to Jo Helle-Valle for invaluable discussions and fruitful inputs throughout the process and on earlier versions of this manuscript. The research was funded by the New Media Practices in a Changing Africa project, financed by the Research Council of Norway (grant no. FriPro 240714).

Ardis Storm-Mathisen is Research Professor at Consumption Research Norway and Faculty of Education, Oslo Metropolitan University. Her research has focused on issues of gender, identity and vulnerability among children, youth and families in relation to their everyday, digital media-related practices, currently as Principal Investigator for Relink (Building resilient households through interdisciplinary and multi-level exploration and intervention), a project funded by the Research Council of Norway. She conducted fieldwork in Botswana between 2015 and 2018, giving special attention to gender relations and the lives of the young. During this research she was affiliated to the Centre for Gender Research, University of Oslo as a senior researcher and a visiting researcher at the University of Botswana.

Notes

1. Pinterest is a social media app that invites you to 'explore lifestyle inspiration', 'discover over 100 billion possibilities for every part of your life' (https://play.google.com/store/apps/details?id=com.pinterestandhl=en_US) (accessed 10 December 2017).
2. According to the Botswana Poverty Assessment report, the Gini coefficient was 60.4 (at last measure in 2009), the richest 20 per cent of the population owned 65 per cent of the country's income, whereas 19 per cent lived below the poverty line of 1.25 USD a day (World Bank, 2015). The report finds that whereas regional and educational differences explained most of the inequality, employment explained less, and 'the gender component had almost no effect on "between" inequality, suggesting that factors other than gender differences impact total inequality' (ibid., p. 37).
3. I similarly use the term 'dynamic' (a general term for interactional processes), 'factor' (an element in such dynamics) and 'concerns' (what people's acts are oriented to) as descriptive concepts, hence of properties belonging to the field of study.
4. The fieldwork was undertaken from August 2015 to April 2016 and from October to November 2017 and 2018 by Jo Helle-Valle and myself. For further information about the wider study, see www.mediacfrica.no.
5. These included a web survey open to all Batswana and two enumerated stratified door-to-door surveys (i) in households (with household head or representative) and (ii) among individuals (interview with the household member present that was most familiar with ICTs). Both surveys included photo documentation and were conducted in the capital (N = 170 x 2, December 2015) and in the particular village (N = 200 x 2, January 2016).
6. Services were offered from 1998 by two mobile operators – Mascom (the leading operator) and Vista (now Orange) – on backbone services of Botswana Tele Communications (BTC). A liberation of the market took place in 2006 and allowed all operators to develop their own backbone services. A third operator – beMobile (BTV) – started services in 2008 (Esselaar and Sebusang, 2013).

7. Names and certain characteristics are changed to protect these people's identity.
8. The father of her boys had married another woman and the father of her daughter was deceased.
9. However, there were some variations on the more specific questions (ibid.).
10. See also de Bruijn (2014) for a discussion of such complex dynamics.
11. Kusimba makes a similar point when addressing how mobile money transfers reveal the importance of hearthhold networks and have opened new pathways towards 'gifts that keep on giving' (Kusimba et al., 2016, p. 277).

References

Botswana Communications Regulatory Authority (Bocra). 2017. *Annual Report 2017.* http://www.bocra.org.bw/sites/default/files/documents/BOCRA%20AR%202017%20DIGITAL%20FINAL.pdf (accessed 15 December 2018).

Bourdieu, P. 1986. 'The Forms of Capital', in J. Richardson (ed.), *Handbook of Theory and Research for the Sociology of Education.* Westport, CT: Greenwood, pp. 241–58.

Christian Michelsens Institutt (CMI). 1988. *Botswana: Country Study and Norwegian Aid Review.* Bergen: DERAP Publication no. 235.

Comaroff, J.L., and J. Comaroff. 2001. 'On Personhood: An Anthropological Perspective from Africa', *Social Identities* 7(2): 267–83.

Carmody, P. 2012. 'The Informationalization of Poverty in Africa? Mobile Phones and Economic Structure', *Information Technologies & International Development* 8(3): 1–17.

De Bruijn, M. 2014. 'Connecting in Mobile Communities: An African Case Study', *Media, Culture & Society* 36(83): 319–35.

Deen-Swarray, M., A. Gilwald and A. Morrell. 2012. *Lifting the Veil on ICT Gender Indicators in Africa: Evidence for ICT Policy Action.* Policy Paper 13. Research ICT Africa. https://www.researchictafrica.net/publications/Evidence_for_ICT_Policy_Action/Policy_Paper_13_-_Lifting_the_veil_on_gender_ICT_indicators_in_Africa.pdf (accessed 15 April 2016).

Esselaar, S., and S. Sebusang. 2013. *Understanding What Is Happening in ICT in Botswana: A Supply- and Demand Side Analysis of the ICT Sector. Evidence for ICT Policy Action.* Policy Paper 1. Research ICT Africa. https://www.researchictafrica.net/publications/Evidence_for_ICT_Policy_Action/Policy_Paper_1_-_Understanding_what_is_happening_in_ICT_in_Botswana.pdf (accessed 15 April 2016).

Flyvbjerg, B. 2006. 'Five Misunderstandings about Case-Study Research', *Qualitative Inquiry* 12(2): 219–45.

Giddings, C., and A.J. Hovorka. 2010. 'Place, Ideological Mobility and Youth Negotiations of Gender Identities in Urban Botswana', *Gender, Place and Culture* 17(2): 211–29.

Griffiths, Anne M.O. 1997. *In the Shadow of Marriage: Gender and Justice in an African Community*, Chicago: University of Chicago Press.

Guyer, J. 1995. 'Wealth in People, Wealth in Things: Introduction', *Journal of African History* 36: 83–90.

Helle-Valle, J. 1997. *Change and Diversity in a Kgalagadi Village, Botswana.* Oslo: Senter for Utvikling of Miljø (SUM), University of Oslo.

———. 2010. 'Language-Games, In/dividuals and Media Uses: What a Practice Perspective Should Imply for Media Studies', in B. Bräuchler and J. Postill (eds), *Theorising Media and Practice.* Oxford: Berghahn Books, pp. 191–211.

Helle-Valle, J., and A. Borchgrevink. 2018. 'Household Histories and Methodological Triangulation', *Forum for Development Studies* 45(2): 191–215. doi:10.1080/08039410.2016.1260049.

Hope, K.R. 2001. 'Population Mobility and Multi-Partner Sex in Botswana: Implications for the Spread of HIV/AIDS', *African Journal of Reproductive Health* 5(3): 73–83.

International Telecommunications Union (ITU). 2017. *Measuring the Information Society Report 2017*, vol. 1. Geneva: ITU.

Kusimba, S., Y. Yang and N. Chawla. 2016. 'Hearthholds of Mobile Money in Western Kenya', *Economic Anthropology* 3: 266–79.

Latour, B. 2005. *Reassembling the Social: An Introduction to Actor-Network-Theory.* Oxford: Oxford University Press.

Lefko-Everett, K. 2004. 'Botswana's Changing Migration Patterns. Migration Policy Institute, Profile, September 1', https://www.migrationpolicy.org/article/botswanas-changing-migration-patterns (accessed 15 December 2018).

Miller, D., E. Costa, N. Haynes, T. McDonald, R. Nicolescu, J. Sinanan, J. Spyer, S. Venkatraman and W. Wang. 2016. *How the World Changed Social Media.* London: UCL Press.

Ministry of Finance and Development Planning. 2009. *National Development Plan 10 (2009–2016). Volume 1.* Republic of Botswana: Ministry of Finance and Development Planning.

———. 2016. *Draft: National Development Plan 11. April 2017–March 2023. Volume 1* [September 2016]. Republic of Botswana: Ministry of Finance and Development Planning. http://extwprlegs1.fao.org/docs/pdf/bot175398.pdf (accessed 10 November 2017).

Peters, P. 1983. 'Development Cycles and Historical Process: A Critique of Recent Research on Women in Botswana', *Journal of Modern African Studies* 10: 100–122.

Southern Africa Development Community [SADC]. 2015. 'SADC Gender Protocol Barometer 2015 Botswana'. https://genderlinks.org.za/programme-web-menu/publications/sadc-gender-protocol-2015-barometer-botswana-2015-06-25/ (accessed 16 April 2017).

Slater, D. 2013. *New Media, Development and Globalization.* Cambridge: Polity Press.

Statistics Botswana. 2016. *Selected Statistical Indicators 1966–2016: Enabling Stakeholders Formulate Policies, Plan and Make Decisions.* http://www.statsbots.

org.bw/sites/default/files/publications/Selected%20Statistical%20 Indicators%201966-2016-%20Sept%202016.pdf (accessed 15 April 2017).

———. 2017. *Botswana Household Access & Individual Use of Information & Communication Technologies Report-2014*. http://www.statsbots.org.bw/ sites/default/files/publications/Botswana%20Household%20Access%20 %20%26%20Individual%20Use%20of%20Information%20%26%20 Communication%20Technologies%20Report%202014.pdf (accessed 27 May 2017).

Storm-Mathisen, A. 2016. 'Grasping Children's Media Practices: Theoretical and Methodological Challenges', *Journal of Children and Media* 10(1): s.81–89.

———. 2017. 'Gender Representations and Identity Constructions among Young Teenagers in Botswana: Exploring the Influence of Media', in D. Lemish and M. Gotz (eds), *Beyond the Stereotypes? Images of Boys and Girls, and Their Consequences*. Gothenburg: Nordicom, pp. 173–81.

———. 2018. 'Visual Methods in Ethnographic Fieldwork: On Learning from Participants in Ethnographic Fieldwork', *Forum for Development Studies* 45(2): 261–86.

———. 2019. 'New Media Use among Young Batswana: On Concerns, Consequences and the Educational Factor', *Journal of African Media Studies* 11(2).

UNDP. 2016. *Briefing Note for Countries on the 2016 Human Development Report Botswana*. http://hdr.undp.org/sites/all/themes/hdr_theme/country-notes/BWA.pdf (accessed 11 September 2017).

World Bank. 2015. *Botswana Poverty Assessment*. Report No. 88473-BW. http:// documents.worldbank.org/curated/en/351721468184754228/Botswana-poverty-assessment (accessed 27 August 2017).

———. 2016. *World Development Report 2016: Digital Dividends*. http://www. worldbank.org/en/publication/wdr2016 (accessed 7 April 2017).

PART III

Localities and New Media

CHAPTER 6

The Public Inside Out

Facebook, Community and Banal Activism in a Cape Town Suburb

Nanna Schneidermann

What we share on social media has until recently been celebrated as a potential catalyst for activism and reimagining political agendas in a changing world. In the context of South Africa, platforms like Facebook and Twitter are increasingly playing a role in formal politics, protest movements and elections (Bosch, 2018; Steenkamp and Hyde-Clarke, 2014). Social movements have organised through and around social media campaigns, most prominently the student protest movements #rhodesmustfall and #feesmustfall, which called for decolonisation and justice in tertiary education and protested increases in university fees (Bosch, 2017; Nyamnjoh, 2016). The movement #zumamustfall emerged after President Zuma reshuffled the cabinet under allegations of state capture, leading to national protest marches in April 2017 (Nkuna et al., 2017). Perhaps a precursor to the global #metoo campaign, a group of feminist intellectuals used #menaretrash to rally against violence against women, femicide and toxic masculinity in the wake of another murder of a young black woman in Johannesburg, spreading to a national focus in news media and magazines in the first months of 2017. Around the same time, social media also played a central role in a political scandal when the premier of the Western Cape, Helen Zille, tweeted that colonialism wasn't all bad, and was met with a 'shit storm' of accusations of racism and worse (Petrus, 2016). These few examples suggest that social media in South Africa are in remarkable ways tools for activists in mobilising and organising offline activities and sites for activism in themselves, setting agendas in the news and the nation.

More recently, platforms such as Facebook have come under criticism for their role in American and international politics, manipulation of voters in election campaigns and in surveillance and privacy breaches. Although these cases show social media, and Facebook in particular, as catalysts of change and as sites for reimagining political futures, these changes are dystopian ones where nefarious actors and opaque interests work to conspire against democracies and nations by entrenching political divides and hate among users (Del Vicario et al., 2017; Ernst et al., 2017). In this chapter, however, I will argue that far more mundane online activist practices also shape everyday politics of being, working and making one's way in the New South Africa. Furthermore, these everyday social media practices are also place-making and community-making practices that put notions of race and urban space at stake in the post-apartheid city.

When I moved to a coastal suburb of Cape Town called Muizenberg in 2016, I became a member of several groups on Facebook focusing on the Muizenberg area, and also followed profiles on Instagram and Twitter that portrayed and discussed Muizenberg. Hanging out in the physical space of the suburb, I wondered about the role of social media in making Muizenberg Muizenberg. With the vantage point of the Facebook group Muizenberg Notice Board, I here use the local ideal of community as a lens through which to explore banal online activism (Postill, 2011; Smith, 2011) as a mode of political contestation in the New South Africa. Group members share posts about local events, businesses and personal adverts, but the most commented posts are personal, testimonial narratives about personal experiences of living in Muizenberg. Three cases from December 2016 and January 2017 demonstrate how unremarkable events become the basis for mobilising and contesting ideas about 'community': litter in public spaces; petty crime; and unaccompanied children in public spaces. A central concern in posts, and for the group's administrators and local politicians, is who and what belongs in the area, and how to deal with transgressions of boundaries, with the issue of race always looming in the background. A derivative concern is how such problems can legitimately be articulated and shared in an online group with more than seven thousand members. Online local politics are shaped by everyday concerns, and in Muizenberg these concerns revolve around the ideal of 'community' and what membership affords those traversing, living in and doing business in Muizenberg. The spatial and racial segregation of Cape Town is reformulated by practices of banal activism on social media, and these contestations of community and belonging may be even more profound than more spectacular online activism as they use personal experience and affect to turn the public inside out.

The Notice Board

The posts on the Facebook group Muizenberg Notice Board resembled the kinds of posts one might find on the notice board at the local supermarket: events at the nearby theatre, people looking for jobs or a room to rent, advertisements for a yoga class and a new pizza place. It could be people seeking recommendations for a plumber or artisanal birthday cakes. Some people were looking to sell a fern or had found a stray dog or cat in the streets. Many posts took seriously what was going on in 'the community' and the consequences of events or initiatives for the well-being of the area. Posts of this kind could contain links to news websites or other websites, but many were personal posts written as narratives or testimonials by members of the group. The narrative posts attracted the most likes and comments, and some became sites of debate.

Muizenberg seems to have always been a place of significant encounters that confronts questions of boundaries and belonging. Sitting in the nook of False Bay on the eastern side of the Cape of Good Hope, between Simon's Town and Cape Town, the seaside village is known for three things: it was the site of battle between the British and the Dutch in 1795, when South Africa became a British colony (for the first time); it was the ultimate holiday destination for the colonial elite in the early 1900s when people like Cecil Rhodes, George Bernard Shaw, Rudyard Kipling and the Oppenheimers strolled the beaches; and it is the epicentre of South Africa's surfing culture.[1] It is an infrastructural node for commuters to the Cape Peninsula and for those travelling to and from the Cape Flat townships of Strandfontein, Mitchells Plain and Khayelitsha. Joy Owen's ethnography of Congolese migrants' lives in Muizenberg in the mid-2000s describes how the once attractive beachfront had deteriorated over the decades and how post-apartheid Muizenberg was at times referred to as a 'ghetto' inhabited by lower-middle-class whites, coloured and black Africans as well as a growing number of immigrants (Owen, 2015). Since then Muizenberg has in many ways been restored to its former glory, with a new beachfront bustling with surfers, bars and restaurants and the village gaining a reputation as being home to 'creatives' – artists and activists. In the 2011 census, the central Muizenberg village was home to just over 5500 people, 49.9 per cent of them identifying as white, 23.2 per cent identifying as Black

African, 18.4 per cent as Coloured, 2 per cent as Indian or Asian and 6.6 per cent as Other. The larger Muizenberg area includes, apart from the village, the partly informal settlement of Vrygrond, home to over fifty thousand people of black, coloured and migrant backgrounds. It also includes the suburban Lakeside and various gated estates and condominiums near the beach. In this way, Muizenberg represents a kind of micro-cosmos of Cape Town's characteristically spatialised inequality, and an apt case for exploring how social media shapes place-making in the New South Africa.[2]

Attached to the Muizenberg Notice Board Facebook group was a five-page PDF file outlining the Community Standards of the group. It read: 'Muizenberg is a wonderful eclectic mix of cultures, outlooks of life, socio-economic classes, political views and traditions. ... This board is there to serve all the members of the Muizenberg Community as an online public notice board via social media platforms'. The local notion of community was central to many posts in the group, and in the following I explore online activism on the Notice Board as practices of sharing and boundary-drawing around 'community' in a city characterised by extreme inequality and spatial segregation.

Danielle[3] started the Muizenberg Notice Board group on Facebook in 2015, thinking that just her own friends would join. She was of coloured background and had lived in Muizenberg most of her life.[3] Now in her late twenties she was married with two children and had a marketing job in a small company. The group soon had over two thousand members. Danielle could often monitor what was going on in the group during the day while at the office, but as the group grew, she decided to advertise on the group for help. She enlisted four group members as administrators of the group ('admins'), along with a group moderator. Although they never met in person, they started a separate group chat for the admins to discuss issues related to the management of the group. The six of them drew up a formal constitution, the Community Standards, formalising the rules of the group and guidelines for use and membership. When I moved to Muizenberg in November 2016, the group had just over seven thousand members.

Membership and posting were the two instruments of governance that the admins had at their disposal regarding the group.[4] 'Generally we don't have to regulate', said Amy of her work on the group. She was in her mid-fifties, white, and had lived in Muizenberg for over ten years. 'You keep an eye on things ... and then if things get out of hand then you just instantly delete it. We don't police it that heavily.'

Amy had become an admin after being involved in several discussions about race and racism on the Notice Board. She saw her role as a natural extension of being an active resident in Muizenberg and her lifelong engagement with social justice: 'I think having a social media group is very important and very valuable, but having one that is riddled with racism is of no value whatsoever. So for me to keep it a racist-free space is something I'd consider important. And you know, homophobic, racist and gender things, you know all kinds of hate speech'. She had noticed that Facebook groups for the neighbouring suburbs, where the population was more affluent and homogenously white, were in general less sensitive to race issues. In Muizenberg, however, it seemed to constantly be present in some way.

Advertising on the Muizenberg Notice Board was allowed but regulated. On Mondays and Wednesdays, local businesses or others delivering goods and services in the Muizenberg area were allowed to post adverts on the group's 'wall'. Advertisements shared on other days and about goods and services not related to the Muizenberg area were deleted by the admins and the poster could be removed from the group. Private persons were allowed to advertise yard sales or individual items for sale or to recommend the services of local companies at any time.

John, a white man in his forties, who had also responded to Danielle's call for fellow admins for the group, policed advertising fiercely, as he saw the forces of the market as the main threat to the community of the group. 'Your profit does not trump my community spirit!' he said, 'and I think it takes a lot of admin'ing, a lot of strong admin'ing, to keep it in line and going. But it is fulfilling. And also I get a joy out of going "delete" and "block"'.

The admins in the group also excluded posts and posters who shared explicitly party-political views or named politicians, whether local or foreign. 'It just polarises your community, and that leaves a very sour taste', said John. Danielle laughingly remembered the day of the presidential election in the US in 2016. Group members alerted her to intense activity on the group page, and new posts and threads of comments about Donald Trump and Hillary Clinton kept emerging on the site. 'Luckily it was a quiet day at work and so I sat there, and I was just watching this political post go from nought to like four hundred comments in like ten minutes, and I was like: "Don't you work? Like, what are you doing the whole day, fighting with people on Facebook?"' The admins conferred in a separate chat group and decided to close all posts in the group for comment, and also closed the group to new members for the day.

The admins distinguished between posts on party politics and posts on municipal council work. They considered issues of the ward council, such as leaking water pipes, public disorder or roadworks, non-political, practical issues which the community as a whole had interests in solving.

Muizenberg was part of ward 64, and at times members of the Facebook group would tag the local councillor in their posts as a way to get a response from the municipality about their issues. The ward councillor said in an interview that she was struggling to form a strategy towards social media communication. She saw obvious potential in communicating with her constituency online, but at the same time it was tiresome to be expected to respond to all kinds of issues ad hoc by being tagged and getting messages on social media, rather than using official communication channels. Boundaries drawn around what kinds of problems and issues are non-political, 'council work' issues, and which issues are party political, in this way became part of the politics of constituting the community.

The practices of the admins in 'policing' the group ran along three axes: discrimination, market forces and party politics. They point to how everyday practices of adding members or blocking comments on posts shape the idea of community as a particular online space existing between public and private spaces, between personal lives, formal governance and market interests. Control of membership, inclusion and exclusion in the group, cut across the practices of policing racism, advertising and political posts on the Muizenberg Notice Board.

Community: Between Private and Public

On a scorching hot January day, John and I were sorting through the list of profiles of those who had recently applied to become members of the Notice Board group. I asked him who was eligible to become a member. Tapping his tablet with experienced fingertips, he explained that people, organisations, events and businesses having to do with the Muizenberg area were welcome. 'So that's the community,' he concluded, 'it's literally everyone and everything and that spirit that we have here'. Like in many other contexts in South Africa, the meaning of the term community was taken for granted as an ideal form of social life: an ahistorical homogenous group of people defined by shared location and interests or culture – the spirit John was talking about. Yet everyday life in Muizenberg was set in a specific historical context among divergent groups, using the physical spaces in different ways, and the boundaries of community in Muizenberg were contested on the Notice Board.

The administrators sought to thoroughly screen the applicants to the group. Several times a week, Amy and John went through the Facebook profiles of those seeking to join the group, and sometimes there were hundreds. Their criteria were that there should be an obvious connection to the Muizenberg area, and that those seeking to join must be real people, organisations or businesses. Furthermore, admins tried to avoid admitting profiles that were likely to not follow the rules of the group, trying to make sure that members had a kind of online moral personhood.

John would spend an hour or more going through applicants for the group while on the treadmill at the gym. He visited the Facebook profile of each applicant and assessed whether or not this was a 'real' or a 'fake' profile. Over time and with experience he had developed a list of interlinked criteria: the age of the profile, the number of friends, the number of photos and the stated hometown. Social bonds weighed most heavily. If the applicant had several friends who were already group members, they were likely to be 'real' people. Profiles with no photos or profile images not of a person were suspect, as were profiles with very few 'friends' or with thousands of them. But 'real' profiles too could end up being seen by admins as insincere or inappropriate for members. If they did not follow the rules of sharing in the group, they were blocked and deleted. As the group grew, the admins no longer gave warnings or second chances as it became impossible to keep track of who had already received them.

The notion of community outlined in the documents of the Muizenberg Notice Board and by John above emphasised diversity and openness; the admins in practice saw their task as protecting the 'community' against a seemingly endless onslaught of threatening forces that did not share the moral values of the community. However, what, where and who the community could be was shaped by these protective measures. To help contextualise the Muizenberg Notice Board as a self-conscious online community, I will here etch out some of the ways in which the concept has been used to stabilise relations between place, people and politics in Muizenberg and South Africa. While it is beyond the scope of this text to give an exhaustive review of the use of the concept of community (see Amit, 2002, 2010), I highlight how 'communities' have in different historical moments been seen as objects of interventions, sites of resistance, and as service providers to the state in South Africa.

During the apartheid era, the concepts of community and community development formed part of the language of ethnic and racial segregation. The then Department of Community Development was responsible for implementing the 1950 Group Areas act, which divided Cape Town into racially segregated areas and led to the forced removal and resettlement of black people in the city in 'townships' (Thompson et al.,

2017). Categorising urban residents as 'communities' turned them into objects of state interventions as legible, discrete groups based on race.

This history of racial segregation and forced removals of black residents from desirable areas to other locations and townships during apartheid, under the Group Areas Act, has also shaped Muizenberg. It was classified as a White area, but according to residents today, Muizenberg was never strictly segregated, and over the years, waves of immigrants settled there. Joy, a local activist of British descent who had lived in Muizenberg since the 1950s, remembered: 'Muizenberg hasn't been just one colour. We were never really divided, except people divided themselves'. After the Russian Revolution, a significant number of Jews settled in Muizenberg, and the village became divided along other lines than just colour, between white Jews and white Christians.

The notion of community also became part of the resistance against apartheid in South Africa. In the Black Consciousness movement, 'the community' described spatially circumscribed residential entities such as townships (Thornton and Ramphele, 1988, p. 35). In this logic, communities were seen as constituted by shared political interests and therefore pre-existing within areas where residents were oppressed. This concept of community as a naturalised homogenous political entity became a point of departure for black civic associations emerging in townships and other deprived areas in the 1970s and 1980s, and they became central sites for the struggle against the apartheid regime. Here the community takes shape as a political formation against the state, part of the movement to make township areas, and the city, 'ungovernable'.

Despite the obvious tension inherent in the concept of community in South African politics, it remains central to policy-making as well as everyday talk of urban political and development after apartheid. According to the 1996 Constitution, recognised as one of the most progressive in the world, municipalities must provide 'democratic and accountable government for local communities' and must facilitate 'the involvement of communities and community organisations in the matters of local government' (Constitution of the Republic of South Africa, 1996, section 152).

In a review of policy documents in the post-apartheid era, Thompson et al. (2017) observe that the concept of community is fluid and used to describe a wide array of phenomena: 'community is pretty much whatever national policy-makers define it to be in any given context … The tendency is to fall back on the idea of a homogenised community projected in national legislation and policy, living in contiguous space, with a collective identity, a recognised leadership and common needs' (Thompson et al., 2017, p. 7). They find that in a range of policy initiatives, 'the community' features as not just an object of intervention of the state but as collaborators in processes of participatory government.

Neighbourhood watches are perhaps the most apt example of how community has moved from a territory of government to being a means of government (Rose, 1996, p. 335) in the South African context. They represent 'community participation' in the production of security in many South African neighbourhoods through an apparent commitment to place and what might be termed neighbourly relations. This securitisation of the idea of community resonates in Muizenberg. The Muizenberg Improvement District and the Muizenberg Community Safety Initiative collaborate with state agencies such as the police, as well as private security contractors, to provide safety for residents (Bénit-Gbaffou, 2009). Long-time residents will tell of the bad old times in the 1990s when the centre of the village in Muizenberg was dominated by drug trade and gangsters, derelict and abandoned houses in the village left to be occupied by vagrants and recent immigrants from other African countries and other marginal existences. But then they tell of how the area has been gentrified and revived by the shared efforts of community associations, new types of residents like artists, intellectuals and small-scale entrepreneurs, and the public authorities. For John, the local neighbourhood watch groups had been instrumental in the revival of Muizenberg as a community: 'As soon as you start making crime difficult like that, it starts moving out of the area and then the area can start rejuvenating. That's sorta what's happening here'. Social control of shared spaces is thus routinely considered a task of the community in the context of urban South Africa, somehow operating in the spaces between the state and personal security (Buur and Jensen, 2004).

Looking at these different invocations of community suggests that the ubiquity of the idea does not correspond to the existence of objective, discrete groups within the urban setting. Rather, the idea of shared spaces overlaid with shared social identities has powerfully animated politics in places characterised by extreme inequality and disparity as an ideal of social life. Steffen Jensen (2004) analyses how different political actors in a Capetonian coloured township continually engage and attempt to stabilise what and where 'the community' is, as well as who gets to legitimately represent it and make claims on its behalf. Following LaClau (1996), Jensen points to the need for understanding community as an empty signifier through which different groups negotiate claims to authority (Jensen, 2004). That is, community is not a naturalised homogenous and continuous existing socio-spatial entity which is the basis for politics in Cape Town, but a shifting horizon of social action at once 'constitutive for and constituted through' local politics (Buur and Jensen, 2004). These dynamic processes of boundary-making were central for the Muizenberg Notice Board.

In local activism in Muizenberg, the notion of community was at once taken for granted as objectively existing and as something to strive for, maintain and remake; an ideal for sociality between the private spaces of homes and families and the public spaces of municipal politics and state governance. Although the apartheid infrastructures that separated residents in the Muizenberg area still shape how people experience and use the shared spaces, the idea of community conjures what is shared between residents, beyond simply being present in the same place. In Muizenberg, some of these dynamics played out as contestations of community through digital infrastructures on the Muizenberg Notice Board Facebook group.

The admins of the Muizenberg Notice Board defined and protected the community against what they saw as destructive forces: the market, racism/discrimination, party politics and insincere membership. By policing these forces, the admins conceptually etched out a space that constituted community in the group. Yet these forces were continually contested by the posts in the group. Posters frequently problematised what could be taken for granted about the community, by contesting who belongs, how to belong, where boundaries are drawn, what actually is shared. Going through the newsfeed during the festive season, the last few weeks of December 2016 and the first weeks of January 2017, three interlinked issues featured prominently on the Notice Board as problems that needed solving in the community. The first issue was litter in public spaces; the second unaccompanied children in public spaces; and the last petty crime and theft. These posts became sites of debate about what and who belongs in the community, who has the right to use public spaces in the area and how, and how such contested belongings and claims can be addressed.

Litter in Public Spaces

Around the end of the year, Muizenberg's beaches become crowded with Xhosa families and others of African background. They travel to the beach, traditionally on New Year's Day, to wash away the old year and enter the new one refreshed. These days on the beach are holidays of merrymaking and fun. But the influx of, some say, fifty thousand people from other parts of the city is not unproblematic. The beaches become intense points of convergence between tourists, surfers, local residents and black Capetonians from other parts of the city, many from the former township areas and informal settlements adjacent to Muizenberg village. One reoccurring issue on the Notice Board was the litter left behind by the many visitors. The threads about the litter on the beach seemed to have two sides – those who argued that the many visitors and their litter were an annoyance and that this should not be allowed, and those who argued that the beaches are public goods to be enjoyed by all.

Posts on the theme of litter on the beach were not only about the people who leave behind the litter, but also about those who prevent it and clean it up. The Muizenberg Improvement District and the Muizenberg Community Safety Initiative were actively involved in confiscating alcohol from incoming patrons and cleaning up litter in public spaces. Some had posted the interventions as events on Facebook and advertised them on the Notice Board for local residents to join in. On 2 January, a woman who is a resident and a local business owner posted a humorous post about the massive amounts of litter usually left behind: 'I went out to walk my dog by the beach this morning and self-righteously brought a bag for litter, gloves and my fishing net to pick up as much rubbish as possible. BUT THERE WASN'T ANY TO PICK UP!!!! Thanks those who have participated in picking up the rubbish. Well done by volunteers, and the city cleansing department'. She went on to describe how she had greeted the many workers and volunteers who were cleaning up the public outdoor areas and that she had thanked them. They had been grateful for the recognition. 'This makes me so happy. Let us make this year a year for a greener Muizenberg.'[5]

In the posts about the influx of black Capetonian residents to Muizenberg beach over New Year, community as ideal sociality in spatial form works as a boundary-expressing symbol (Cohen, 1985, p. 15). The posts contested who had the right to use shared spaces in Muizenberg and the morally acceptable ways to be and interact in these spaces. The idea of community worked as overlaid processes of geographical, social and moral boundary-drawing around what are perceived as shared spaces – the beach and enjoying leisure time there. In turn, for the admins, these posts also put at stake how such boundary-drawing could legitimately be expressed: '…and then of course that always becomes about race', added John, who was himself white, with a sigh. Arguments would erupt about whether or not black South Africans were leaving litter on the beach due to their skin colour or cultural background. One poster suggested that the visitors were 'behaving like monkeys', and other members attacked her for invoking racist and apartheid stereotypes, but many other posts were more subtle in articulating 'us' and 'them'. Amy kept an eye on these kinds of posts: 'There's a lot of rubbish on the beach, it is predominantly black people [coming to the beach over New Year]. And people [who post in the Facebook group] will start saying "*they*", you know. And we just delete it. Those few days after Christmas you're on the board all the time'.

Children in Public Spaces

Around the same time, a series of posts about unaccompanied children on or near the beach appeared on the Notice Board. Just before New Year, a woman posted a question: 'I'm seeing a lot of ambulances and police at the bridge at the vlei,[6] what is going on?' In the comment section it soon became clear that one or more young children had died while playing around the bridge. Some said they had been jumping off the bridge into the shallow water. Initially comments sought to assign responsibility for the deaths: the parents should have been present; the children from townships who do not know how to swim should not be near water; passers-by who had seen the children blamed themselves for not having stopped them. The tragedy was also shared as a newspaper article in the comments, and it emerged that the two boys were cousins, six and eight years old, and came from the informal settlement in Vrygrond neighbouring Muizenberg village. The posts and comments about the deaths then turned from discussing responsibility to expressing condolences and sympathy. Dozens of comments poured in with crying emojis, 'OMG so sad' and prayers and thoughts for the families of the children. The following weekend several memorial pictures of the dead boys were shared in the group, as their families held funerals and memorial services. Comments in the Facebook group described the boys as 'little angels' now 'sleeping in heaven'.

Danielle who had started the Notice Board mentioned the drowning incident as drawing forth the positive sides of the group, moral support and sympathy in times of crisis: 'You see people just coming together, with the help and – if an accident has been reported, like they sympathise with you. ... You saw everyone come together in the comments, it is all: "Rest in peace", like, it was cute. ... It was still going on weeks later, it was still comments like: "How is the family doing?" and stuff'. The dynamic shifts in the content of posts and comments about the accident with the children highlight the fluid nature of community on the Notice Board. A year later I met the mother of one of the drowned boys, and it did not seem that the sympathies had turned into material support. She was not herself a Facebook user, and struggled to provide for her other children, living in a shack in the informal settlement of Vrygrond, while fighting a losing battle against addiction to alcohol and crystal meth (locally known as *tik*).

Members of the Notice Board reflected on the status of unaccompanied children in public spaces and morally included the family of the drowned children in the community, and this to Danielle was an expression of the strength of the community. But the moral online 'coming together' did not mean that the community manifested itself in tangible ways for the bereft families for whom the emojis on the group had cried. The community in its outpouring of sympathy confirmed the moral belonging among the Facebook group members, while inadvertently exposing the rifts of inequality across space, race and class and the exclusion of poor black people from the space that makes up Muizenberg.

Petty Crime and Theft

A few days into January, a woman posted to the Muizenberg Notice Board a testimonial about being attacked and robbed at the local shopping centre. She described coming out of the supermarket with her groceries and being held up by a group of youths with knives as she was walking to her car. Her story emphasised the fact that several people walked right past her while she was being robbed, but they did not intervene. The comments expressed sympathy, and some called for more 'security' at the shopping centre because this was not the first time that someone had been robbed or attacked in the parking lot. Some speculated that the cause of these incidents was the proximity to the poor area of Vrygrond, while others blamed the many (black) young men who loitered around the entrance to the shopping area, as well as the many (black) men who spent their days sitting at the roadside of the adjacent M5 highway, many of whom were also residents of Vrygrond.

As the comments came in, some began to call for a boycott of the shopping centre until the security problem was resolved, and suggested meetings with the management of the mall and the chain stores within it. 'We need to take our communities back', wrote an elderly white woman. 'They rob their own people all these years, and getting away with it, and now they are going after bigger targets', wrote a coloured woman. Here, like with the litter on the beach, black poor people were evoked as a generic category of destructive, intrusive outsiders to the community.

Other posts in the following weeks documented experiences of local residents and tourists who had been mugged while walking on the beach or in shopping areas around Muizenberg. Some of these posts were shared immediately after the crime happened and described the incident, the scene and the perpetrators with the aim of warning others. These posts were met with outpourings of sympathy but also intense debates about how to address the appearance of the perpetrators. Some members of the board objected to using the racial categories used by the apartheid regime and accused those who did describe their assailants as 'coloured', 'African' or simply 'BM' (Black Male) of being racist. The admin Amy understood the concern and explained to me that it is racist to identify people only by 'race': 'If you post that there is a suspicious looking African man walking down the street, well, what is it that makes him look suspicious? That he is black? That he has a knife in his hands and blood dripping off his shirt? ... You know there are still South Africans who immediately they see a black person in a suburban area, they say: "What are you doing here?!" They can't for the life of them imagine that the person actually lives there'. The apartheid regime, its language and the spatial segregation according to 'race' appeared to still haunt the debates on the Notice Board in 2017.

Danielle was frustrated by the debate and logged off for the day: 'I was just like, with the group: I am done, I have seen it all'. She was less concerned about the problem of race in the Facebook group than her white fellow admins: 'I don't think it was that. That racist. ... But then people got a bit too emotional about it'. As a woman of colour herself, she seemed set on pragmatically moving on from the structural legacy of apartheid: 'The thing is, everything is always gonna be about race, so – what's the point, like...'.

Danielle would rather have focused on how the Notice Board had been a site for showing the positive sides of Muizenberg. 'There's crime everywhere. As long as the community stands here the way it used to, then that's cool, that's actually the most important part.' An instantiation of the community coming together, for Danielle, was that residents through the Notice Board and WhatsApp groups had formed walking groups that met by the beach and walked together, decreasing the risk of being mugged.

Banal Activism: Turning the Private Inside Out

Here I wish to stay with Danielle's observation that on the matter of racism, some group members were 'a bit too emotional' in their shared posts. The personal experiences and emotions of residents in the Muizenberg area were at the centre of the contestation of community in the cases I have brought forward here. At times, the posts attracted dozens of comments with similar kinds of content: emotions, other personal experiences or moral judgements of the original post and its posters. It is easy to dismiss these genres of self-writing and commenting on social media as effects of global neoliberalism turning affect into political currency.

As Bystrom and Nuttall (2013) observe about contemporary artistic expressions and activism in South Africa, 'publics of intimate exposure' are emerging as political practice in South Africa. Their mediated context ties in with globally circulated media forms like soap operas, reality television, YouTube, art and literature, but they are rooted in and given meaning by the specific context of post-apartheid South Africa (Bystrom and Nuttall, 2013; see also Bystrom, 2013). Where the formal public sphere is dominated by spectacular aesthetics of activism (Ndebele, 1994), other, less remarkable spaces emerge in which affect and subjectivity dominate the forms of public expression. This turn to the personal and intimate is perhaps a necessary move after the apartheid regime in which the individuality of the self was denied by racial categories (Hamilton, 2009, p. 368). Opening the spaces between private and the public sites of communication in social media may be driven by attempts to redefine relations of social action to reach beyond race, but, as Danielle remarked, it is difficult to escape. Social media and groups like the Muizenberg Notice Board are in their own way a public site of intimate exposure with political significance.

Daniel Miller and colleagues have aptly defined social media as 'the colonization of the space between traditional broadcast and private dyadic communication' (Miller et al., 2016). In the space between the completely public traditional broadcast, such as television or radio, and the private one-to-one communication, like a phone call, the internet has given rise to a plethora of sites, platforms and apps. By focusing on the uses rather than the specific infrastructures or functionalities of sites and platforms, this definition asks us to explore how people associate with one another, things and ideas in these newly colonised media spaces. One characteristic of social media is what we might call 'scalable sociality' (Miller et al., 2016) along two axes: from the most private to the most public; from the smallest group to the largest group.

In the context of South Africa, it is worth noting that the introduction of internet-enabled mobile phones and smartphones has significantly increased internet use: 9.1 per cent of the population used the internet in 2008, rising to 34 per cent in 2011. In 2016, more than 50 per cent of South Africans were internet users.[7] Since most people access the internet on their mobile phones by buying data by the megabyte, 'light' platforms like WhatsApp and Facebook Zero (a version of Facebook based on text, for free use) are for some the main options to get 'connected'. The messaging platform WhatsApp is the most used social media platform in the country, followed by Facebook (fourteen million monthly users in 2016), Twitter, LinkedIn and Instagram.[8] In Muizenberg, using Facebook seemed to be a leisure activity associated with the consumption of data, something to do for entertainment during free time and when bored at work, or in restaurants or coffee shops where there might be free WiFi. During my fieldwork I also interviewed residents of Vrygrond, the poor area of Reconstruction and Development Programme (RDP) housing and informal settlements in Muizenberg. Though some had Facebook profiles, residents in the area mainly used the internet on their phones to chat to their families and friends on WhatsApp as well as to follow group chats like community and church groups.

Yet the newly colonised spaces between private and public in social media are sites for intimate exposure that should not be dismissed as politically irrelevant, and I suggest seeing the Muizenberg Notice Board as a site of banal online activism. Smith coined the term 'banal activism' to describe Tory Party members' retreat to 'practices that scholars of Western politics tend to overlook because they more often resemble the mundane activities of paperwork and petty bureaucracy' (Smith, 2011, p. 2) in the wake of a historical defeat in Scotland in 1997. By looking at the 'discursive artefacts' that the party members produced – leaflets, brochures, surveys and the like – Smith analyses political knowledge practices that might have remained invisible to conventional analytical approaches to political activism (2011, p. 7). While the 'banal activism' of my fellow residents in Muizenberg on the Facebook Notice Board was not formal political activism, the turn to petty issues and familiar, seemingly safe practices in the face of complete defeat on the political scene might resonate with the general political context in South Africa. Many of the residents I met in Muizenberg were disenchanted with formal politics at both the national and regional level. Retreating to a focus on a smaller scale and engaging with 'community' as existing in the realm between private and public, activism in everyday, personal forms of expression might be etching out new spaces for hopes for political change.

When trying to understand the internet as a site for activism, there is much value, John Postill claims, in studying these kinds of 'banal activism', the activism of 'seemingly mundane issues' (2008, p. 419; 2011). In his examination of how the internet is localised by residents in the model neighbourhood of Subang Jaya in Kuala Lumpur, he uses the term as a lens through which to understand their engagements with the development of the area both online and offline. Taking up this perspective on online activism requires us not only to place activism in context, but to approach activism *as* context, something completely normal and everyday.

Postill (2008) dismisses the usefulness of social scientific concepts of community versus network in the study of online activism and, inspired by Bourdieu, proposes the idea of a 'field of residential affairs'. In the Muizenberg Notice Board, community itself was the explicit aim and means of action, and should not be dismissed from the discussion of the banal activism of the Facebook group members. Community as an ethnographic concept was constitutive of the field of residential affairs, as it 'signal[s] fields of complex processes through which sociality is sought, rejected, argued over, realized, interpreted, exploited or enforced' (Amit, 2002, p. 14). Thus, the Muizenberg Notice Board adds a Capetonian perspective to online banal activism and digital localisation in neighbourhoods worldwide. As residents contest community as the basis for social relations in shared space on the Muizenberg Facebook group, the juxtaposition of scalable sociality in social media and in community demonstrates a capacity to turn the public and private inside out. The banal online activism of Muizenberg seems to point to how what we share on social media entails a moral encompassment (Miller, 2012, p. 158) that gives these sharings political significance. Residents' affect-driven and personal stories on the Muizenberg Notice Board are, I suggest, experiments with community that emerges in everyday experience rather than conventional political rhetoric. This kind of banal online activism paints a messy picture of urban sociality after apartheid, one that by necessity encompasses tensions between different forms of inclusion and exclusion, with 'race' at the centre.

Community and Sharing Space in a Divided City

In the banal online activism of the Notice Board, what seems to animate the sharing of personal experiences is a concern for the community as an ideal of urban sociality. The narrative posts do not only describe boundaries and breaches of community, they also describe the norms from which the breaches happen. What might loosely be termed as mundane middle-class values in the Facebook group become the nexus upon which to base human-spatial relations in the city. The ability to participate in and express opinions about mundane middle-class activities is what allows residents to be members of 'the community'. In the stories shared in the cases above, particular everyday activities are the vantage point: taking one's dog for a walk, taking one's family out for leisure activities, going shopping at the shopping centre, or taking a leisurely walk on the beach. When these mundane middle-class activities are interrupted or breached, there is a basis for mobilising, discussing and negotiating human-spatial relations in the name of community welfare. There are some things, people and ideas that are out of place in Muizenberg and they need to be removed or alter the way they exist in the space there. In all three cases, the adjacent black, poor and partly informal settlement of Vrygrond in implicit or explicit ways provides the discursive and imaginative ground, a generic Other, for drawing these boundaries: the many black guests coming down for Christmas, the unsupervised children who died, and the unemployed black men waiting at the roadside. While the relationship between Muizenberg as distinct from Vrygrond was rarely questioned on the Notice Board, more abstract discussions were raised about how to deal with race, class and space in a post-apartheid city. The ideal of community and the unquestionable objective of wanting to have a 'community' puts at stake but somehow also entrenches the violent ways in which the city continues to be racially, economically and socially divided.

The contestation of community sociality on the Muizenberg Notice Board group is, I have suggested here, part of wider currents of turning the private and the public inside out, of making the political personal, in the political realms of the New South Africa. It is so in unremarkable and mundane ways, often enforcing middle-class norms through the concept of the community. Yet it is also a space in which these norms are challenged and discussed, a space of scalable socialites in which residents can engage looming issues of race and territorial marginalisation in a public forum.

Although the turn to affect in unspectacular sites of public deliberation offers no clear solution to co-existence and community, perhaps the focus on the personal, the intimate, is an attempt at 'rebuilding the self' and a site of hope for creating new kinds of connections to others (Bystrom and Nuttall, 2013, p. 323). Seeing the Muizenberg group as a site in which affect and emotion play a role expands the notion of banal online activism to capture how the people who post and share about mundane suburban issues draw lines of inclusion and exclusion through the post-apartheid geographies of Cape Town. But such a view also points to the awkward and uneasy aspects of these practices. The admins of the Muizenberg Notice Board seemed to be aware of the complexities of being and making community online in one of the world's most unequal cities. Danielle, who had founded the Facebook group, summed up how she felt about the seemingly irreconcilable forces involved in sharing space by suggesting a tagline for the group: 'Muizenberg – complicated, but okay', she laughed.

Acknowledgements

I would like to thank residents and friends in Muizenberg with the hope that they will continue to hold the community spirit high, as they engage with the difficult questions of sharing space in Cape Town. Thanks to MediAfrica colleagues, Francis Nyamnjoh, Steffen Jensen and James Siguru Wahutu for their comments on previous drafts of this chapter, to Shari Thanjan for her unwavering support, and to the Norwegian Research Council for financial support for fieldwork in South Africa and for supporting the overall project, New Media Practices in a Changing Africa (grant no. FriPro 240714).

Nanna Schneidermann was previously a postdoctoral researcher in the MediAfrica project in the Section for Development Studies at Oslo Metropolitan University and at the University of Cape Town Department of Anthropology. She is currently Assistant Professor in Anthropology at Aarhus University.

Notes

1. As the chairwoman of the local historical society notes, this version of the history of Muizenberg leaves out the history of what went before the colonisation of the Cape.
2. See https://census2011.adrianfrith.com/place/199050 (accessed 20 September 2019).
3. Names have been changed to protect the identity of research participants. Racial categories are difficult and tension fraught in the context of South Africa. I try here to use the categories used by my interlocutors themselves when self-identifying and identifying others.
4. The group was within the Facebook platform called a 'closed group'. The content of the group was accessible to members and only members could 'post' in the group's newsfeed. It was a two-step process to become a member: the user who wished to join applied by clicking the 'join' button on the group page and an admin then accepted, ignored or rejected the new member. The admins could delete posts and comments and they could close posts for comments so that the post remained visible but users could not add comments.
5. Quotes from the Facebook group have been anonymised by paraphrasing.
6. Vlei is a South African term for pond or marshlands.

7. See http://www.internetworldstats.com/af/za.htm (accessed 20 September 2019).
8. See https://businesstech.co.za/news/general/128584/massive-rise-in-facebook-users-in-south-africa/ (accessed 20 September).

References

Amit, V. 2002. 'Reconceptualizing Community', in V. Amit (ed.), *Realizing Community: Concepts, Social Relationships and Sentiments.* London: Routledge, pp. 1–20.

———. 2010. 'Community as "Good to Think With": The Productiveness of Strategic Ambiguities', *Anthropologica* 52(2): 357–63.

Bénit-Gbaffou, C. 2009. 'Who Controls the Streets? Crime, "Communities" and the State in Post-Apartheid Johannesburg', in F. Locatelli and P. Nugent (eds), *African Cities: Competing Claims on Urban Spaces,* vol. 3. Leiden: Brill Publishers, pp. 55–81.

Bosch, T. 2017. 'Twitter Activism and Youth in South Africa: The Case of #RhodesMustFall', *Information, Communication & Society* 20(2): 221–32.

———. 2018. 'Digital Media and Political Citizenship: Facebook and Politics in South Africa', in B. Mutsvairo and B. Karam (eds), *Political Communications in Africa: From Mandela to Magufuli.* London: Palgrave.

Buur, L., and S. Jensen. 2004. 'Introduction: Vigilantism and the Policing of Everyday Life in South Africa', *African Studies* 63(2): 139–52.

Bystrom, K. 2013. 'Johannesburg Interiors', *Cultural Studies* 27(3): 333–56.

Bystrom, K., and S. Nuttall. 2013. 'Introduction: Private Lives and Public Cultures in South Africa', *Cultural Studies* 27(3): 307–32.

Cohen, A.P. 1985. *The Symbolic Construction of Community.* London: Psychology Press.

Constitution of the Republic of South Africa. 1996. http://www.justice.gov.za/legislation/constitution/SAConstitution-web-eng.pdf (accessed 20 September 2019)

Del Vicario, M., F. Zollo, G. Caldarelli, A. Scala and W. Quattrociocchi. 2017. 'Mapping Social Dynamics on Facebook: The Brexit Debate', *Social Networks* 50: 6–16.

De Villiers, J. 2017. 'SAHRC to Investigate Helen Zille's Colonialism Tweets', *NEWS24,* 21 April. http://www.news24.com/SouthAfrica/News/sahrc-to-investigate-helen-zilles-colonialism-tweets-20170421 (accessed 1 February 2018).

Ernst, N., S. Engesser, F. Büchel, S. Blassnig and F. Esser. 2017. 'Extreme Parties and Populism: An Analysis of Facebook and Twitter across Six Countries', *Information, Communication & Society* 20(9): 1347–64.

Hamilton, C. 2009. 'Uncertain Citizenship and Public Deliberation in Post-Apartheid South Africa', *Social Dynamics* 35(2): 355–74.

Jensen, S. 2004. 'Claiming Community: Local Politics on the Cape Flats, South Africa', *Critique of Anthropology* 24(2): 179–207.

Laclau, E. 1996. *Emancipation(s).* London: Verso Books.

Miller, D. 2012. 'Social Networking Sites', in H. Horst and D. Miller (eds), *Digital Anthropology.* Oxford: Berg Publishers, pp. 146–61.

Miller, D., E. Costa, N. Haynes, T. McDonald, R. Nicolescu, J. Sinanan, J. Spyer, S. Venkatraman and X. Wang. 2016. *How the World Changed Social Media.* London: UCL Press.

Ndebele, N.S. 1994. *South African Literature and Culture: Rediscovery of the Ordinary.* Manchester: Manchester University Press.

Nkuna, L., P.P. Frassinelli and C. Runciman. 2017. 'Survey Sheds Light on Who Marched gainst Zuma and Why', *Mail and Guardian,* 22 April 2017. https://mg.co.za/article/2017-04-22-survey-sheds-light-on-who-marched-against-zuma-and-why (accessed 30 January 2018).

Nyamnjoh, F.B. 2016. *#RhodesMustFall: Nibbling at Resilient Colonialism in South Africa.* Bamenda: Langaa RPCIG.

Owen, J. 2015. *Congolese Social Networks: Living on the Margins in Muizenberg, Cape Town.* Lanham, MD: Lexington Books.

Petrus, T. 2016. 'Globalism vs Culture(s): A Critique of Transculturalism and the One World, One Culture Globalist Narrative in Africa', *International Social Science Journal* 66(219–20): 39–48.

Postill, J. 2008. 'Localizing the Internet beyond Communities and Networks', *New Media & Society* 10(3): 413–31.

———. 2011. *Localizing the Internet: An Anthropological Account,* vol. 5. Oxford: Berghahn Books.

Rose, N. 1996. 'The Death of the Social? Re-figuring the Territory of Government', *International Journal of Human Resource Management* 25(3): 327–56.

Smith, A. 2011. *Devolution and the Scottish Conservatives: Banal Activism, Electioneering and the Politics of Irrelevance.* Oxford: Oxford University Press.

Steenkamp, M., and N. Hyde-Clarke. 2014. 'The Use of Facebook for Political Commentary in South Africa', *Telematics and Informatics* 31(1): 91–97.

Thompson, L., C. Tapscott and P.T.D. Wet. 2017. 'An Exploration of the Concept of Community and Its Impact on Participatory Governance Policy and Service Delivery in Poor Areas of Cape Town, South Africa', *Politikon* 45(2): 1–15.

Thornton, R., and M. Ramphele. 1988. 'The Quest for Community' in R. Thornton, E. Boonzaier and J. Sharp (eds), *South African Keywords: The Uses and Abuses of Political Concepts.* Johannesburg: David Phillip, pp. 29–39.

CHAPTER 7

From No Media to All Media

Domesticating New Media in a Kalahari Village

Jo Helle-Valle

Introduction

This chapter discusses the social significance of media in a village in the Kalahari over a period of almost three decades. In this formulation lie the following ambitions: I want to provide an overall, nuanced description of the village's media ecology; I apply a historical perspective; and I want to say something about media's impact – in what ways and to what extent the changes the village has gone through are caused by new media. The chapter rests on three analytical premises: to understand media's social significance, one needs to study media practices; practices are always particular and embedded; and in order to say something meaningful about its significance, we need to confront the issue of causality.

As a result of Africa, like the rest of the world, having gone through a media revolution, research interest in media's impact on development processes has exploded. This interest rests on an idea that new media makes a difference, that it does something with society that would otherwise not have taken place. This constitutes two challenges: to establish what changes have actually taken place, and to link media's role to these changes. If we are content with statistical approaches, these challenges should not be insurmountable, as long as the numbers are available. Historical data sets and creative uses of regression analysis might give indications of media's impact on social development. However, the value of this approach rests on the assumptions that media can be treated as a variable, and that the quantitative data are available and reliable. I will return to these issues shortly, but to state my position: quantitative data from Africa are notoriously unreliable (Jerven, 2015), and it makes little analytical sense to treat media as a variable. We should definitely make use of numbers, where they are available – although critically and selectively – but they give meaning only when they are used against the background of intimate, ethnographic knowledge.

To emphasise ethnographic knowledge means to insist on the specificity of practice, that two situations that appear at first sight to be similar cannot necessarily be analysed as such. Thus, generalisation is problematic. On the other hand, as ethnographic knowledge implies taking the actors' points of view seriously, to ascertain whether *they* see the situations as similar and hence act accordingly, such approaches deliver the key to grasp patterns and understand changes. Returning to the theme discussed here, we need solid knowledge of the fabrics and workings of a given social site, both from before the media revolution and after. If a researcher wants to study the impact of media, without solid historical knowledge of the given locality, s/he is faced with a crushing methodological challenge: how to know what changes have actually taken place. Without data for real diachronic comparison, one is left making logical inferences ('new media play this or that role in contemporary social life, hence without these media sociality must have been more like …', and so on) or relying on narratives – on people's accounts of how it was before, as compared to now. I will in no way dismiss these as methods and analytical strategies but they obviously have their weaknesses. The ideal situation is to have been doing fieldwork at the same site before and after the introduction of new media – thus enabling a direct comparison between two relevant social situations (cf. Holy, 1987).

I am in the fortunate position of having done fieldwork in the same location 'before and after'. I conducted my first fieldwork in a village in the Botswana part of the Kalahari in 1990 and my – so far – last field visit was in 2018.[1] This gives me a personal experience of the changes that have taken place. I have seen gradual, and abrupt, changes occurring over a period of nearly three decades. This provides me with insights that enable me to better understand the interrelatedness of various types of changes, as well as the various mechanisms that have generated changes. And – just as importantly – it has also enabled me to see facets of sociality that have not changed.

However, being in such a fortunate position in no way solves all the challenges related to understanding new media's roles in a changing sociality. For one, media are not one entity – they are newspapers delivered from the capital to certain outlets, then read by relatively few villagers; TV programmes watched on TV sets inside households; individuals using Facebook and WhatsApp; texting on SMS; and RFID (Radio Frequency IDentification) tags clipped into the ears of cattle – to mention just a few. Thus, one term covers a heterogeneous set of materialities and practices. Moreover, we cannot isolate media and measure their impact on sociality because media are by necessity parts of wider practices. Media are means, which means that they are put to uses that have nothing to do with the devices themselves. Thus, to understand the social significance of media, one needs to anchor media uses to the specific socio-cultural and practical contexts of which they are part. For this reason, media cannot be treated as a discrete variable.

Secondly, there is the problem of causality. Quantitatively oriented researchers happily map and measure causality (although there is much to be said about how they do it). However, social scientists who are hermeneutically oriented, like myself, are wary of using the term. Our position is that there are such infinite numbers of practices that together constitute such a complex web of interrelated forces that the issue of causality is best left in peace. However, as I have argued elsewhere (Helle-Valle, 2019), wilfully ignoring causality is to throw the baby out with the bath water. Although we acknowledge that searching for causality in the sense that the hard sciences and economists relate to it is a futile and misplaced endeavour, this does not mean that we should leave it out altogether, because we do actually propose causalities all the time, we just disguise them through the use of vague phrasing. What I propose is to introduce the idea of 'tendential causality' (see ibid., and the introductory chapter in this volume) – not to postulate absolute, mechanical causality but to focus on how certain outputs will *tend* to emerge from certain inputs. For instance, that it is usually the resourceful who will benefit from a new technology like ICTs, that weak governance will *tend* to hamper the full economic potential of new media, and so on. These are reasonable assumptions but they are not laws in a scientific sense and their truth content needs to be investigated.[2]

My ambition is to apply this mode of reasoning in my presentation of the village's media ecology – to suggest some media-related *social mechanisms* (Hedström and Swedberg, 1998) that can help explain how the village has changed and what media's roles are. I will do this by describing how the village was almost three decades before this chapter was written, then describe it today, and then present some media-relevant numbers as well as ethnographic data. I will use these data to suggest some types of social mechanisms or dynamics that contribute to understanding the causative role of new media.

Before I start on this, I need to provide some facts about this chapter's methodological foundation. I have done in total almost two years of fieldwork in this particular village.[3] On my first visit, I also conducted a comprehensive survey of all the households in the village (n=442). This covered a wide range of topics, some of which provide relevant information for understanding the media situation. In 2016, my colleague Ardis Storm-Mathisen and I conducted a new survey in the village, in which some questions were related to the 1990 survey and some more specifically oriented towards the media situation.

Background and the Village

Botswana is a special country in Africa. It was one of the poorest and is now one of the wealthiest on the continent. This is due to two factors: firstly, vast amounts of minerals, principally diamonds, and increasingly also tourism are behind a steadily growing economy (National Development Plan [NDP], 2016); and secondly, four decades of uninterrupted civilian leadership, with low levels of corruption and state malpractice, progressive social policies and substantial capital investment have created one of the most stable regimes in Africa. A significant trait for the context of this chapter is that Botswana is a very rich state but has a relatively poor population. Moreover, the wealth is among the most unevenly distributed, with a Gini coefficient of above 60 (World Bank, 2017). This situation is to some extent countered by an impressive system of social services: everyone over the age of sixty-five is eligible for an old age pension, there is an efficient system of destitute allowances, drought relief programmes are in operation more often than not and health services and education are free (NDP, 2016).

For many years, the government has put high priority on investing in ICT infrastructure (Botswana Government, 2016, p. 80; Esselaar and Sebusang, 2013). This has led to a relatively well-developed ICT infrastructure. However, the use of this infrastructure is relatively low, especially in remote areas such as the village described here, first of all because the cost of telephone and internet services is such that parts of the population cannot afford more than sporadic use of new media (e.g. Research ICT Africa, 2017; see also Storm-Mathisen and Helle-Valle's chapter in this book).

The village from which this chapter draws its ethnographic data is Letlhakeng, a sub-district capital, approximately 120 km from the capital. Despite its size and its administrative status, most Batswana consider it to be remote and backward – a Kgalagadi village. On my first visit, in 1990, it took almost four hours by car to reach the village from the capital. It was a large village by African standards, housing about 3500 people, but relatively small by Botswana standards.[4] There were few cars on the dirt roads into and in the village, no sewage system, no electricity, only a few schools and some government offices. There were three television sets in the whole of the village, two in schools and one belonging to the household of the richest man in the village. However, as there were no TV signals, they only functioned as screens for VHS players. Due to the lack of electricity, the sets could be watched only to the sound of noisy diesel aggregates. In the schools they were used infrequently, to show tapes of educational programmes for children; in the household it was used for watching films and South African soap operas.

Newspapers were rare and always a day old. The only paper was the government's *Daily News*, brought in from the capital, arriving one or more days late but distributed for free. However, functional literacy was relatively low, and the stories in the paper were of little interest to villagers, so newspaper consumption was low.

Telephones were also rare. Some, but not all public offices had one, but their use was restricted to a few members of staff. A handful of private households had one too but the service was expensive and unreliable. Thus, for most villagers, dialogical contact with the outside – for instance the regional capital, the national capital and South Africa – had to be made either by travel or by letter.

Radios were the most common ICT in the village. According to our survey conducted in November 1990, 44 per cent of the households owned a radio. Thus, it was common to hear radios playing when walking around in the village during the day, even though only one station was accessible, broadcasting news and mostly Botswana and South African music (Helle-Valle, 1997).

Arriving in the same village in the 2010s is a very different story. Paved roads bring you from the capital in less than two hours, there is now road lighting (powered by solar batteries), and a sewage system exists, although most households are still not attached to it. The village has grown to about eight thousand people. While the visual impression in the 1990s was a village consisting mostly of traditional round huts with thatched roofs (*rondavel* and *sesowa*) but with some modern buildings in between, the overall visual impression in the 2010s is a lot more mixed – almost exclusively one-storey buildings, but now a large number of 'modern' brick buildings with corrugated iron or slated roofs, as well as a handful of huge commercial buildings. Electricity wires criss-cross the air above people and buildings. Thus, on the face of it, the site has been transformed from a sleepy, remote village to a semi-urban site.[5]

As to the media situation in the village, the meagre access a few decades back has been supplanted by a rich and varied assortment of information platforms and content. In the 2010s, four or five different Botswana papers, as well as a few South African ones, can be bought in many of the several dozen shops in the village. While radio use and ownership has only marginally increased (households owning a radio increased from 44 per cent to 58 per cent between 1990 and 2016), TV ownership has exploded. In 2016, 54 per cent of the households owned a functioning TV set (up from 0.2 per cent in 1990). And, of course, mobile phones – which did not exist in 1990 – are now available to almost every adult in the village (for a more detailed account, see Storm-Mathisen and Helle-Valle's chapter in this book).

These are some tangible facts about the village that constitute the basis for this chapter – the same site separated by almost three decades. However, to explain this transformation, and more specifically to expound on the effect of a new media ecology on sociality, is an entirely different issue. As I have already pointed out, I have no illusions of providing a concise and exact account of media's roles. What I will do is to approach this empirical and analytical challenge by providing different accounts – perspectival angles, one might say – of media practices in the village. I will do this by first giving some facts (to the extent that statistical material can be given such a flattering characterisation) about who uses what kinds of media for what purposes, and then discuss how these different practices amount to overall media-related fields of practice.

But first I must expand on the analytical foundation of this endeavour.

Analytical Premises

Media are both (information and communication) technologies – material objects and networks – and mediators of meaningful messages (content). This 'double articulation' (Silverstone et al., 1992, p. 28) implies that media's social significance is both as tangible objects and as means to mediate 'texts'. This has several analytical implications. As high-tech, material objects, they must be purchased and the technology needs to work. As a medium, they need to be put to some use – something needs to be mediated. The material aspect is in no way insignificant. A new smartphone is expensive to buy, beyond the means of many, and to use the phone of course costs money. Moreover, mobile phones need electronic signals to function, which are not available if one moves a couple of kilometres out of the village. Thus, practicalities shape use.

As mediums, media are mediating something. The extent and ways in which media are put to use by people are also linked to their everyday concerns. Therefore, in order to see the social significance of media, we need to look at how they relate to people's life worlds. To have such roles, media need to be conceptually and practically *domesticated* by their users; in cultural terms they must be tamed, in practical terms they must represent some kind of added value (Silverstone et al., 1992). In other words, we cannot take for granted that new media are actually put to use, nor can we predict how and to what ends they are used. The analytical implication of this is that (i) in order to understand the social significance of media, we need to look at their uses; and (ii) we need to understand the uses media are put to by way of focusing on people's perspectives and concerns (cf. Helle-Valle, 2010). The first amounts to approaching media from a practice perspective (cf., e.g., Bräuchler and Postill, 2010), the second requires ethnographic methods. In other words, we need to apply what Morley (2009) labels a non-media-centric media study, emphasising the fact that media are used for heterotelic purposes.

Media Use in the Village

The village consists of about eight thousand people living in approximately 1200 households. We have survey data on all types of media technologies, from newspapers and radios to computers, tablets and mobile phones. The general trend is an increase in ownership, access and consumption. However, a conspicuous trait is the almost total dominance of the mobile phone as a device for digital media. Very few own other digital technologies (like computers and tablets) and about 97 per cent of all internet traffic takes place on mobile phones (Central Statistics Office, Botswana [CSO], 2013).[6]

The signal coverage for mobile telephony is good in the village proper but one cannot travel far before signals disappear. Our own survey, conducted in 2016, showed that 96 per cent of the households in the village owned at least one mobile phone, and the average number of mobile phones in households was 3.5, with almost four sim cards. Fifty-eight per cent of the respondents stated that they can access the internet on their own phone. On the other hand, a negligible number of villagers own computers or tablets.

Households' average cost for mobile use was 200 Pula a month,[7] while their total cost of ICT services was 235 Pula. The lion's share of the cost difference between the last two figures is television expenses. In fact, more than half of the households in the village had TVs. Ninety per cent agreed with the statement 'I cannot live without my mobile phone'. However, if we break it down to what they use their phones for, more interesting patterns appear. While only 37 per cent said that they used their phones for work-related activities,[8] and 13 per cent stated that they used the internet for work-related activities, 81 per cent said that they used their phones for communicating with kin and 40 per cent stated that they used the internet to this end. There are some obvious weaknesses in these numbers, as they do not state how much new media are used and how important they are for such purposes. Nevertheless, the figures are a clear indication of new media being more important for networking than for directly productive activities. Other numbers underscore this: 75 per cent of the respondents stated that they used mobile phone-based money transfer services ('mobile money'), 53 per cent used their phones regularly to receive or give gifts, 87 per cent used their phones to keep in touch with family and kin and 75 per cent said they used their phones for romance.

That mobile phones are used for strengthening networks is not especially surprising, but it is interesting nevertheless. In the 1990s I found that a dominant strategy in the village was to diversify in order to minimise risks (Helle-Valle, 1997, pp. 94ff), a typical orientation in peasant economies (Lipton, 1982; Sahlins, 1974). I contend that the uses of mobile phones that we find today directly reflect this orientation among the villagers. If anything, new media generate networked societies (Castells, 2010) – the speed, coordination and mobility of digital media are ideal for a population that is routinely exposed to misfortune (droughts, animal sickness, etc.). In such an economic ecology, establishing and maintaining networks through regular interactions and gift giving is the best insurance. Thus, social capital can in dire times compensate for dramatic fluctuations in economic capital (Bourdieu, 1977, p. 183; cf. also Evans-Pritchard, 1940, p. 85). Our numbers give some support to this contention: the most commonly cited activities for which villagers use their phones are funerals (86 per cent) and marriages (87 per cent). These are core kinship rituals and crucial arenas for signalling allegiance. In a local community in which most of those you interact with are related to you, it is crucial that you show your commitment to the moral community by actively attending such rituals. In fact, as in the case of funerals, which I will return to below, these rituals seem to have increased their symbolic position in the village.

In other words, our survey results, as well as our fieldwork data, show that new media are more important in managing social capital than economic. However, an important point to make is that if we take capital conversions into the analysis, we find that the economic significance of new media is in fact greater than the survey data account for. This is because it facilitates the flows of different forms of capital in ways that smooth out the ups and downs of economic uncertainty and hence have a preserving effect on (good) sociality. There are numerous mechanisms by which social capital – the networking, which is importantly facilitated by new media – is converted into economic or cultural capital. One important example is migration: finding a job outside the village (preferably in the capital or in the diamond mines in Botswana) in the old days was a laborious and uncertain task because one either had to travel in person to these sites to seek employment or depend on messages from acquaintances about an available job. These messages had to be in the form of letters sent by the postal service or giving word via a third person travelling to the village (cf. Schapera, 1947). Thus, it could take a long time before the villager showed up and the job was by that time often taken by others. Today, however, digital communication technology enables a person looking for work to receive word immediately. Thus, the network provides the relevant information, and the technology speedily transmits it.

Digital Divides?

Thus far I have presented media-relevant frequencies and suggested some mechanisms that link them to sociality. What about ownership and usage distribution? Both our ethnographic experience and survey data tell us that there are two important factors that generate inequality in media use: age and class.

Looking at age first, our survey data reveal that while 84 per cent of those younger than forty years can access the internet from their phones, only 4 per cent of those aged forty or older can do so. Turning to class, we used education as an indicator of class position. In households that had at least one member with tertiary education, almost 90 per cent had access to the internet via their mobile phone, while only about half of those households without tertiary education could do so. These are highly significant correlations (with Chi square scores of 0.0 and 0.014 respectively).

While the age differences suggest differences in competence (as we find all over the world), the class differences are of course also related to resources. Purchasing a smartphone is outside the economic reach of a substantial part of the village population. Moreover, airtime is expensive. A report from Research ICT Africa (2017, p. 13) warns that the oligarchical structure of the telecommunication sector in Botswana hampers the ICT revolution. The price profile is such that you pay for every byte you use and every minute of a call you make. Thus, for the less resourceful villager, having a smartphone in no way guarantees that you can actually use it. We found that airtime is a current concern among individuals. It is a scarce resource, and not infrequently it served as currency in many informal relationships. The value of this currency was further enhanced by the fact that free WiFi networks were almost non-existent in the village. Botswana has had a system of educational hubs spread around the country, called Kitso centres. In the village analysed here, the Kitso centre no longer existed but its functions were taken over by the village library. Inside, there were computers that could be used for free for thirty minutes, or one could access the WiFi network. However, the WiFi connection was of very low quality and the staff at the library closely monitored the use of the stationary, cable-connected computers, which made many users uncomfortable. Thus, as Larkin (2008) reminds us, media use requires working infrastructures and signals, and malfunctioning is just as significant as its functioning (see also Parks and Staroielski, 2015).

Another challenge for the poorer segment of the village is charging their phones. Our survey tells us that 54 per cent charged their phones at home – which reflects the number of households in the village that have electricity. Thus, for those without electricity in their homes, charging is obviously a practical problem and for some it also represents an additional cost.

Surprisingly, we find no significant gender difference in ownership and uses of new media. Our ethnographic data showed no discernible differences in ownership, amount or type of uses and our survey data confirmed this. The latter tells us that while 91.8 per cent of males own a phone, 91.4 per cent of women own one. It was found that 9.5 per cent of males and 5.2 per cent of females never use social platforms like Facebook. Moreover, 15.4 per cent of males and 24.5 per cent of females never use mobile money. None of these differences are statistically significant. The only use-aspect that shows statistical significance on gender is whether the person's phone can access the internet. Here we find a weak significance in that 67.4 per cent of males have a smartphone while only 50.4 per cent of females have such a phone.[9] It is also worth mentioning that all respondents held that new media are equally important to men and women.

Concerns and Institutions

Much of what has been presented above points to concerns that motivate individuals to domesticate these new technologies – foremost social and economic. It is now time to link media use more explicitly to such concerns. Obviously, they are diverse and they vary, depending on personal dispositions and social position. While some of the factors are personal and idiosyncratic, and hence difficult to handle from a sociological point of view, there are *areas* of concern that are universal – such as economic, educational, political, health and socio-existential concerns. For that reason, they often become institutionalised in some form or another. Given the very limited space a book chapter allows, I have chosen to approach villagers' concerns via the institutions that reflect such concerns. I am not arguing that, for example, the educational system is designed to fulfil people's desires. Not at all. Institutions are created to fulfil defined socio-political goals, with national, regional and/or social segments' interests in mind. What I am claiming is that such concerns are for a large part expressed in sociologically significant ways through local institutions. For instance, most local parents have a strong interest in letting their children have as good and as much of an education as possible, and when acting on those concerns they are forced to relate to the educational system. In other words, the concerns are those of the villagers, and the framework within which these concerns by necessity are enacted are local institutions. Based on my fieldwork experience, I have chosen the following institutions as central to discuss how media affect village sociality: local and regional government offices; the local health system; and the educational system.[10]

The Educational System

The village has two primary schools and one junior secondary school. They all had what were termed computer labs. In the primary schools these consisted of three or four computers, while the secondary school had an impressive, large room with several dozen computers. However, none of the labs had any computers that worked. In the primary schools, this was explained by the poor quality of the computers. We were told that the good computers went to urban schools while those distributed to the rural schools were leftovers from urban schools and government offices. In the case of the secondary school, the computers looked relatively modern but the problem was infrastructure and maintenance. Thus, the secondary school is a good example of the often vast distance between plans and official accounts (cf., e.g., Mutula et al., 2010; UNESCO, 2016) on the one hand and reality on the other. According to records, the school had solid ICT capacity. Moreover, the staff had initially told us that the school had a modern computer lab with an impressive number of machines, all connected to the internet. However, visiting the lab revealed quite another reality: the computers were there but there were no students. In fact, the lab had been closed for months because they had no staff to service the machines. In addition, the internet connection (a satellite dish) was out of order, and had been so for the last year. The school's two computer teachers therefore had to teach pupils in their classrooms about how the computers could have worked.

For the most critical voices, this is just one example of the poor quality of education locally. This has led to a 'brain drain' – typically the most gifted (and resourceful) students are sent by their parents or guardians to schools in urban centres that presumably will give their children a better chance of getting grades that will allow them to pursue tertiary education.

Local and Regional Administration Offices

All villagers relate, directly or indirectly, to public services. These are of many different kinds. We find offices that provide services for those who cultivate, for those who own domestic animals, for those who ask for destitute allowances and for various forms of support programmes for the underprivileged, to mention just a few. Moreover, the Land Board is extremely important as it allocates residence plots and cultivatable land for free to locals, which is becoming increasingly important as land is becoming more valuable. These institutions are thus meant to cater for people's economic concerns. However, new media played hardly any role in these institutions. Most offices had computers but no working data server and few printers. Thus, employees mostly write documents by hand and file them in cabinets. If they have the time and motivation, they will also write them into their computers, but this would have no current organisational advantage as their computers were not linked to servers that could bring their documents into some sort of efficiency-generating system. The mismatch between plans and reality here had serious practical repercussions. A system that was organised and staffed on the presumption that it was digitalised and hence efficient suffered greatly by not having access to these ICTs. All administrative procedures took much longer than was expected and the result was devastating for villagers. For instance, an application to the Land Board normally took several years. For young people who wanted to start farming or rearing animals, this had demoralising effects – keeping their lives in the village on hold for years, in a state of un- or underemployment.

Village Clinic

More than a decade ago, the Ministry of Health introduced a digital patient data system in which all patient data are to be entered into a secure database, enabling any authorised health worker to access them from wherever he or she is. For Botswana, with a sparse but highly mobile population, this system represents a great leap forward both in terms of service and costs. According to official records, the system is up and running but the fact is that the village clinic did not have access to the system. The clinic matron could not give a good explanation for why it was not connected. Employees conveyed that they had been promised this long ago but nothing had so far materialised. (This situation is echoed nationwide in Sebina and Grand, 2017.)

Again, the consequences are grave for villagers. It is common for them to move regularly between cities, villages and areas where they have their lands for cultivation, and to be able to be effectively serviced by the health system is crucial. This is especially important for those with HIV. The prevalence in the district is almost 20 per cent and the patients depend on regular supplies of antiretroviral treatment (ART). Moreover, as with the local administration, the health care system is organised and staffed on the presumption of digitalised handling of information. When this is not the case, patients suffer. It was a common complaint among villagers that the time it took to be admitted for care at the village clinic was far too long.

Complex Assemblages

So far I have looked at different aspects of media practices in the village individually. However, the complexities of (local) sociality are high, meaning that if we look at more complex, composite fields of practice, the overall social effects are impossible to predict. Putting together all social aspects into one, unifying picture is a great challenge. I have no pretention of doing so here; the chapter format does not allow it. Instead, I want to present two examples of how different mechanisms are activated within given fields of practice in such ways that the aggregated consequences cannot be predicted.

Burials

In 'the old days' – before technology to store dead bodies over a longer period of time was available to people in the village – funerals were swift events. The hot climate meant that the body needed to get in the ground within a few days after death. Funerals were an important social affair, and ideally all relatives were supposed to take part. However, due to the short time span between the death and the funeral, and the high degree of mobility among people, many did not make it to the ritual.

In 1990, the technology of placing the corpse in a cooler was available to villagers. This required, however, that the corpse was transported to a funeral home in the regional capital, a couple of hours' drive eastwards. The main reason for spending money on the services of funeral homes was that this gave relatives and friends around the country time to attend. The number of attendants was an expression of the standing of the deceased, thus it was important for the family to mobilise all those who felt an obligation to be present. However, communication was a problem. In cases where relatives lived elsewhere, the challenge was to communicate the death in a reliable manner and as quickly as possible. Very few had access to a telephone. In some cases, the family of the deceased had access to a phone, and knew of a phone that could be called, informing someone at the other end who knew the relative in question about the death. This person would then perhaps have to travel by bus to another village to deliver the message face to face. In cases where the relative was not too far away, a family member might him/herself travel by bus to inform them of the death, and in some instances they needed to communicate by letter. These changes in technology had three significant effects. First, the time span between the death and the funeral increased dramatically; two weeks was not uncommon. Secondly, the cost of a funeral process increased significantly. The cost of keeping the body in a cooler was substantial, the services of the funeral homes likewise, and the fact that a lot more people gathered at the funeral meant more mouths to feed, hence higher expenses. (Giving gifts at funerals was common but it did not compensate for the increased expenses.) In addition, these cost-driving mechanisms were exacerbated by the many deaths due to AIDS.

Today, with the massive use of mobile phones, the time needed to gather relatives and friends to a funeral has decreased. As a rule, people are notified within the first day as they are reachable on mobile phones. Thus, one could expect that expenses for funeral home services would decrease. However, in the meantime the ideas about what a proper funeral is have radically changed. It is now no longer acceptable to bury someone without the assistance of a funeral home. The requirements are new and more elaborate. In 1990 it was not absolutely necessary to bury the body in a coffin, and in any case most of those who did settled for a simple one that was crafted in the village. Now, in contrast, it seems that a more professionally produced coffin is a given. These are not available in the village and will normally be provided by/through the funeral home. Moreover, our latest field visits revealed another cost-driving novelty, namely photos. Hiring a professional photographer for the ritual, as well as printing expensive-looking leaflets with (sometimes photoshopped) pictures of the deceased is fast becoming the norm. (For a similar discussion on funerals and new media in Uganda, see Vokes, 2018.)

Due to these increased expenses, many poorer households/families find that funerals can be a serious burden on the household economy. To take one example: Mpho, a single mother of three, was born into a poor household and received no education above primary school. Through hard work over many years, she had built herself up to a decent economic standing. In 2007 her mother died. Although Botswana's social services can pay for funerals for the poorest, Mpho did not fall into a destitute category, and in any case it was a matter of pride to her to arrange a funeral that properly honoured her mother. The result was that all the money she had saved during the years was spent on the funeral. Moreover, because she depended on her mother to take care of her children while she worked (her work was quite some distance from the village), she also had to quit her job. Thus, her mother's death changed her from an independent, self-reliant woman (with crucial support from her mother) to a poor one who had to rely on destitute work and help from near and distant relatives.

In other words, although new technologies could have meant quicker and cheaper funerals (lower funeral home expenses), new ideas about what constitutes a proper funeral have increased the expenses significantly. What further drives the expenses related to burials are their symbolic importance. As with weddings – where the aim is not to get away with minimal expenses and few cattle paid as bride price – the funeral's lavishness is a strong public signal not only of the socio-economic standing of a family group but also of its moral status. Thus, arranging a stingy funeral lessens the group's social and cultural capital.

The changing practices and expectations related to funerals demonstrate that although new media might be a significant part of changing practices, they are always part of wider assemblages that include actors and other materialities. Thus, the constellation of the many different actors and actants interacting in a complex landscape of different dynamics and mechanisms makes the social outcome unpredictable.

Cattle and RFID Technology

Another example of the unanticipated consequences of media practices are RFID tags[11] that are inserted into the ears of cattle. The background for these are the recurring problems of foot and mouth disease that threaten to jeopardise Botswana's beef trade agreement with the EU. This prompted Botswana to introduce RFID tagging of cattle as early as 2001 as a means to control the disease. Through these identity tags, animal movement as well as sales can be effectively monitored (Government of Botswana [GoB], 2011). Today almost all cattle in Botswana are identified by RFID tags. This makes a big difference for every cattle owner, even though it is not necessarily clearly visible to them. For one, Botswana Meat Company (BMC) usually offers the best prices when farmers sell their animals, but they require the beasts to be tagged. Moreover, this tagging system has greatly improved the monitoring of cattle in general, leading, among other things, to better veterinary services. And not least, the introduction of this ID system has meant that Botswana has been able to continue its trade agreement with the EU, a fact that greatly benefits all cattle owners. An additional effect, which was not anticipated, has become evident. Due to the close monitoring of all cattle with the RFID tag, there has been a dramatic reduction (60 per cent) in cattle thefts (Practical Action, 2004). Given that cattle theft was mentioned as one of the main problems involved in practising animal husbandry in our survey in 1990, this is no small improvement.

However, if we look in more detail at farmers relating to these technologically driven services, the picture becomes much more diverse, contradictory and interesting. Let me use Gaimelwe, a villager I have known since 1990, as an example. He has lived a rather typical life for his generation: he has no education beyond primary school, he worked for many years in the gold mines in South Africa, he is divorced and he struggles to build and maintain a herd of cattle. He invested what he managed to save from his work in South Africa (which was not much as he has always been fond of women and beer) in livestock. However, this herd has fluctuated between a few dozen and almost zero over the years. Drought, insufficient access to water, sickness and theft have repeatedly led his herd to the brink of extinction. He is now over seventy years old and owns just a dozen cows.

Most, but not all of his cows are RFID tagged, and not all his beasts are vaccinated. Why not make use of free services that both aid his beasts' health (thus lowering the mortality rate) and make it possible for him to sell animals to the best buyer – the BMC? Again, the answer lies (partly) in looking beyond the official descriptions to see how the institution really works. The services are not free; there are small costs here and there. For instance, the RFID tags have to be bought and paid for by the farmer himself, and for some unexplainable reason they are not purchasable in the village. He has to travel to the capital to get them. This means that he has to take into consideration the expenses (in time and money) when making the decision to tag his cattle. He acknowledges the fact that not vaccinating his cattle increases the chance of sickness among his animals, and also that it makes it more difficult to sell them at a good price. However, to understand his practices two factors are important. For one, his relationship to his cattle is typically traditional. He does not want to sell them if he does not have to; cattle are much more than objects that can be bought and sold (Schapera, [1953] 1984).[12] This means that it is not particularly important for him to be able to sell to BMC, thus the motivation to spend time and money on travelling to the capital to buy RFID tags is not very high. Secondly, as with many others in his situation, he suspects that the authorities use these tags to survey every farmer's herd so that they can later tax them (which might very well be true). Thus, avoiding the veterinary service is a way to elude state control.

Not all owners hold this attitude to the animal services. The better education and the more capitalist attitude to animal husbandry an owner has, the higher the chances that they will eagerly make use of the services that the government provides. Gaimelwe was not among the most resourceful, and it is thus no coincidence that he never seemed able to build his herd above the bare minimum.

The purpose of presenting these two brief examples is threefold. First, it draws attention to the fact that 'new media' are much more than mobile phones and computers. Infrastructure, detection devices such as RFID and NFC (Near Field Communication technology) are only a few, but important forms of ICT – although largely invisible. Furthermore, it adds new mechanisms to the overall picture of the significance of media for development. And lastly, both examples illustrate the localisation of the global. The global is not somewhere else, or of another nature, but simply causal chains or networks that stretch out in space but with local significance. Local and global are simply analytical abstractions and should not be given explanatory power. Instead, it is by tracing networks and causal links that we discover the factual seamless connections between two constructed concepts. The cow that wanders the bush outside the village with an RFID tag in its ear connects the local (the farmer), the regional (veterinary services), the national (state legislation) and the transcontinental (trade agreement with the EU). In this way, by following actors and networks, we do away with the unfortunate distinction between micro and macro (Latour, 2005, pp. 191ff).

Concluding Reflections

This chapter shows the complexity and many-faceted quality of the village media ecology. Media – as technology and as medium – are diverse and always connected in various ways to other actors and actants. Data show that mobile phones are almost universally adopted, although economic restrictions keep media consumption down. Significantly fewer access the internet on a regular basis than the number of phones might suggest. This is due to the cost of the devices (not all can afford a smartphone), of airtime and of access to the internet.

Thus, in its own sense, the village has domesticated new media. It has been integrated into the lives of almost all villagers. Its economic relevance is, however, still slight. The bulk of media consumption is tied to networking – keeping in touch with family, sweethearts, kin and friends. However, as these networks are significant for villagers' livelihoods, it is reasonable to label such new media-supported networks as productive, as social capital. As capital, it can be converted to other forms. It can take the shape of cultural capital through, for example, education, and it can be transformed into economic capital by providing information on employment opportunities and business deals. In addition, new media are relevant for cultivators and animal owners in that public services are provided.

Although we can safely say that new media have been domesticated, we find marked digital divides within the village. As expected, age and class are the main dividing lines. More surprisingly, gender does not count for significant differences.

Lastly, villagers' eager uses of new media do not extend to institutions. Villagers still connect with public and commercial institutions mostly in analogue ways. To take one example: by far the most common complaint from youth in the village is the lack of jobs and business opportunities. Un- and underemployment are rampant and are seen as a problem by every villager – old and young, rich and poor. At the same time, there are objectively many opportunities in the form of a wide variety of support programmes financed by the state. Youth programmes finance start-ups of animal husbandry (goats), small businesses and so on. There is a Youth Office in the local administration that deals exclusively with such support. Its main job is to facilitate those in need – to inform them of the kinds of programmes that are available, the requirements for applying, the kinds of documents that need to be provided, how to fill out the application form, and follow up with courses and advice for those who receive funding. In theory, it is a generous set of opportunities for the young. The problem, unfortunately, is that the system is malfunctioning. The young complain that the officers are not available, that the information they get is scant and sometimes misleading and that it can take years before their applications are processed. So what is the problem? Too few employed, complicated and overly bureaucratised institutions and partly incompetent and demotivated staff are all factors that help to explain the poor working of the system. However, a crucial factor is the lack of information and the lack of co-ordinating information. Seeing how the staff work is telling: there is a computer in almost all offices but they are in most cases not connected to the internet or to other machines in the offices. All information must be extracted from paper documents or from non-transferrable documents on the office computer. The application forms must be filled out by hand and, worse, much of the necessary information is not available because they are offline. Thus, the funds are there but many of the prospective applicants do not get their funding due to bureaucratic malfunction. The competence of the staff is crucial but there is no doubt that the most important improvement lies in e-government – using ICTs and the internet to provide efficient governance. Most significant would be self-servicing: online application forms and easy access to all relevant information via the internet. The irony of the situation is that many of the applicants most likely have a higher competence in using these digital resources than the staff who are there to service them.

To borrow terms and perspectives from Latour: in the example above, the associations and assemblages that could have been positively facilitated by digital media are hindered by a lack of appropriate technology, and weak and inefficient ties between actors, and between actors and actants. The transformations envisioned by policy planners have not – yet – been turned into reality. Had useful content been made available to villagers, new media and the internet would most likely have made a difference. As it is now, free internet services are few and of very low quality, while functional internet is too expensive for those who have the most need for it. However, as Gaimelwe's case exemplifies, the social mechanism of the poorer and less educated not exploiting the potential of new media is not simply a question of monetary shortcomings.

He has a phone, he knows that there are possibilities within his reach for improving his own animal husbandry, but his views and way of life seem to prevent him from turning his media competence into a productive practice. Thus, the factors at work here are many and interrelated in complex ways (which reminds us why we should not treat media as a discrete variable), but the aggregate outcome is that, as a rule, the poor let opportunities go by while the educated and more resourceful seem to be able to realise the potential inherent in the technologies. For Gaimelwe the new technologies are – at best – weakly connected to his income-generating practices and therefore do not alter his strategies for making a living, and certainly not his values or perspective on life. In contrast, we met villagers who have fully integrated new media into their animal husbandry, not only by exploiting the veterinary services to the full, and buying and selling animals through various new media channels, but they also seem to have shifted their outlook from viewing their animals as symbols of a good life and hence as objects belonging to an exchange sphere of prestige objects (bride price, etc.) to the commercial sphere (cf. Barth, 1967).

For Letlhakeng, the lack of a fast and functional infrastructure is part of the picture, but more significantly, while new media have become an integrated part of the villagers' social capital, they have not yet become an integral part of the socio-cultural fabric that would have expanded their significance into the local economy. This will without doubt change – not least due to new media and technologies – but how and to what extent remains to be seen.

Acknowledgements

I am deeply indebted to the wonderful, helpful people in Letlhakeng village who did so much to help us in our endeavours. I also thank the participants at the Marrakech meeting in January 2018 for their input on an earlier version of this chapter.

Jo Helle-Valle is a social anthropologist and Professor in the Development Studies Department at Oslo Metropolitan University. He has carried out fieldwork in Botswana, Uganda, Ethiopia and Norway. His main research areas are media practices, gender, local politics and economy, and theoretical issues related to the social sciences. Helle-Valle has served as a Visiting Scholar at Harvard, Oxford, Simon Fraser University, the University of Botswana and Makerere University. He has published in journals such as *Journal of African Media Studies, Africa, Ethnos, History and Anthropology* and *New Media & Society.*

Notes

1. In total I have made eight field trips to the village, but did not visit the village between 1998 and 2012. In retrospect, this pause was fortunate because new media were virtually non-existent in the village in 1998, while it had arrived with full force in 2012. Thus, visiting in 2012 gave me an acute awareness of the novelty of new media.
2. These are arguments put forth by scholars such as Elster (2007), Hedström and Swedberg (1998) and Harré (2009) and are akin to perspectives advocated by Latour (2005).
3. Field visits were undertaken in 1990, 1992, 1993, 1998, 2012, 2015–2016, 2017 and 2018.
4. Historically, demographic patterns in Botswana have been rather unusual: the chief's need to control people generated a pattern of large villages. Seasonal movements to lands and cattle posts had to be permitted by the chief (cf., e.g., Schapera, [1938] 1955).
5. In addition to the striking visual changes, the *sound* of modernity is also striking compared to before. While the dominant sounds in the village in 1990 were human voices and animal noises, the sound of cars and other vehicles is striking in 2017. Moreover, nightlife in 1990 was quiet – except for music from cassette players in the five bars audible to neighbours until 9 p.m. Today, electronically mediated music can be heard all over the village, and long into the night.
6. Although mobile phones are the dominant media device, it is important to acknowledge that a too-close focus on the type of device is of limited value. To take one example: as already mentioned, radios seem to have lost their importance over time. This is true as far as technology is concerned, but it is obvious that a lot of the media content that is associated with the radio is now transmitted by smartphones.
7. At the time of the survey, the exchange rate was approximately 10 Pula for one US dollar.
8. This figure breaks down to animal husbandry (43 per cent), cultivation (47 per cent), small-scale business (31 per cent) and formal employment (32 per cent).
9. However, this gendered difference is mostly a spurious effect. With very few exceptions, villagers define households as male-headed if an adult man is part of the household. This means that female-headed households by emic definitions have fewer producers and hence are poorer. Therefore, the effect we find on ownership of smartphones we first of all attribute to the income gap that follows from this classification and not directly to gender.
10. Political concerns and political institutions would have been a natural candidate to discuss here. These are left out however, simply because new media have not yet become a significant part of this field.
11. RFID – Radio Frequency IDentification – tags are small chips that provide unique identification via a reader (unlike barcodes, for example, which only

identify types of objects, not individual objects). As the reader is connected to a database, almost limitless amounts of information can be attached to each tag.

12. In one conversation we had, he said that he usually knew early in what is supposed to be the rainy season if it was going to be a drought year or not. He had of course experienced drought many times and every time he lost a substantial part of his herd – as they thinned, they became weak and many would then die from some sort of sickness. In addition, selling beasts in the late phase of a drought meant that you got much less as the slaughter weight would be low. I asked why he didn't sell a cow or two before the weight loss set in, so he could use the money to buy medicines and fodder for the remaining ones. Although he was an intelligent man, this logic seemed not to have occurred to him. My understanding is that it was impossible for him to treat cattle as mere commodities, buying and selling them to maximise profits.

References

Barth, F. 1967. 'Economic Spheres in Darfur', in R. Firth (ed.), *Themes in Economic Anthropology*. London: Tavistock Publications, pp. 149–74.

Botswana Government. 2016. *DRAFT: National Development Plan 11. April 2017–March 2023.* http://www.ncongo.info/wp-content/uploads/2017/02/NDP-11.pdf (accessed 15 October 2019).

Bourdieu, P. 1977. *Outline of a Theory of Practice.* Cambridge: Cambridge University Press.

Bräuchler, B. and J. Postill (eds). 2010. *Theorising Media and Practice.* Oxford: Berghahn Books.

Castells, M. 2010. *The Rise of the Network Society*, 2nd ed. Chichester: Wiley-Blackwell.

Central Statistics Office, Botswana (CSO). 2013. *Botswana Information and Communication Technology Statistics 2012.* Gaborone: Statistics Botswana.

Elster, J. 2007. *Explaining Social Behaviour.* Cambridge: Cambridge University Press.

Esselaar, S., and S. Sebusang. 2013. *Understanding What Is Happening in ICT in Botswana.* Policy Paper 1. researchICTbotswana.net.

Evans-Pritchard, E.E. 1940. *The Nuer: A Description of the Modes of Livelihood and Political Institutions of a Nilotic People.* Oxford: Oxford University Press.

Government of Botswana (GoB). 2011. *Livestock Identification and Traceback System (LITS).* http://www.gov.bw/en/Ministries–Authorities/Ministries/MinistryofAgriculture-MOA/Tools--Services/Livestock/Livestock-Identification-and-Traceability/?p_id=3191 (accessed 12 August 2018).

Harré, R. 2009. 'Saving Critical Realism', *Journal for the Theory of Social Behaviour* 39(2): 129–43.

Hedström, P., and R. Swedberg. 1998. 'Social Mechanisms: An Introductory Essay', in P. Hedström and R. Swedberg (eds), *Social Mechanisms: An Analytical Approach to Social Theory.* Cambridge: Cambridge University Press, pp. 1–31.

Helle-Valle, J. 1997. *Change and Diversity in a Kgalagadi Village, Botswana.* Oslo: SUM, University of Oslo, Dissertations and Theses, no. 1/97.

———. 2010. 'Language-Games, In/dividuals and Media Uses: What a Practice Perspective Should Imply for Media Studies', in B. Bräuchler and J. Postill (eds), *Theorising Media and Practice.* Oxford: Berghahn Books, pp. 191–211.

———. 2017. 'Media Culture in Africa? A Practice-Ethnographic Approach', in W. Willems and W. Mano (eds), *Everyday Media Cultures in Africa: Audiences and Users.* New York: Routledge, pp. 27–46.

———. 2019. 'Advocating Causal Analyses of Media and Social Change by Way of Social Mechanisms', *Journal of African Media Studies* 11(2): 143–161.

Holy, L. 1987. 'Introduction. Description, Generalisation and Comparison: Two Paradigms', in L. Holy (ed.), *Comparative Anthropology.* Oxford: Basil Blackwell, pp. 1–21.

Jerven, M. 2015. *Africa: Why Economists Get It Wrong.* London: Zed Books.

Larkin, B. 2008. *Signal and Noise: Media, Infrastructure, and Urban Culture in Africa.* Durham, NC: Duke University Press.

Latour, B. 2005. *Reassembling the Social: An Introduction to Actor-Network-Theory.* Oxford: Oxford University Press.

Lipton, M. 1982. 'Game against Nature: Theories of Peasant Decision-Making', in J. Harriss (ed.), *Rural Development: Theories of Peasant Economy and Agrarian Change.* London: Hutchinson University Library.

Morley, D. 2009. 'For a Materialist, Non-Media-Centric Media Studies', *Television & New Media* 10(1): 114–16.

Mutula, S., B. Grand, S. Zulu and P. Sebina. 2010. *Towards an Information Society in Botswana.* ICT4D Country Report.www.thetha.org.

National Development Plan (NDP). 2016. *DRAFT National Development Plan 11. April 2017–March 2023.* Gaborone: Government Printer.

Parks, Lisa, and Nicole Staroielski (eds). 2015. *Signal Traffic: Critical Studies of Media Infrastructures.* Urbana: University of Illinois Press.

Practical Action. 2004. *Cattle Tracking in Botswana.* https://practicalaction.org/cattle-tracking-in-botswana (accessed 21 April 2017).

Research ICT Africa. 2017. 'Botswana Telecommunications Limp a Decade after Policy Changes' *Policy Brief 1: Botswana.* https://researchictafrica.net/polbrf/Research_ICT_Africa_Policy_Briefs/2017%20Policy%20Brief%201_Botswana%20.pdf (accessed 1 October 2019).

Sahlins, M. 1974. *Stone Age Economics.* London: Tavistock Publications.

Schapera, I. 1947. *Migrant Labour and Tribal Life: A Study of Conditions in the Bechuanaland Protectorate.* London: Oxford University Press.

———. 1955 [1938]. *A Handbook of Tswana Law and Custom,* 2nd ed. London: Frank Cass.

———. 1984 [1953]. *The Tswana.* London: KPI.

Sebina, P., and B. Grand. 2017. 'Records Management and Open Data in Healthcare Provision in Africa: Reflections and Lessons for Botswana', in K. Moahi, K. Bwalya and P. Sebina (eds), *Health Information Systems and the Advancement of Medical Practice in Developing Countries,* pp. 1–10. https://

www.igi-global.com/book/health-information-systems-advancement-medical/173017 (accessed 23 June 2019).

Silverstone, R., E. Hirsch and D. Morley. 1992. 'Information and Communication Technologies and the Moral Economy of the Household', in R. Silverstone and D. Hirsch (eds), *Consuming Technologies: Media and Information in Domestic Spaces*. London: Routledge, pp. 15–31.

UNESCO. 2016. *ICT Literacy Policy: BOTSWANA*. Study and Report by Botswana IFAP Committee, 9th session of the Intergovernmental Council for the IFAP, 30–31 May 2016, UNESCO Headquarters, Paris.

Vokes, R. 2018. 'Before the Call: Mobile Phones, Exchange Relations, and Social Change in South-western Uganda', *Ethnos* 83(2): 274–90.

World Bank. 2017. *GINI Index*. https://data.worldbank.org/indicator/SI.POV.GINI?locations=BW (accessed 20 November 2017).

AFTERWORD

The Electronic Media in Africa, with an Addendum from Mauritius

Thomas Hylland Eriksen

When, around 2003, my household finally abandoned the landline, it had long since fallen into disuse. In the end, it felt as if the only people who occasionally rang us up on it were salesmen bent on interrupting family dinners or scammers claiming, in heavily accented English, to work for Microsoft. It was the end of an era and represented the loss of a hub. All household members save the cat now had their own telephones, and all seemed to prefer the privacy and comfort of an easy chair or a bedroom to the exposed nature of the hallway. Yet there was a sense of loss; never again would I pick up the phone to hear a tiny voice asking if my son or daughter were at home. A few years later, this development was replicated in the collective withdrawal from *le petit* écran, now replaced by the even smaller screens of laptops and (heaven forbid) smartphones. My wife, my children and I could easily spend time in the same room, but consuming four different kinds of content through earplugs. So, building on personal experience, I have strong reasons to believe in the potentially transformative character of new media on social relationships. Yet certain things people do are simply magnified and strengthened by the new technologies. Before the text message, schoolchildren might send each other secret notes in class; they can now do so without the risk of being caught out by the teacher. If they so desire, they may even get an audience larger than one. But how do societies and kinds of relationship differ in this domain? What do Africans, differently positioned, in different countries, do? In this book, some answers are offered, and new questions for further exploration are raised.

The Internet in Africa

According to Internet World Stats (2018), internet penetration in Africa was 35.2 per cent at the beginning of 2018, while the figure for the rest of the world was 58.4 per cent (global penetration, including Africa, was 54.4 per cent). Among the countries covered in this book, coverage for the Democratic Republic of Congo was just 6.1 per cent (the figure for Kinshasa is certainly much higher), while internet saturation in Botswana was 39.6 per cent, Zambia 41.2 per cent and South Africa 53.7 per cent. At 63.4 per cent, Mauritius, about which I have some reflections in the second part of this Afterword, ranks above the global average. However, these figures say little about usage patterns, and there are obvious methodological problems concerning the reliability of the data. What does it actually mean that someone has access to the internet, if money is scarce and connectivity dodgy? As noted by Helle-Valle in this book, even if nearly all adult villagers have a mobile phone, most can use their internet connection only occasionally because that is all they can afford; coverage is also uneven, especially in rural Africa. And how can one be certain that several people do not share one internet connection? And how can one even trust the figures produced by way of statistical methods with no hands-on contact with the people involved? Helle-Valle and Storm-Mathisen have a thing or two to say about this in the introduction to this book. Yet, even if taken with a large pinch of salt, the numbers I have quoted do indicate great disparities between countries, even if they say nothing about the unequal access within countries.

Regarding mobile phones, the data indicate that saturation is virtually complete in the more affluent African countries, such as South Africa, Mauritius, Seychelles and Botswana, but also in Kenya, while about 40 per cent of the population in DRC and 74 per cent in Zambia had mobile phones a few years ago (World Bank, 2017). Again, there are methodological problems here, since the percentages refer to the number of subscriptions, not to the number of people who have a subscription. So, in some countries, the saturation is well above 100 per cent. There is little doubt that the mobile phone, transformed into the smartphone since 2007, has transformed everyday life – for those who have one – around the world; but it is no less obvious that these changes have taken place in different ways, for reasons of economy, social organisation, network types, political regimes, scale and cultural values. One should nevertheless be wary of simple generalisations, and as pointed out by Vokes and Pype (2018), it cannot simply be assumed that the internet leads to time–space compression; time–space expansion is also a way of looking at it – space is expanded, and time becomes flexible in new ways. The editors' critique of quantitative methods in the introduction to this book, which generate the kind of data I have just referred to, is timely and important, and the ethnographic method shines not least in its ability to reveal what is unique, tangible and urgent in human life-worlds. Yet macro perspectives and statistics are necessary for the small-scale ethnography to make full sense, and besides, it is sometimes necessary to generalise before making caveats and adding nuance, lest we end up as theoretically impoverished butterfly collectors. Briefly, then, the African countries covered in this book share a number of features, showing that the conditions for internet use, and use patterns, differ in sub-Saharan Africa from the situation in the North Atlantic world, or in the Arab world for that matter, where the use of social media and instantaneous communication in general during the so-called Arab Spring in 2011 (which almost immediately turned into autumn except in Tunisia) has often been mentioned as revolutionary, both in technological and political terms.

General Features of the African Internet

Drawing on the previous chapters in this book and other research (such as the *Ethnos* special issue edited by Pype and Vokes, 2018), it is possible to distil a number of features that are peculiar to Africa and which contribute to shaping people's usage, as always at the risk of overgeneralising, but with the aim of framing a conversation about internet diversity. Even if the material at hand is close-up and ethnographic, it makes little sense with no reference to the structural level.

First of all, money is scarce to most Africans. This means that people have to regiment and ration their use of social media. Although prices have declined sharply, the expense of buying access, and sometimes to replace a broken phone, has to be weighed against other necessities including, in many cases, food.

Secondly, the typical African state is weaker than in the North Atlantic area, the exception in this book being Schneidermann's chapter starting with a friendly wave to James Scott (Chapter 4), which shows how the South African state actively uses the new communication technologies, in an almost Foucauldian way, to create a virtual panopticon. As a rule, however, innovations in internet use in Africa have not emerged from state agencies, but through start-ups and civil society initiatives, the most famous example of the former probably being the Kenyan M-Pesa payment system. Moreover, the weakness of the state also precludes effective policies in realms such as taxation (of global companies), improved efficiency in bureaucratic routines, protection of personal data and so on. As a result, the African internet emerges mainly in the intersection between business interests and civil society, with less interference and regulation from the state than elsewhere (one need only think of the ban on Facebook in China for a contrast).

Thirdly, mobile telephony and internet use have become widespread more recently and faster in Africa than elsewhere in the world. As late as 2005, the proportion of sub-Saharan Africans with internet access was estimated to be about 2 per cent (bar South Africa; see Eriksen, 2014). At the time of this writing (2019), the percentage is estimated to be about 35 per cent. As noted by Willems in her chapter, whereas just a hundred thousand Zambians had mobile phones in 2000, the figure in 2016 was twelve million! The role of transcontinental African traders and the increased availability of affordable, mainly Chinese, smartphones has been explored ethnographically by Mathews (2012) and Yang (2012). Although these trading links are financially risky, they can also be lucrative, and have been decisive for mobile telephony and the spread of the internet in Africa. Mathews (2012) estimates that about 20 per cent of the mobile phones sold in Africa were at the time bought by itinerant African traders in the ramshackle wholesale hub Chungking Mansions in Hong Kong, while Yang (2012) states that more than half the African traders who come to Guangzhou go bankrupt and never return. This was in the early 2010s, however, and the world has seen a lot of change since then.

Fourthly, owing to the weakness of state institutions, interaction and transactions in the informal sector are more significant in Africa than elsewhere. The material presented in this book, again with the exception of the South African case, shows that internet use tends to be network-based rather than hierarchically ordered.

Fifthly, use of new technologies is never uniform or predictable. As shown in Paula Uimonen's pioneering study of internet use in three South-East Asian countries, there were distinct imaginaries about this then brand-new technology in Malaysia, Laos and Thailand (Uimonen, 2001). In Malaysia, the internet was mainly associated with business and political discussions; in Thailand, the gaming possibilities were at the forefront; while the poorer and more authoritarian Laotian case showed that the web was being used, largely by exiles, to promote alternative political ideas and to criticise the government. Røhnebæk (2005) showed that internet cafes in south Indian villages, intended to help farmers monitor produce prices and young adults to apply for grants and admission to universities, ended up largely being used by young men and adolescent boys to surf on porn sites. Edvardsen (2005) described, in her research from Tanzania, how an internet-enabled computer meant to facilitate access to knowledge, donated to a school by an international NGO, sat behind glass in a locked cupboard in the headmaster's office. Other creative uses of the new technologies could have been foregrounded – for example, in this book, Nigerian scammers are barely mentioned – but the general point is that people everywhere tend to use new information technologies as extensions or expansions of activities in which they were involved before the internet, such as sexually tinged networking with men (Pype), market trading (Willems), keeping kin and other networks going (Storm-Mathisen), reciprocity and rituals (Helle-Valle). This is not to say that the new technologies do not induce changes, and as this book shows, they affect both time and space in important ways – social circles can be expanded, constant availability enables new ways of timing activities, and so on. Yet at the same time, frantic change in one area should not lead to the assumption that everything changes at the same speed or direction (Eriksen, 2016). If kinship is socially, economically, politically and existentially important, as is the case in most of Africa, it does not necessarily cease to be important owing to the introduction of an information technology which may in principle enable people to transcend kinship ties easily. This is an empirical question, and there is great variety. In rural China, social media have enabled many young villagers to develop a sense of privacy for the first time (Miller et al., 2016), while some of the Batswana described by Helle-Valle in this book use new media to strengthen rather than weaken kin ties.

Finally, discourses about new media differ significantly across continents and countries. For example, the North Atlantic controversies around surveillance, identity theft and data ownership are far less visible in most of Africa, where the official discourse concerns the potential of new media to stimulate economic growth and informal discourses tend to focus on pricing and availability of services as well as possible forms of networking through new media. The concern about platformisation and corporate appropriation of biographical and private details, raised by Willems in this book, seems to be shared by few of her informants.

Mauritius and Modernity

I would now like to move on to an empirical case, which might add some perspectives to the analyses and ethnographies of the previous chapters. Some of the most interesting questions about new media concern their potential for allowing transformations of social and cultural worlds. Do internet-based services and mobile phones increase people's social capital, and to what extent is this capital being converted, for example into political or economic capital? Does the flexibility and deterritorialised nature of new media strengthen social networks at the expense of weakening traditional corporations? Or, phrased differently, do people in general use these media to strengthen already strong ties, or to fan out into a large quantity of weak ties (Granovetter, 1973)? What are people's fundamental concerns, and to what extent do new media facilitate their pursuits of important goals in life?

Unlike the vast majority of human societies, the Indian Ocean island-state of Mauritius (current population 1.2 million) has been modern since its inception. By this, I do not mean that modernity, as a cultural style, has pervaded the island since it was settled in the early eighteenth century, but that its economy and political arrangements, as well as the composition of its population, are the results of distinctively modern processes, being part and parcel of the European colonial adventure. Strategically located in a succession of colonial empires ruling the island, the very *raison-d'être* of Mauritius was transnational in nature and commercial in intent, first as a transit and trade hub, later as a plantation colony (Eriksen, 1998). The constituents of its uprooted population, with origins ranging from Bretagne to Canton, from Madagascar to Bihar, could yearn for their respective homelands, but they were forced to create their history anew in a foreign land. They had left their past behind and were subsequently forced to reconstruct it from myth and memory, or to create something entirely new instead. They did both. This is why Mauritius, in spite of its geographical location *en route* between Africa and Asia, is a classic New World country.

Mauritius, a small but profitable cog in the huge machinery of colonialism, came of age and developed under the full floodlight of modernity. Its history is mainly a written one, the development of its complex population, economy and political institutions known from archival sources. Building on no pre-existing traditional arrangements, this society was modern from day one.

That the structural features of Mauritius (colonial administration, slavery, trade, eventually sugar production on a large scale etc.) were part of the modern world does not, however, imply that its inhabitants had a modern frame of mind based on individualism and openness to change. Until well into the twentieth century, most Mauritians were illiterate. Indentured labourers and their descendants lived in villages which in some ways replicated Indian village life, with the exception, though, that they were wageworkers and smallholders, integrated into the incipient capitalist world system. This was also the case for the descendants of slaves, who would soon begin to engage in a variety of monetary activities following liberation in 1839. However, kinship remained important as an organising principle, with some variation between the ethnic groups due to their differing history. The omnipresence of the monetary economy from an early stage nevertheless testifies to some degree of cultural modernisation; money is individually obtained, can be divided, pooled, spent and saved, and primarily serves to create relationships between individuals, not groups.

Diversification of Diversity

A fully-fledged modernity in the cultural sense, referring to mentality rather than social structure, has developed unevenly and incompletely in Mauritius, as in many other parts of the world including most of Europe. The sugar industry led to some degree of individualisation because it created jobs for individuals not groups, and lifted persons out of their village and kinship networks. Education and the growth of mass media similarly expanded people's awareness of the surrounding world and contributed in no small way to social mobility. A non-white indigenous middle class began to emerge. However, modernisation (in the cultural sense) took a huge step forward in the 1980s, when manufacturing and tourism exploded as sources of employment and revenue.

In the 1970s, V.S. Naipaul had infamously, in his characteristically sarcastic manner, described Mauritius as a place that everybody wanted to leave – stagnant, overpopulated, drab (Naipaul, 1973). Arriving on the island for the first time in the rainy season of 1986, I read, on one of my very first days in the field, about a SOFRÈS opinion poll which indicated that more than half of Mauritius's adults were hoping that their children would emigrate. Unemployment was officially hovering around the 20 per cent mark.

Less than a year later, on the eve of my departure, the leading newspaper *Le Mauricien* reported that the country was now importing Malaysian construction workers. Unemployment was almost negligible. The year 1986 was an extraordinary year, the year of a beginning tourism boom and an industrial revolution which brought not least thousands of young women to the factory floor. Returning to do more fieldwork in 1991–92, some of my old friends were already complaining about stress, reminiscing about the 'good old days' when you always had time on your hands. By then, many middle-class Mauritians already had mobile phones, and less than a decade later, the same people would be online.

The social worlds of working-class Mauritians would also change fast in the last decades of the twentieth century. Large numbers of young women were employed in the textile industry, both genders in the growing tourism business, and Mauritius established itself as a so-called middle-income country.

As early as 1991, the then foreign minister Jean-Claude de l'Estrac spoke about *le deuxième phase*, the second phase of industrialisation, highlighting finance and IT as a natural development from reliance on sugar first, then manufacturing and tourist services. By the early 2000s, a hi-tech hub called Cybercity was being built at Ebène, between the town of Rose-Hill and the university and research centres at Le Réduit. Catering for banking and information industries, with tall office buildings (by Mauritian standards) and busy lunch cafes, it may perhaps resemble a miniature Singapore, as was the intention. Yet, like the African countries presented previously in this book, Mauritius remains mainly an information society rather than a knowledge economy, with sugar, manufacturing and tourism by far exceeding information services and technology development in revenue. The lofty dreams promoted in the early 1990s seem, for the time being, to have been an instance of what Morozov (2013) criticises as 'technological solutionism'. Digitisation of the state has been sluggish, few IT start-ups have been successful, and there is little trace of the 'texting like a state' phenomenon discussed by Schneidermann in this book.

On the other hand, large numbers of Mauritians have become avid and versatile *users* of the new technology. Switching almost seamlessly between French, English and the vernacular Kreol Morisien (a French-based Creole), Mauritians have a visible and active online presence on social media, on blogs and so on. The printed media, of which Mauritius has a great deal considering its small population, went online early, and some have relinquished print altogether.

A question that needs to be raised concerns whether the recent online presence of many Mauritians, not least young people, leads to the strengthening and extension of existing social relationships and social groups, or the establishment of new ones. Answers are by necessity tentative and based on impressions and anecdotal evidence, since no ethnography on this subject exists yet (although Eisenlohr [2015] has studied religious temporalities among Mauritian Hindus with a focus on new media). My interest in these remarks lies primarily in the realm of ethnicity, which has defined politics and social relationships in Mauritius for decades.

To return to the restructuring of the Mauritian economy and some of its implications, the new arrangements and opportunities in the labour market, along with steadily improving educational achievements in the population, also entailed new options for identification. Women increasingly had their own money, and they were exposed to social complexities they had never encountered before. Workplaces where employees routinely worked alongside people from other ethnic groups, and took their lunchbreaks with them, became quite common. Some predicted, if not the slow demise of ethnicity in Mauritius, then at least its reduced importance; and I seem to recall that I was indeed one of them. In predicting the emergence of a society less dominated by ethnicity, we were partly right, but at the same time, we overestimated the role of economic arrangements, underestimating the importance of kinship, religion and political patronage. It can nevertheless be argued that a main line of tension in Mauritian society today, as was the case in the late twentieth century, can be drawn between ethnic and non-ethnic life-worlds, strategies and outlooks, and that this is a tension in which many individuals find themselves caught while trying to negotiate their way through the practical challenges of everyday life. The official ideology of the country is multiculturalism, meaning the peaceful coexistence of and compromises between delineated ethnocultural groups, but there is also interculturalism, cosmopolitanism and indeed unreformed individualism to be found for those who search for it. In this, Mauritius is different from most of continental Africa in the sense that there is an ongoing, continuous discourse, private as well as public, about the nature of group identity, options and alternatives – about the meanings of the word 'we'. I now turn to considering the role of media and electronic communication in the forging of collective identities in contemporary Mauritius.

From Printed to Electronic Media

The history of media in Mauritius differs in striking ways from the situation described by Helle-Valle for Botswana, which again reminds us that Mauritius is different from continental Africa. The first newspapers on the island were published in the late eighteenth century, and there was hardly any 'no media' period, although the media's reach into rural districts slowly gained pace during the twentieth century. By the 1970s, radio and to some extent newspapers had penetrated even the remotest rural villages.

Considering its small scale, Mauritius has a very diverse and vibrant media sphere, comprising not least a broad range of printed publications. Although sectional interests certainly exist in the media, they purport to represent, often with considerable success, society as a whole, and most overt political interests in the country can be heard through the press. The main newspapers have consistently campaigned against communalism (ethnic favouritism), they have debated uneven development – for a while using the controversial term 'le malaise créole' to designate the marginalisation of the Creole ethnic group – and exposed corruption. The role of the media, and not least the printed press, in forging a sense of Mauritianness should not be underestimated.

The official media sphere of Mauritius – print, TV, radio – is generally orderly and takes on the dual responsibilities of creating a shared identity while simultaneously allowing dissent and disagreement to surface.

As in virtually every country in the world, it is much harder to generalise about the electronic jungle, or cybernetic ecosystem if you like, than about the ordered landscape of the printed press. If the world of the internet is a jungle, that of the printed media is a park. Sprawling and diverse, ranging from blogs to tweets and Facebook discussions, Mauritian internet use shares many features with that in European countries.

Since the turn of the millennium, the internet has changed in character. From being primarily a medium of information, it has been transformed – increasingly – into a medium of communication, through the introduction of the blog, Facebook, discussion forums on news sites and so on. There exists a plethora of websites which represent diasporic and scattered communities, some of them with nation-building ambitions, such as diasporic Kurdish and Tamil Sri Lankan websites (Eriksen, 2007). There are websites for diasporic Hindus (not least based in the Americas), for Chileans in exile and for Muslims in Europe. Unlike the older, but still modern information technologies, internet communication is not confined to place. One can thus create *de facto* virtual communities on the web. For diasporic and scattered groups, this possibility has been used widely in recent years in order to enhance their community.

On this background, and with the complex history of Mauritian identities as a backdrop, it is worthwhile to investigate how Mauritians use the new internet, previously known as Web 2.0, to build networks and community.

There are a number of Mauritian blogs in French, English and Kreol; most of them appear to be updated far too rarely to function as discussion sites, and only a handful deal with current issues such as language policy and politics, one outstanding exception being Malenn Oodiah's *Projet de société* (Oodiah, 2018), which is regularly updated with articles elaborating the author's visions for a green, modern and equitable future Mauritius. At the same time, it seems clear that the Mauritian blogosphere, as Mauritian Facebook use, strengthens rather than weakens Mauritian identity. This apparent paradox was described as early as 2000 by Miller and Slater in an early study of internet usage in Trinidad. They found, briefly, that the Trinidadian internet – far from creating new, fragmented, transnational, virtual identities – in fact contributed to strengthening family values, existing social networks and national identity. In the Mauritian case, blogs and discussions suggest a similar pattern. Some talk about their holidays and family life, clearly with friends and acquaintances in mind; those who discuss politics do so in a distinctively Mauritian way, with language policy, communalism, economic issues and corruption being the main topics. In general, shared conversations about common concerns that transcend social and economic boundaries are facilitated through new media, and it should also be kept in mind that Mauritians are passionate about politics and the future of their society. To some, weak ties are forged; to others, already strong ties are strengthened. There is an interesting contrast here not only to African societies, where the online conversation about societal issues is limited, but also to those North Atlantic societies where the public concern with online hate speech and echo chambers has been on the rise. Online Mauritian discussions about politics and the economy tend to bring people closer together, not further apart.

Many also use electronic media, especially texting and Snapchat, for building other kinds of ties that would have been difficult to create offline. A familiar feature of new media almost everywhere, electronic flirting and intimate conversation can be a means of escaping from parental or spousal control, especially for women. While these relationships do not carry with them ambitions comparable to nation-building projects, they nevertheless contribute to weakening kinship ties and opening up possibilities for new kinds of social relationships.

Of course, the mediascapes (Appadurai, 1996) in which Mauritians find themselves vary greatly, from the highly educated urban middle class to the rural planter. However, the difference should not be exaggerated: many of the students at the University of Mauritius have a rural background, and they tell me that everyone they know is active on social media.

In a little-known essay based on a Munro lecture delivered at the University of Edinburgh, Leach (1977) argued that all modern societies are by definition pluralistic.[1] Rather than the replication of similarity, modernity represents the organisation of diversity, as pointed out already in 1964 by Anthony Wallace (Wallace, 1970). In Mauritius, with its colonial heritage cementing an ethnic division of labour and subsequent politicisation of ethnicity, diversity is nothing new. Yet, as I have suggested, the new media situation, which enables people to disembed themselves from community-based identities, at least at the discursive and symbolic level, may contribute to a situation of super-diversity, described by Vertovec (2007) as a 'diversification of diversity' in that individual variation becomes more important than group boundaries. There is no reason to assume that such a development will take place automatically, as recent developments in Europe and the Middle East have shown, where new media are actively being used for primordialist purposes. Yet new media open up a field of possibilities that were previously not on the cards.

As noted above, in the early 1990s, some researchers and commentators believed in the imminent decline of ethnicity and communalism in Mauritius. A quarter of a century later, the situation has not changed dramatically, but the cosmopolitan, or post-ethnic, middle class – where intermarriage is relatively uncontroversial, and where ancestral identities are not seen as imperative – is more established now, representing a counterweight to the group or community-based way of thinking and acting. Yet communities are well and thriving in most of the island. Moreover, even if communalism and ethnic identities may appear to be weakened through the cross-cutting communication taking place through mobile phones and social media, one should keep in mind the important distinction between saying and doing, between attitudes and action. People may well be cosmopolitan on Facebook and communally oriented in their everyday pragmatics.

The perspectives from media and communication studies on identity are illuminating, but ultimately limited. Even if the Mauritian web, including the blogosphere, Twitter and Facebook, were totally colour-blind, this would not necessarily have an impact on the actual functioning of Mauritian society. As noted, political discussions on Facebook, of which there are many, generally come across as open and inclusive. Mauritius being a small-scale society, the people discussing usually know each other offline, or are at least aware of each other, their political views, their party allegiances if applicable, and so on. Discussions shift between French, English and Kreol, and it is not uncommon that all three languages are used, for effect, in the same post.

And yet, as long as crucial resources – work, security, support of various kinds – flow through kin and ethnic networks, no amount of tolerance and colour-blindness can make ethnicity irrelevant. Too much is at stake. Mauritianness as an overarching identity can be strengthened through the growth of new, electronic communities, just as Kreol as a shared language makes it easy for Mauritians to discover their Mauritianness the moment they are confronted with foreigners. At the same time, for the new identities to be societally important and transformative, the structural arrangements of society, from politics to the labour market, from marriage practices to informal interaction, currently saturated by ethnic practices, will also have to change.

What Is at Stake?

As this Mauritian sketch has indicated, people use social media differently in Mauritius compared to the continental African countries surveyed in the previous chapters. At one level of analysis, this difference can be put down to variation between concerns: while Mauritians are convinced that their society would be better (and, in many cases, they themselves would be better off) if the relationship between ethnicity and politics were changed, the continental Africans encountered in this book are concerned with networks, money and kinship. However, at another level, it may be argued that the focus on identity, both individual and collective, evident in the Mauritian case, signifies something qualitatively different. Marinated in the often enforced individualisation and uprootedness characteristic of modernity, Mauritians constantly interrogate their personal and collective identities, asking what it means, entails and implies to be 'I' and 'we'. A form of personhood is apparent which recalls theorists of late modernity such as Bauman (2000) and Giddens (1991). The scarce resource, that which is at stake for many Mauritians in their online identities, is a secure sense of self and a sense of belonging in a society that could be bewilderingly complex even before the electronic revolution.

There is no simple evolutionary story about the relationship between electronic media and identities, personal and collective. Whereas McLuhan wrote prophetically about the global village in the 1960s (McLuhan, [1964] 1994), Castells (1997), in his influential work about the emergence of the network society, prefers to speak of customised cottages. Both were right, and one might even get a few things right by talking about global villages in the plural. The internet and the smartphone are what we make of them, but we do not deal with them in a vacuum. These technologies are simultaneously transformative and conserving; they offer new opportunities and options, and they can also be used to strengthen existing social forms, which are nevertheless being transformed through the powers released by deterritorialised, electronic communication technologies. As social scientists working with qualitative, mainly ethnographic methods, the best we can do may not be merely to describe and analyse uniqueness and diversity, but to show how the uniqueness of specific settings speaks to something more general, in this case merely what it means to be a human being and what the contemporary world is like.

Acknowledgements

I would like to thank the other contributors for enlightenment and pleasure in Marrakesh and the editors for incisive comments.

Thomas Hylland Eriksen is Professor of Social Anthropology at the University of Oslo, a member of the Norwegian Academy of Sciences and the Humanities and an External Scientific Member of the Max Planck Society. His recent work has focused on accelerated change and globalisation, disseminated through several books including *Overheating* (2016) and *Boomtown* (2018). He is currently writing about the smartphone.

Note

1. Thanks to Nigel Rapport for alerting me to this text.

References

Appadurai, A. 1996. *Modernity at Large*. Minneapolis: University of Minnesota Press.

Bauman, Z. 2000. *Liquid Modernity*. Cambridge: Polity.

Castells, M. 1997. *The Rise of the Network Society*. Oxford: Blackwell.

Edvardsen, C.H. 2005. 'Internett i afrikanske skoler?', in T.H. Eriksen (ed.), *Internett i praksis*. Oslo: Spartacus, pp. 93–110.

Eisenlohr, P. 2015. 'Mediating Disjunctures of Time: Ancestral Chronotopes in Ritual and Media Practices', *Anthropological Quarterly* 88(2): 281–304.

Eriksen, T.H. 1998. *Common Denominators: Ethnicity, Nation-building and Compromise in Mauritius*. Oxford: Berg.

———. 2007. 'Nationalism and the Internet', *Nations and Nationalism* 13(1): 1–18.

———. 2014. *Globalization: The Key Concepts*. London: Bloomsbury.

———. 2016. *Overheating: An Anthropology of Accelerated Change*. London: Pluto.

Giddens, A. 1991. *Modernity and Self-Identity*. Cambridge: Polity.

Granovetter, M. 1973. 'The Strength of Weak Ties', *American Journal of Sociology* 78(6): 1360–80.

Internet World Stats. 2018. 'Internet World Stats: Usage and Population Statistics'. https://www.internetworldstats.com/stats1.htm (accessed 7 April 2018).

Leach, E.R. 1977. *Custom, Law and Terrorist Violence.* Edinburgh: Edinburgh University Press.

Mathews, G. 2012. 'Neoliberalism and Globalization from Below in Chungking Mansions, Hong Kong', in G. Mathews, G.L. Ribeiro and C.A. Vega (eds), *Globalization from Below: The World's Other Economy.* London: Routledge, pp. 69–85.

McLuhan, M. [1964] 1994. *Understanding Media: The Extensions of Man.* London: Routledge.

Miller, D., and D. Slater. 2000. *The Internet: An Ethnographic Approach.* Oxford: Berg.

Miller, D., E. Costa, N. Haynes, T. McDonald, R. Nicolescu, J. Spyer, S. Venkatraman and X. Wang. 2016. *How the World Changed Social Media.* London: UCL Press.

Morozov, E. 2013. *To Save Everything, Click Here: The Folly of Technological Solutionism.* New York: Public Affairs.

Naipaul, V.S. 1973. *The Overcrowded Barracoon.* New York: Knopf.

Oodiah, M. 2018. *Projet de société: Construire et vivre ensemble.* http://projetsociete.blogspot.com (accessed 6 April 2018).

Pype, K., and R. Vokes (eds). 2018. 'Chronotopes of Media in Africa', Special Issue, *Ethnos* 83(2).

Røhnebæk, M. 2005. 'Hvis Internett er svaret, hva er spørsmålet?' [If the Internet Is the Answer, What Is the Question?], in T.H. Eriksen (ed.), *Internett i praksis.* Oslo: Spartacus, pp. 111–40.

Uimonen, P. 2001. *Transnational.Dynamics@Development.Net: Internet, Modernization and Globalization.* Stockholm: Department of Social Anthropology.

Vertovec, S. 2007. 'Super-Diversity and Its Implications', *Ethnic and Racial Studies* 30(6): 1024–54.

Vokes, R., and K. Pype. 2018. 'Chronotopes of Media in Sub-Saharan Africa', *Ethnos* 8(2): 207–17.

Wallace, A.F.C. 1970. *Culture and Personality.* New York: Random House.

World Bank. 2017. 'World Development Indicators'. http://databank.worldbank.org/data/reports.aspx?Id=5494af8e&Report_Name=Mobile-penetration-# (accessed 7 April 2018).

Yang, Y. 2012. 'African Traders in Guangzhou: Routes, Reasons, Profits, Dreams', in G. Mathews, G.L. Ribeiro and C.A. Vega (eds), *Globalization from Below: The World's Other Economy.* London: Routledge, pp. 154–70.

Index

www.ingramcontent.com/pod-product-compliance
Ingram Content Group UK Ltd.
Pitfield, Milton Keynes, MK11 3LW, UK
UKHW021837100926
8556IPUK00004B/395

9 781789 206616